Affectionately dedicated by a grateful son to
the memory of his distinguished father,
who encouraged from childhood
the pursuit of excellence and
a fond respect for God's
other creatures.

CLIMBER'S GUIDE
TO THE
ROCKY MOUNTAINS
OF
CANADA
SOUTH

by

WILLIAM L. PUTNAM
and
GLEN W. BOLES

Based on earlier editions by
James Monroe Thorington

Published by the
AMERICAN ALPINE CLUB
and the
ALPINE CLUB OF CANADA

SIXTH EDITION

CONTENTS

INTRODUCTION

This edition of the Climber's Guide to the Rocky Mountains of Canada represents a substantial revision from past issues. In compiling this, the editors have been mindful of the need to maintain a measure of continuity, but have set out to make this volume responsive to the climbing needs of the 1970's. Nevertheless, it will be clear that the hand and words of Palmer and Thorington are still with us. This volume represents the current edition of a work begun in 1921 as the first alpine climber's guide in North America, and the editors are pleased that half a century later, Dr. Thorington has continued to provide important guidance to the endeavor he brought to life.

It is impossible to recount the names of all who have assisted in this edition, in conversation, correspondence, correction and abuse. To assign a priority among the more prominent would be unfair, but this volume, for all its remaining faults would not be what it is without the help so generously given by David Michael, Pat Boswell, Brian Greenwood, Charlie Locke, Hans Gmoser, Arnör Larson, Dave Jones, Dave Fisher, Tony Daffern, Millie Fadgen, Steve Roper, Allen Steck, and Jim Tarrant. A special word of thanks is due Ed Cooper, who provided the bulk of the very high quality photographs herein, including the covers.

The sponsoring clubs are the respective national organizations of mountaineering in North America and have underwritten this endeavor as they have other guidebooks, publishing efforts, training programs and many other works of service to the public.

Use of this Book

The basic arrangement is from south to north, although it is obvious that certain allowances have been made for the width of the area covered. In any case, that which is adjacent on the ground will be found adjacent in this text. Peaks are to be found under the group heading, or can be rapidly located using the index.

Data on passes, including the streams draining each side, the altitude, the adjacent summits, the watershed traversed and the nature of trails, will be found in a separate appendix, and is not given in the text itself.

Each peak listing includes its altitude and locational data, along with any references which may be particularly useful with respect to early attempts, etc. The route of first ascent is given next, along with such evaluation (NCCS) as is possible to obtain and concluding with any references which are particularly pertinent to this route. Other routes are given in geographic order, clockwise around the mountain, and containing the same evaluation and references.

This book does not attempt to give a pitch by pitch route description, for to do so would destroy the sense of adventure, which we seek in the mountains. It does, however, give sufficient data to get one surely to the base of the climb, sufficient landmarks that the user can stay on the route, time checkpoints for evaluating progress, and descent data of importance. We assume the user to be of sufficient intelligence to get out of this volume all that we have put into it.

Please, if unfamiliar with this region, **read the full introduction** before setting out further.

Geographic Span

This volume is one of a pair and encompasses the alpine territory from the 49th Parallel to the line of the North Saskatchewan River and Howse Pass. Peaks to the north of that line will be found in the companion volume to be published one year hence.

Every named peak in excess of 9000 feet, and below that altitude when of mountaineering importance, is included. Also included is every unnamed peak that exceeds 10,000 feet, and an exhaustive index with all place names of mountaineering importance in the area covered.

An extensive mountain area is included within various national parks. Waterton Lakes contains 220 square miles in

Alberta, adjacent to the International Boundary. Banff, with an area of 2585 square miles, lies in Alberta between Palliser and Sunwapta Passes. Most of the Park is included within this volume. Immediately to the west of the southern part of Banff Park, in British Columbia, one enters Kootenay Park with 587 square miles. This park is traversed by the Banff-Windermere Highway (Route 95). Yoho, also in British Columbia, contains 507 square miles, much of which can be reached by road from Field or the Blaeberry River. The Lake Louise-Jasper Highway traverses below many of the frontal peaks from Lake Louise northwards. Only a portion of the peaks accessible from this highway are covered by this volume.

Topography

It is important that persons unfamiliar with these mountains understand the nature of the bedrock and peculiarities of topography. Fundamentally, this is an area of severely glaciated, sedimentary rock, much of it flat lying, although folded and thrust-faulted to the NE. Certain formations, particularly within the Cambrian and Devonian, offer excellent rock by local standards. However, those who are familiar with the nature of bedrock in such areas as Yosemite, the Dolomites, Laurentians, Chamonix or Shawangunks will need a serious readjustment of climbing practices and standards when on severe faces in the Rockies. Basically, this is not an area of sound rock, and **all routes are subject to rockfall** in varying degrees of danger (CAJ 50–90).

The principal glaciation in the Canadian Rocky Mountains occurs on or near the Continental Divide and lies in the area covered by the companion volume. While substantial glaciers do exist in the area covered by this volume, along the Divide peaks, in those to the west, and in a few cases certain of the Frontal Ranges, there is nothing comparable with the extent of the Columbia Icefield and its adjacent neve regions to the north. In general, snowline is to be found at an altitude of 9000' to 10000', depending on exposure. This, of course, means that only on the more protected reaches of the higher peaks will there be permanent snow. The glaciers extend down to a lowest limit of approximately 6000' and without exception,

7

all have shown considerable recession within the last 50 years.

Users of this book should note that snowfall is not constant from year to year, and that many routes are dependent on snow depth and cover. The descriptions assume average snow levels as best as the editors can determine. With greater or lesser amounts of snow the routes may vary immensely in difficulty.

The main drainage is comparatively simple. East of the Continental Divide it is largely through the Bow River and its tributaries; and to the west, the major portion is through the Kootenay River system.

The Frontal Ranges, both north and south of the Bow River, form distinct and separate climbing areas, in which snow or ice has been of little mountaineering importance. For the most part the climbing has been done on limestone or dolomite, some of which is of a relatively high and durable order (AAJ 17-84). The bulk of the climbs in the Frontal Ranges are of two fundamentally different types. Most of the peaks were originally climbed by their generally gentle southwest slopes, which are largely comformable to the dip of the strata and littered with talus and scree. When approached from the northeast, however, these same peaks generally present spectacular cliffs, one of which exceeds 1500' over a continuous distance of 7 miles. Approaches to some of the peaks in these groups are easy over roads and trails maintained by the various park and forest authorities. However, even where trails are non-existent, due to the substantially drier nature of these areas, travel is easy, for the forest is less luxuriant, although timberline remains at essentially the same level as in the mountain areas to the west.

The groups west of the main watershed are not nearly as accessible, and in many ways resemble the Interior Ranges in their lush vegetation and higher precipitation. Roads and trails are maintained in many of the valleys and access is easier now than in years past.

References and History

Many of the older and superfluous references have been eliminated from this edition, since they are not responsive to modern climbing due to glacial recession or changes in access. The scholar who wishes to consult these in older volumes will find them; the climber of modern schools will have no need. Although the editors have reviewed every line of this text for its current accuracy, some anachronisms may remain. Where no recent data is available, such will be obvious by the antiquity of the references cited. In such cases due allowance must be given for glacial recession and changes in access.

While the editors have researched all sources, it is possible that certain climbs and routes may have escaped our attention; lack of mention herein is not proof-positive that an ascent has never been made.

With the introduction to each group is a map showing sufficient of the peaks and other landmarks to aid in locating others. However, for detailed data, we suggest purchasing maps on a scale of 1:50000 from the Department of Mines and Technical Surveys (615 Booth Street, Ottawa) which at $1.00 apiece are an investment well worth the expenditure. With each group introduction will be found the code numbers by which the appropriate sheets should be ordered. In certain locational descriptions will be found a six-digit number. This is to be used with the military grid system which is explained on these maps. An additional source of excellent maps is the B. C. Dept of Lands and Forests in Victoria which publishes a series for most of that Province on a scale of 1:125000.

In the introduction to each group we include the pertinent road and trail information to provide access. However, for those who wish more detailed information, the *Canadian Rockies Trail Guide*, a hiker's manual, is available at many locations in these mountains. This is an admirable guide to the trails of the National Parks in these ranges and furnishes for most such areas much more detail than is given herein.

Peaks named in **bold face** type have been officially adopted by the Canadian Permanent Committee on Geographic Names. Those given in *(italics)* are alternate or former applications.

The early white travellers were associated with the Northwest Company — geographers, explorers and traders.

David Thompson crossed the Howse Pass in 1807 and a host followed after his opening of the Athabaska Pass in 1811 (CAJ 16–194). David Douglas' ascent of Mt Brown under winter conditions in 1827 attracted later mountaineer-explorers, although they failed to substantiate the great elevations attributed to peaks of that area. Accurate knowledge was much advanced by the Palliser expedition (1857-60) sent out by the British government to search for railroad routes. Dr. James Hector established basic nomenclature, retained by modern maps. The Frontal Ranges were traversed from north to south in 1859 by the hunting party of the Earl of Southesk, whose route (uncertainly described in his *Saskatchewan and the Rocky Mountains;* London, 1875) can now be identified. Further historic information, where appropriate, is given in the group introductions or under specific peaks.

The literature pertinent to the exploration and early mountaineering in the Rocky Mountains of Canada is most extensive and, to a degree, inseparably bound up in part with that of the Hudson Bay and Northwest Companies, in other part with the explorations for and construction of the Canadian Pacific Railway. In addition, there are many volumes that deal tangentially with mountaineering, being primarily concerned with hunting or related fields. The most pertinent volumes, however, are the following:

Stutfield, H. & Collie, J. N., 1903, — *Climbs and Explorations in the Canadian Rockies.* This, to some extent, overlaps and interlocks with Outram.

Outram, James, — 1905, *In The Heart of the Canadian Rockies* covers climbs made in the area generally south from Sunwapta Pass.

Wilcox, Walter D., 1909, — *The Rockies of Canada.* This is the second of two volumes, dealing largely with the southern portions of the range.

Coleman, A. P. *The Canadian Rockies,* 1911, details a number of trips on foot and horse over several years from both sides of the range.

Burpee, Laurence J. *Among the Canadian Alps*, 1914, deals largely with non-technical climbs in the northern portions of the range.

Thorington, J. M., 1925, *The Glittering Mountains of Canada* is largely an account of its author's first trips in this area but contains much historic data of interest to scholarly mountaineers.

Kain, Conrad *Where the Clouds Can Go*, 1935, written with the assistance of Dr. Thorington, an excellent autobiography of Canada's most famous guide.

Frazer, Esther *The Canadian Rockies*, 1969, a capsule summary of many of the more intriguing explorers and mountaineers and their principal exploits.

Other references herein are abbreviated as indicated:

AJ — Alpine Journal, London.

CAJ — Canadian Alpine Journal, Banff, Alberta

App — Appalachia, Boston, Massachusetts

VOC — Varsity Outdoor Club, UBC, Vancouver, B. C.

AAJ — American Alpine Journal, New York, N.Y.

Harvard — Journal of Harvard Mountaineering Club, Cambridge, Massachusetts

Access and Services

The Alpine huts are described in the appropriate introductions, but the mountain traveller should not count on obtaining much more than shelter, and must always arrange for his own provisions.

Professional guides, whose experience includes the entire range, may be secured through the Association of Canadian Mountain Guides, or through the office of the Alpine Club of Canada in Banff, Alberta.

In recent years the number of climbing centers in the Canadian Rockies has expanded with the opening of new roads. The traditional routes of approach have in many cases changed from those noted in some of the references. Helicopters are frequently used for mountain base camps outside the National Parks, or where roads and trails are lacking. These can be chartered by phone, and are based at airports in Calgary, Edmonton, Golden and other points. The greater increase in accessibility to these areas is not an unmixed blessing, for many wilderness values have been destroyed, with significant improvement in access being attained in only a few areas. Pack-train travel for mountaineers now has entirely disappeared.

Horses were used in the Canadian mountains by the earliest travellers and fur-traders, who crossed the Continental Divide through Howse, Athabaska and other passes during the 19th century. Throughout the construction of railroads through Kicking Horse and Yellowhead Passes, horses brought in supplies. Packtrains were retained after railroad completion for mountain exploration and hunting parties. Until the 1940's there were few roads and one gained the lateral valleys by wilderness trails. The major rivers, were unbridged except by rail, and distances were so great that it was practically impossible for climbers to maintain themselves and reach far-away peaks by backpacking. Horses solved the problem for half a century before highways, and helicopters made them obsolete.

The packtrain was a pleasant method of travel, with pic-turesque outfitters Tom Wilson, Bill Peyto, Jim Simpson, George Harrison and others, operating from the Canadian Pacific, and Curly Phillips, on the Canadian National. Banff, Lake Louise and Jasper were the usual starting points. Even toward the end of the era one could have a climbers' packtrain for $10 per day per man, including saddle-horses for the entire party, all provisions, guide, cook, packer and wrangler. The party that went to the Columbia Icefield in 1923, for instance, included two tourists, a climbing guide, outfit personnel of four, and twenty horses.

One could be out for a month and never see another party. Life on the trail was pleasant, as men like Collie, Coleman, Wilcox and others had discovered long before. One had the quiet peace of the forest, with scarcely a sound save rushing water, bird songs, horse-bells and perhaps the distant rumble of an avalanche. It is usual for modern climbers, who have no experience of such days, to look down on this life of long ago; but those who have never seen a long packtrain swimming the North Saskatchewan or descending the ice of the Saskatchewan Glacier, or have never camped on the Castleguard Meadows with campfire smoke rising toward Mt. Bryce and the sunset, have missed great moments. Horses are still used by hunting parties and for supplying some of the annual camps of the Alpine Club of Canada, but the days of leisurely travel by packtrain vanished with the coming of roads, speeding motors and the fumes of gasoline. Nostalgia for the past is not to be despised; the pity is that it will not return.

Comparison Climbs

UIAA Grade	Area	Peak	Route
III—	Canadian Rockies	Assiniboine	North Ridge
	Colorado Rockies	1st Flatiron	East Face
	Valais	Matterhorn	Swiss Ridge
	Yosemite	Gunsight	
III	Tetons	Symmetry Spire	Normal
	Valais	Zinal Rothorn	Normal
	Dolomites	Cina Piccolo	Normal
	Yosemite	Sunnyside Bench	Normal
III+	Tetons	Grand	Exum
	Valais	Zinal Rothorn	South Ridge
	Mt Blanc	Dent du Roquin	via Colonnes
	Canadian Rockies	Eisenhower Tower	Grassi
IV—	Selkirks	Uto Peak	SW Ridge
	Valais	Weisshorn	Schalligrat
	Canadian Rockies	Mt Louis	Route one
	Yosemite	Glacier Point	Terrace
IV	Purcells	Pigeon Spire	West Ridge
	Dolomites	Campanile Basso	Normal
	Bernina	Piz Badile	North Ridge
	Tetons	Symmetry Spire	Durrance
IV+	Cascades	Mt Rainier	Liberty Ridge

13

UIAA Grade	Area	Peak	Route
	Canadian Rockies	Mt Eisenhower	Brewer Ridge
	Dolomites	Cima della Madonna	Spigolo Velo
	Yosemite	Footstool	East Side
V−	Purcells	Snowpatch	Normal
	Black Hills	Devil's Tower	Durrance
	Canadian Rockies	Yamnuska	Red Shirt
	Yosemite	Arrowhead Spire	South Arete
V	Cascades	Baring	North Face
	Tetons	Grand	North Ridge
	Kaisergebirge	Fleischbank	East Face Dulfer
	White Mountains	Cannon Mtn	Sam's Swan Song
V+	Black Hills	Devil's Tower	Wiessner
	Dolomites	Cima Piccolo	Gelbe Kante
	Yosemite	Washington Column	Direct
	Purcells	Bugaboo Spire	East Face

Ratings

Some routes in this book are given rating values by the Decimal system. In an attempt to correlate all the rating systems, the UIAA has suggested that guidebooks adopt a common usage. The tables below give comparisons.

UIAA	Decimal	NCCS	British
I	I	FI	Easy
II	2 & 3	F2	Moderate
III−	4	F3	Moderately Difficult
III	5.0		
III+	5.1	F4	Difficult
IV−	5.2		Very Difficult
IV	5.3	F5	Severe
IV+	5.4		
V−	5.5		
V	5.6	F6	Very Severe
V+	5.7	F7	
VI−	5.8	F8	Hard
VI	5.9	F9	
VI+	5.10	F10	

Unfortunately, while all systems of grading are intended to give standard and concise information, such can be misleading. Therefore, we urge the user to read the whole description before deciding a climb is within his powers. The multiplicity of classification systems also leads to some confusion. Each new system that has come into use has not expunged use of older ones, resulting in climbers occasionally using parts of various systems of grading, without meaning to do so.

This text uses the Numeral system (as in Roper's Yosemite Valley Guide) and the Decimal system for individual pitch ratings. These will be found, where given, at the end of each route description. Grade I implies a climb normally taking only a few hours; Grade II, half a day; Grade III, most of a day; Grade IV, a long day; Grade V, more than one day; Grade VI, several days. All times given in this text are from the initial point indicated.

In many instances in this text will be found ratings other than as described above. It will be recognized that the editors are not personally familiar with each and every route described herein; we have, therefore, not ascribed to ourselves knowledge superior to the individual contributors, nor have we taken liberties with ratings assigned by them.

Registration is mandatory for all climbs in the National Parks, which includes almost all the more popular areas. This process is greatly simplified by self registration boxes in many locations which can be found by making inquiry at any Park entrance. Climbers should be sure to check out after completing the stated climbs.

Alpine Huts

Here are listed all the alpine huts in the area covered by this volume. Further data is under the specific areas served by each.

ACC huts are for the use of members of the Alpine Club of Canada and their guests only. It is important that a member of the Huts Committee be notified of intention to use the huts, so that overcrowding may be avoided. Local rules posted in each hut must be observed. Garbage must be packed out. All climbing must be reported to a responsible climbing authority, generally Park Wardens or the R.C.M.P. Newcomers should check for local conditions. Hut fees — Members $1.00 per night. Non-members $2.00 per night. Under 16 years of age $.50 per night. Keys can be obtained from the Club office, Banff, Alberta.

ACC ELIZABETH PARKER — 6800. In meadow ¼ mile W. of Lake O'Hara. Locked. One large and one small sleeping building. Large cabin has foam-covered area for 14 people and three stoves with adequate utensils, etc., coal oil lamps and Coleman lamp. Small cabin, bunk sleeping area for 8 people. Wood scarce.

Accessible on foot from Lake Wapta on Trans-Canada Highway, 7 mi — 4 hr; or by Brewster bus from Lake Louise to Lake O'Hara. Summer only.

ACC FAY — 6700. In Prospectors Valley up from Marble Canyon. One room and a sleeping loft for 12 people. Mattresses are deteriorating, new wood stove, utensils but no lantern. Poor shape.

Accessible from: Marble Canyon, Tokumm Creek and Prospectors Valley. True right hand of first creek before Kaufmann Lake. Cross creek before tree line. Hut is off the creek in heavy timber. 9 mi — 7 hr. **Due to be removed in 1973.**

ACC STANLEY MITCHELL — 7000. In the Little Yoho above Takakkaw Falls. Locked. Large living room plus kitchen. One large sleeping loft with foam for 26 people and one small extension with foam for 6 people. Three wood stoves, 2 Coleman lanterns and all utensils.

Accessible from: (1) Takakkaw Falls, up Yoho River on true right hand side to Laughing Falls, thence up true left hand side of Little Yoho River to hut. 7 mi — 4 hr (2) Emerald Lake to Yoho Pass, thence to Little Yoho via High Line Route. 9 mi — 7 hr.

ABBOT PASS — 9598. In Abbot Pass, National Parks. Two bunk rooms, six people apiece and a living-cum cooking room. Oil stove and Coleman (spastic). Mattresses and blankets. Utensils.

Accessible from: (1) Lake Louise, Plain of Six Glaciers and Deathtrap — 5 hr (2) Lake Oesa via Lake O'Hara and extensive scree — 5 hr.

ASSINIBOINE — 8700. Above Lake Magog headwall, Provincial Parks. Bunks for 12. Gasoline stove. 2 hr from lake. Ascend towards scree fan, bear right to ledge leading right (W), then switch left, passing snow patches to gentle gully leading to easier grade at top of headwall.

BALFOUR — 8100. Directly in Balfour Pass. National Parks. Burning barrel and biffy.

Accessible from: Bow Hut. Ascend up the Bow Glacier to the N and W of Mt. St. Nicholas. Pass around Nicholas to Nicholas-Olive Col. Descend the Vulture Glacier to Balfour Pass. 9 mi, 5-6 hr.

BOW — 8400 at the foot of the Bow Glacier, directly below Mt. St. Nicholas and ½ mi S. of the actual Bow icefall as seen from the Banff-Jasper Hwy. One large room with sleeping loft for 20 people, and foam for 10. Coleman stove, lantern, a few pots, pans and utensils. Drain sink, cupboards, fuel oil heater and biffy.

Accessible from Bow Lake on the Banff-Jasper Hwy. Cross Lake in winter or contour N side in the summer. Winter: Enter canyon at junction of the creeks which feed the lake. Follow canyon for ¾ of its length. Climb out on the E side and contour past the head of the canyon to the evident cliffs which are split to allow an ascending climb to the upper approach to the Glacier, roughly ¼ mi from the upper icefall of the Vulture Glacier. Ascend obvious steep gullies through cliff band and climb moderate slopes to the Hut. Summer: Climb cliffs at beginning of the canyon on the W side. Ascend diagonally to the SW slopes of scree, cliffs and glacial slabs towards Mt. St. Nicholas. Occasional cairn. 4 hr. 5 mi.

GRAHAM COOPER MEMORIAL — 9300. At the head of the Three-Four Couloir, Valley of the Ten Peaks. National Parks.

One wooden, aluminum-covered structure sleeping 6 people. Coleman stove, and a few pots.

Accessible from: Moraine Lake. Up Three-Four Couloir between Peaks Three and Four.

MT. EISENHOWER — 7400, on the obvious ledge system which traverses the mountain and below the third buttress from the E end. ¾ mi W of the gully, which splits the Tower from the mountain proper. National Parks. One room sleeping 8 people on foam. Coleman stove and a few pots and pans. Water in vicinity.

Accessible from: the Fire Lookout Road, 1½ hr — 2½ mi: or from the Warden's Cabin up trail towards Rockbound Lake approach to the Tower. Traverse the ledge system to the third buttress, 4 hr — 5 mi.

PETER WHYTE — at the foot of Mt. Thompson in Peyto Glacier Area. This is a route continuation of the Balfour area for spring ski touring. Local Ski Clubs. An orange fiberglass igloo with wooden floor for 8 people. One Coleman stove, table, two benches and foam insulated. Burning barrel and biffy.

Accessible from: (1) Peyto Glacier from Peyto Lake on the Banff-Jasper Highway. (2) Bow Glacier, Wapta Icefield, to Peyto Glacier from Bow Lake on the Banff-Jasper Highway.

Metric Conversion Table

Meters	Feet	Feet	Meters
2400	7874	8000	2438
2500	8202	8250	2515
2600	8530	8500	2591
2700	8858	8750	2667
2800	9186	9000	2743
2900	9514	9250	2819
3000	9843	9500	2896
3100	10171	9750	2972
3200	10499	10000	3048
3300	10827	10250	3124
3400	11155	10500	3200
3500	11483	10750	3277
3600	11811	11000	3353
3700	12139	11250	3429
3800	12467	11500	3505
3900	12795	11750	3581
4000	13123	12000	3658

Apology

As the reader will realize, this edition represents a modern revision and correction of its predecessors. Future editions will assuredly follow; like the present one, their accuracy will measure their value. Any publication such as the present one becomes obsolescent even while in the hands of the printer. The scope of the undertaking, moreover, is such that occasional errors and inaccuracies are unavoidable. We have inserted at the end of this work a number of perforated pages. These may be used by readers to rectify possible errors or supply any omitted data for inclusion in later editions.

We urge the users of this guidebook to show greater respect than some of our predecessors for the conservation and perpetuation of the wilderness areas they enter. The expanses of remote country so precious to mountaineers are daily dwindling under the pressure of men and machines.

To the limits of our ability we who frequent the hills should seek to preserve for our successors that which is still our good fortune to find.

WILLIAM L. PUTNAM
GLEN W. BOLES

American Alpine Club   Alpine Club of Canada

113 East 90th Street   Box 1026

New York City 10028   Banff, Alberta TOL OCO

FLATHEAD RANGE
(Blakiston Group)
49° to Tornado Pass

The airline distance from the International Boundary to Tornado Pass is approximately 75 mi. Broadly speaking, thiiss section of the range lies between the drainage of Flathead and Elk Rivers on the W and that of Waterton and Livingstone Rivers on the E. The principal passes crossing the Divide are Akamina, the Kootenay series, Ptolemy, the Crowsnest series — (Tent, Crowsnest and Phillips) North Fork and Tornado. North Kootenay Pass was crossed in 1858 by Lt. Blakiston of the Palliser Expedition. The average altitude of all peaks on the Divide is under 9000', Mt. Ptolemy, the highest peak S of Crowsnest Pass, and Mt. Erris, the highest peak N of that pass, being exceptions. The mountains are of bare limestone, without glaciers or permanent snow, and are seldom visited by climbers. E of the Divide, Mt. Blakiston is the highest summit, while W of the Divide only King Edward and Starvation Peaks surpass 9000'.

This is not an area of significant interest to the alpinist, although it offers much scenic attraction. R. M. Patterson's *Buffalo Head* deals with some of this region and areas to the N; *Trails of Wilderness Wanderer* by Andy Russell deals with other aspects. Trails extend through many of the passes and lumber access roads are not shown on many of the maps, but as in other areas, some trails shown even on recent maps are often illusory. Some of the peaks appear to offer challenging rock climbs. A number of one-day ascents of lesser points are chronicled in VOC 3–69.

From the Crowsnest area, trails also extend N, close to the Divide, and on both sides of it, by which North Fork and Tornado Passes may be reached. Many of the trails are in bad condition owing to fallen timber.

Crowsnest Pass was discovered in the late 1860's by Michael Phillips, an employee of the Hudson's Bay Co. at Fort Sheppard, and later a prospector in the gold rush near Fort Steele.

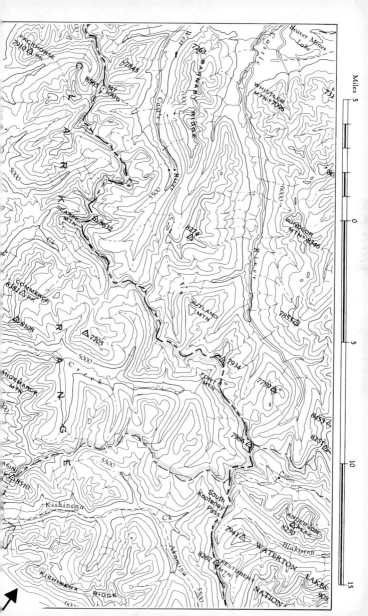

The pass was found during his trapping along Morrisey and Michel Creeks (CAJ *1*–108; *2*, 2–199).
Maps: 82G1; 82G10; 82G15.

King Edward Peak (9220)
One mi S of Starvation Peak, at W end of Kishenena Ridge.

Starvation Peak (9310)
In SW angle of Kishenena Creek with Beavertail Creek. 2 mi N of International Boundary.

Mt. Lineham (8950)
3½ mi N of Cameron Lake; 7 mi SE of Sage Pass.

Mt. Blakiston (9550)
5 mi N of Akamina Pass; S of Blakiston Creek; 5 mi E of S. Kootenay Pass.
F. R. A. July 1942, J. S. T. Gibson, G. Williams. From Blakiston Creek ascend side valley past a waterfall into a high corrie. Turn right above waterfall and up grassy shoulder — 3 hr — to rock of NE ridge. About 1000' of rock and scree to summit ridge, reached without difficulty. A direct traverse along the summit ridge is prevented by a vertical step of 200'. On the right (W) it is possible to descend and traverse around the vertical rocks. Thence up rocks and snow couloirs to ridge about 300' below summit; thence zigzagging ledges and more snow couloirs to top, a narrow ridge with cornice on S. A cairn was found on the summit. In the vicinity of Mt. Blakiston there are few other peaks worth climbing, many being rounded domes with pony trails to their summits.

Mt. Darrah (9036)
4 mi SE of former Corbin Station, CPR.
F. A. 1914, by the Boundary Commission.

Mt. Ptolemy (9228)
Apex of Flathead Range; 3 mi E of Ptolemy Pass; 6 mi S of Crowsnest Lake.
F. A. 1914, by the Boundary Commission.

Crowsnest Mtn (9138)

Isolated peak W of Livingstone Range; 7 mi NE of Crowsnest Pass.

F. A. 1904, T. E. Wilson and two guides, one of whom was *H. Kaufmann* (route unknown) (AAJ *4*–315).

2 — NW Ridge 1905, G. Harrower, P. D. McTavish, L. Stauffer, K. Whimster. From Coleman Station, CPR, follow Oldman River for 5 mi to W; turn N by trail leading to deserted lumber camp (4700). Work above timberline across W slopes to base of cliffs at NW angle. A series of chimneys, penetrates the first cliff belt — 400' — to slopes leading to final dome, 1000' above (CAJ *1*–108).

3 — N Face, 1915, F. W. Godsal. On N a large couloir offers a passage through the cliff belt. Much loose stone (CAJ 7–118).

Mt. Erris (9250)

Highest point between North Fork and Crowsnest Passes; 3 mi S of North Fork Pass.

F. A. 1913, by the Topographical Survey.

Gould Dome (9495)

S of Tornado Pass; 2 mi E of North Fork Pass.

F. A. 1913, by the Topographical Survey. From camp on Dutch Creek ascend ridge NE and climb E face of the mountain.

HIGHWOOD RANGE

These peaks lie entirely in Alberta and are separated from the High Rock Range by the S-flowing Highwood River. The N boundary is the Elbow River, along which a reasonable road (see intro to Kananaskis Group) exists. Access can also be from the Highwood Road. This group can be readily divided into those peaks, dominated by Mt. Rae, known as the Misty Range, and which lie to the NW of the angle between the headwaters forks of the Highwood River, Storm (W) and Mist (E) Creeks; and the main group which lies E of the Misty Range and surrounds in large part the sources of the Sheep River. Trail in Mist Creek passes (7650') W of Gibraltar Mtn to Sheep River Road. Trail up Burns Creek from Sheep River Road to lakes E of Mt. Arethusa. Trail from Kananaskis Road to Elpoca Pass (Elbow Lake), and on to Sheep River Road. Sheep River Road is occasionally closed to vehicles by a gate and at other times is almost impassable (4 fords, the southernmost being critical). Map, 82J10, 82J7.

Mist Mtn (10297)
W of Mist Creek (Highwood River), above its junction with Storm Creek; impressive NE face.

F. A. July, 1946 by three Blayney brothers, D. King. Via basin S of SE ridge. Gain SW ridge at 9200' and follow to summit.

2 — SW Ridge. Oct 1948 by E. H. J. Smyth and party.
From Sheep River and Bighorn Ranger Station, fording and refording river below Gibraltar Mtn to reach disused coal mine, from which a trail leads over to headwaters of Mist Creek. Thence via SW ridge (CAJ 35–44).

3 — SW Ridge. June 1971 by W. D. Gant, *A. Larson*.
From road on Storm Creek (Highwood River) gain SW ridge at 9500'. There join Route 2 and follow SW ridge throughout. 5½ hr up.

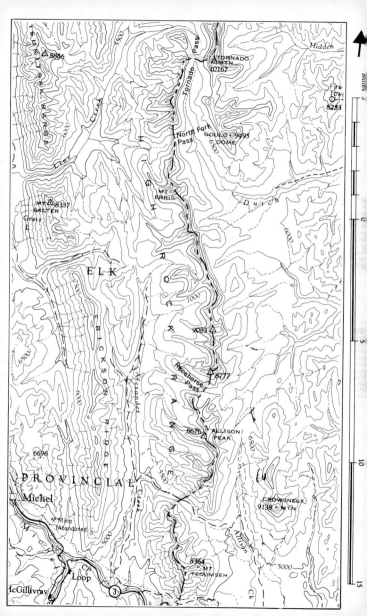

Storm Mtn (10153)

3 mi. NW of Mist Mtn; E of Highwood Pass; between heads of Storm Creek (Highwood River) and Sheep River (CAJ 35–45).

F. A. 1950 by G. Langille, E. H. J. Smyth. From the Kananaskis road at the pass. The main S ridge is gained from the W via a snow couloir N of a prominent gendarme. Thence N, the sharp crest being avoided by reaching a terrace of scree and snow 50' down on the E side. Easy rock leads to summit 400' above.

A July 1971 party kept to crest and descended via SW couloir (W. D. Gant, A. *Larson*) "Perhaps would provide a better ascent route on this rotten mountain."

Mt. Arethusa (9550)

4 mi NE of Elk Pass; NE of Mt Tyrwhitt; E of Highwood Pass.

F. A. June 1971 by W. D. Gant, A. *Larson*. From Highwood road via snow (gone in Sept) gully, on W slopes to SE ridge; scramble. 4 hr up.

2 — SE Ridge. Sept 1972, W. D. Gant, R. Weyand, A. *Larson*. From Burns Lake to Arethusa-Storm col, thence on SE ridge all the way. 4 hr up (under winter conditions).

Mt. Rae (10560)

E of Kananaskis River; 2 mi NE of Highwood Pass. The N drainage (with largest glacier in range E of Divide and S of Bow River) is the principal source of Elbow River (CAJ 35–46).

F. R. A. 1950, G. Langille, E. H. J. Smyth. From Highwood Pass via basin S of peak and steep scree to col (9650) in W ridge, thence to buttress at 10000' and S ridge to summit (cairn without record). Ascent 6½ hr.

In 1948 D. King and party reached the 10000' buttress from Rae-Arethusa col and S ridge after approach from Burns Lake. In Nov 1970 G. Bell and A. *Larson* attained same point with approach from Elbow Lake (Elpoca Pass) via Rae Glacier to

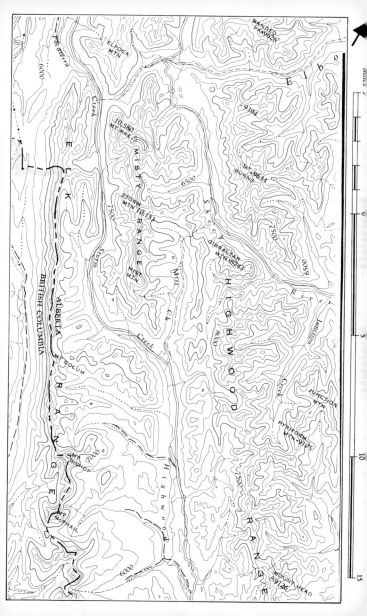

9650 col. 1½ mi E of summit. N of Burns Lakes is a prominent wall (*Gant Wall* — 9150′) facing E. This was climbed from Burns Creek in Sept 1970 by W. D. Gant, *A. Larson*.

Mt. Head (9126)

W of Eden Valley Indian Reserve; N of Highwood River. (This peak appeared erroneously on the Palliser (1860) and many subsequent maps as a point on the Continental Divide. Its historic significance is discussed in CAJ *13*–245).

F. A. circa 1934 by R. Patterson and party. From Wileman Creek via couloir between E and W summits. Rock slides in 1942–43 may have altered this access.

2—SW approach, June 1971, W. D. Gant, *A. Larson*.
Approach via Stony Creek to headwaters. Ascent was via first major rib S of the summit to ridge at 8500′, thence to main NW summit. Easy ascent.

Gibraltar Mtn (8743)

4½ mi E of Storm Mtn; 10 mi W of Sheep River Ranger Station.

An easy ascent from S or W; the E subsidiary summit (8450′) rising above Cliff Creek and prominent in the view from Sheep River road was first climbed in Aug 1970 by W. D. Gant, *A. Larson*, via rock rib at W of N face. 2½ hr from road. Party found cairn on lower point but nothing on main summit.

2—N Face. July 1971, W. Davidson, J. White
Cross river on beaver dam to base of face. Scramble up and left on ramp to gravel ledge and first bivouac. From here traverse down and right ascending past cave on easy slabs. This leads to a long system of dihedrals 200 yards E of the central pillar of the face. The fifth bivouac was on top of this pillar 2/3 of the way up the cliff. From here the route follows the center of the sweeping reentrant directly above the pillar. Three more bivouacs to the summit ridge just right (W) of the summit. This was a **long and severe climb,** the first extended aid climb in the Canadian Rockies. Many pitches were overhanging in their entirety. Descent was via second gully on W ridge. V1, 5.8; A4 A11 belays secured by bolt. 8 lost arrows; 6 knifeblades; 6 Leepers, 22 angles (½″ to 4″).

NE Ridge

5th Bivouac

North Pillar

2nd Bivouac

GIBRALTAR NORTH FACE

J. White

The ascent took 8½ days, complicated in part by bad weather. (CAJ 55–16).

Mt. Burns (9633)

5 mi E of Mt. Rae; between Sheep and Elbow Rivers — a triple summit, the highest in the middle. Entire crest traversed in July 1970 by W. D. Gant. *A. Larson* from Burns Creek via SW approach. Cairn without record on highest point. An easy ascent.

Cougar Mtn (9394)

3 mi NW of Mt. Burns; between heads of Elbow and Sheep Rivers.

Bluerock Mtn (9150)

4 mi E of Cougar Mtn.

Any mountain may be climbed safely under certain good conditions; and there is no mountain which may not be dangerous under other bad conditions.

Leslie Stephen

HIGH ROCK RANGE
(Tornado Group)

This section of the Divide is essentially a single continuous ridge of peaks throughout, comprising the High Rock Range and the Elk Mountains from Tornado Pass to Elk Pass, an airline length of about 45 mi. Almost all peaks are on the Divide.

Tornado Mtn is the highest. The area is drained by Elk River (Kootenay) on the W and by Livingstone and Highwood Rivers (South Saskatchewan) on the E.

Access to the S portion of this group may be had from the trail up Oldman River on the E and from trails in the valleys of Line Creek and Fording River on the W. Further N there is a road along Highwood River on the E and a road up Elk River from Natal which connects with the Kananaskis road (see Joffre Group). This road gives access to the Weary Creek primitive road which is not maintained but goes to Weary Creek Gap. 7 mi S of Weary Creek is a primitive road up Aldridge Creek to Fording Pass which is subject to mud slides in the spring. For the Kananaskis Road (1950) see CAJ 35–18, sketch map. See introduction to Flathead Range for literary refs.

Maps: 82G15; 82J2; 82J7; 82J10; 82J11.

Tornado Mtn (10167)
   E buttress of Tornado Pass. The first peak over 10000′ N of the International Boundary; 70 mi distant from same.
   F. A. 1915 by the Boundary Commission.

Beehive Mtn (9497)
   8 mi N of Tornado Pass, between Tornado Mtn. and Mt. Lyall.
   F. A. 1913 by the Topographical Survey.

Mt. Feuz (*Lyall*) (9684)

10 mi N of Tornado Pass; SE of Mt. Gass; the highest peak between Tornado Mtn and Fording Pass.

F. A. June 1972, Miss J. Brownell, *A. Larson.* From lower Todhunter Creek on W side, gain N ridge at 8300'. 3/4 mi along ridge to summit. 7 hr up. Descent via W ridge to 9100', thence down snow of N cirque. This might be a better ascent route.

Mt. Gass (9403)

NW of Mt. Lyall; between Chauncey Creek and Oldman River sources.

F. R. A. June 1972; Miss J. Brownell, *A. Larson.* An easy ascent from Todhunter Creek via SW slopes in 6 hr.

Mt. Pierce (9350)

One mi S of Mt. Farquhar; the highest point is just W of the Divide.

Mt. Farquhar (9530)

One mi N of Mt. Pierce; head of Cataract River.

Mt. Scrimger (9040)

6 mi S of Fording Pass; 2 mi S of Mt. Etherington.

Mt. Etherington (9440)

4 mi S of Fording Pass; S of Baril Peak; N of Mt. Scrimger.

Baril Peak (9837)

2 mi SE of Fording Pass; E of Mt. Cornwell.

F. A. 1915 by the Boundary Commission.

Mt. Cornwell (9750)

S buttress of Fording Pass: W of Baril Peak.

F. A. 1915 by the Boundary Commission.

Courcelette Peak (9987)

2 mi SSW of Fording Pass; SW of Mt. Cornwell in NE

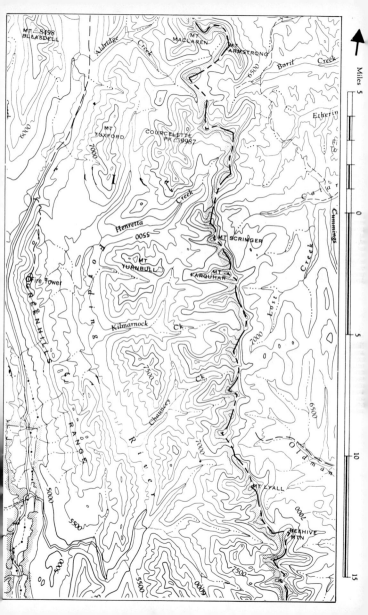

angle between Henretta Creek and Fording River. 2 summits, ½ mi apart.
F. A. 1915 by the Boundary Commission.

Mt. Armstrong (9261)

2 mi NE of Fording Pass; E of Mt. McLaren.
F. A. 1915 by the Boundary Commission.

Mt. MacLaren (9350)

2 mi N of Fording Pass; NW of Mt. Armstrong.

Mt. Muir (9050)

One mi E of Weary Creek.
F. A. 1970 by M. H. Benn, T. Sorensen.
From camp at Weary Creek Gap via W ridge. No difficulties, easy day (CAJ 54–80).

Mt. McPhail (9460)

One mi N. of Weary Creek Gap; the S peak of the Elk Mountains; S of Mt. Bishop.
F. A. 1970 by M. H. Benn, T. Sorensen
From camp at Weary Creek Gap via ENE ridge. 4 hr to summit over varied scrambling (CAJ 54–80).

Mt. Bishop (9350)

4 mi NW of Weary Creek Gap; NW of Mt. McPhail; SE of Mt. Loomis.

Unnamed (9050)

One mi S of Mt. Loomis
F. A. 1970 by M. H. Benn, T. Sorensen, E .Wagner.
Good trail in Loomis Creek to E.

Mt. Loomis (9260)

2½ mi NW of Mt. Bishop; between Elk and Highwood Rivers.

Mt. Storelk (9450)

5 mi SE of Elk Pass; SE of Mt. Tyrwhitt.
F. A. 1915 by the Boundary Commission.

Mt. Tyrwhitt (9428)
E buttress of Elk Pass; NW of Mt. Storelk.
F. A. 1915 by the Boundary Commission.

And why should not English convicts be sent to work in the Rocky Mountains?

A. R. Porter

Judging from our experience in the mountains, the only really dangeruerous animals are the black fly, the mosquito and the bull-dog (Fly).

A. P. Colman

FRONT RANGES

This fine cluster of peaks, about 15 mi long, lies mostly on the Divide between Elk and South Kananaskis Passes. The Joffre Group occurs at a sharp angle in the Divide where it transfers from one element of the parallel series of ranges that constitute the typical formation of the Rockies to the next westerly element. The culminating point is Mt. Joffre. The Italian Group is completely on the B. C. side and lies S of the Joffre Group in a ridge extending 12 mi towards Connor Lakes. S of Mt. Minton this group links with the Harrison Group to the SW.

Glaciers are numerous and extensive on the higher slopes and here the snow and ice scenery so characteristic of the loftier portions of the Canadian Rockies may be said to fully begin, thence extending almost continuously to the Sir Alexander Group, 280 mi to the NW.

Kananaskis Pass was explored by Capt. Palliser in 1858, and may have been crossed earlier by James Sinclair.

Ed il Re ci manda a dire che si trova sui confine e ha bisoqno di noi alpini per potarsi avanzar.

Alpini Song

ITALIAN GROUP

Culminating in Mt. Abruzzi, and entirely on the B. C. side, this is a ridge with local divide between White and Elk Rivers. To the SW of Mt. Minton it joins with the widespread but ill-defined Harrison Group. Most popular access has been traditionally by the Elk Pass to Petain Creek (see intro to Joffre Group). However, the new Elk-White Road (see Harrison Group) gives much access to the SE wing of this group which contains some little frequented country reaching in excess of 9000' over sustained distances. A primitive road and trail goes approximately 7 mi up Cadorna and Abruzzi Creeks from the Elk River road. Soft ground at Elk River. A road and trail in White River passes along the W side of these peaks, connecting through Sylvan Pass with the trail in Joffre Creek. The S portions of this group have been reached by good going in Forsyth Creek to the Connor Lakes. (Accessible by old road up Forsyth Creek from W side of Elk River).

There are still a number of unclimbed peaks, exceeding 10000', in this spectacular looking group, but due to the poor quality of the rock and the fact that the group is not very accessible, climbers have shied away. Map 82J6.

Mt. Ingram (9020)
2 mi E of lower Connor Lake; 7 mi SSE of Mt. Marconi.

Quarrie Ridge (9650)
This irregular area of unvisited high country lies N and E of Quarrie Creek (Elk River). Five distinct areas exceed 9000' in the 4 mi N towards lower Cadorna Creek. The mining access road (washed out in 1971) on the E side of Bleasdell Creek gives some access.

Mt. Minton (10010)
One mi S of Mt. Marconi, with glacier intervening.

Mt. Marconi (10190)
4 mi S of Mt. Abruzzi; between Forsyth Creek (Elk River)

and White River. No glaciers are shown on recent maps, on or near the Divide N of the International Boundary until Mt. Marconi (Lat 50° 22'), a distance of 97 mi. Permanent snow, however, occurs considerably further S (see Mt. Washburn).

Mt. Connor (9640)

2 mi SE of Mt. Abruzzi; E of head of Forsyth Creek (Elk River). S of Mt. Connor on a long ridge E of the Connor Lakes extending to Mt. Ingram are 6 distinct summits exceeding 9000'.

Mt. Lancaster (10350)

One mi SW of Mt. Abruzzi; a double summit on ridge extending toward Mt. Marconi.

Mt. Abruzzi (10717)

At head of Forsyth Creek, between Elk and White Rivers; SE of Mt. Cadorna.

F. R. A. Aug 1929 by Miss K. Gardiner, *W. Feuz.* From camp at a lake (6850') on the W side of the peak, the S ridge was gained and followed to the summit on which a collapsed cairn was found. Descent by N face and glacier. Ascent 5¼ hr; descent 3 hr (AJ *42–72;* CAJ *18–3l).*

Mt. Cadorna (10320)

2 mi NNW of Mt. Abruzzi; S of Cadorna Lake (6270'); E of White River.

F. A. Aug 1929 by Miss K. Gardiner, *W. Feuz.* From camp on White River 6 mi S of Sylvan Pass, the SW arete was attempted, but on account of difficulty was abandoned for the S face, which was then ascended diagonally to the SE arete, this ridge being followed — one hr — to the summit. Ascent 7¾ hr; total time, 14 hr (AJ *42–72;* CAJ *18–31).*

Mt. Swiderski *(Diaz)* (10350)

NW of Mt. Cadorna; Between it and Mt. Battisti.

Unnamed *(Battisti)* (10280)

N of Mt. Cadorna; between Cadorna Lake and White River.

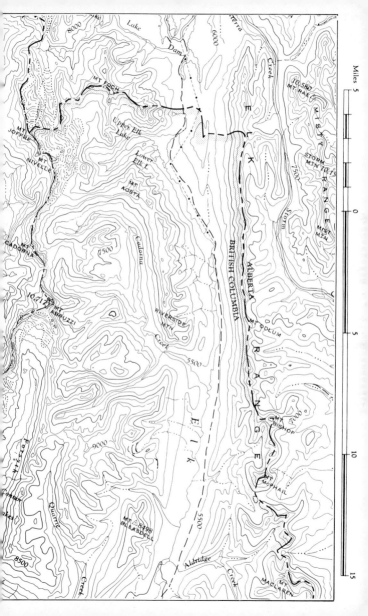

F. A. July 1964 by J. A. Bennett, W. S. Frantz, M. C. Godfrey, W. R. Joyce, W. L. Louis, *P. Fuhrmann*. From Cadorna valley (camp on S side of Coral Pass at timberline), via the hanging glacier on the NE face, gained from the main glacier over loose rock bands to its left. The left edge of the ice was ascended to its convex snow cap. A direct line was then taken through the last 400′ of rock faces to the summit^ (5¼ hr from camp) Descent by series of rappels (AAJ *14*–439; CAJ *48*–189; frontispiece, marked photo).

Unnamed (*Stiletto*) (9760)
1/2 mi N of Battisti; between Cadorna Lakes and White River (CAJ *48*–188).

People must adapt their thinking to the changed condition. Of course, no one should go off into wild flights of fancy, or make plans unwarranted by the objective situation, or stretch for the impossible.

Chairman Mao

JOFFRE GROUP

This group is sometimes referred to as the "French Military Group." These peaks are on or near the Divide and lie NW of Cadorna Creek. On the NE flanks of the group lie the attractive Kananaskis Lakes, while across the Divide to the S are the smaller Elk Lakes whence Elk River flows. The W flanks of the group are drained by White and Palliser Rivers.

This is another group not often visited because the rock leaves much to be desired. Periodically Mt. Joffre is climbed; usually the parties follow the S shoreline of the Upper Kananaskis Lake, then up past Hidden Lake to camp at Aster Lake. This trip can take up to 9 hr, since there is much bushwacking and deadfall along the way. It is advisable to keep to the left side of the creek (CAJ 48–182).

The best route of approach is S from the Trans-Canada by way of roads along Spray or Kananaskis (better) Rivers to Elk Pass. Alternatively one can approach from the S, by the highway from Coleman. 2 mi S of Elk Pass, at a small ranch, a good trail turns W and along the E shore of Upper Elk Lake terminating on the gravel flats at its S end, the site of the 1964 ACC camp (2 hr from Kananaskis Lakes). High camps are not required for peaks on or within the Elk Lakes watershed. To reach the Petain Glacier it is advisable to stay close to the creek and pass the headwalls on the right (E) of the waterfalls. Last timber is at the crest of the highest wall.

From the W a road from the sawmill at Canal Flats leads up Kootenay and Palliser Rivers, draining the W flanks of the group. Albert River is 34.8 mi from the sawmill, branch road goes 12 mi more up Albert River. Main road continues to Joffre Creek. A trail up Joffre Creek gives access to the W slopes of many summits and connects through Sylvan Pass to the White River.

From the E use the Kananaskis (Highwood) road; see CAJ 35–88, and sketch map facing p 48. Another route, used since

1952, starts from Natal and follows the power-line maintenance road E of Elk River to Elk Pass — 70 mi. A trail leads up from the dam at Upper Kananaskis Lake with branches to both of the Kananaskis Passes but is best via the N for connections to LeRoy Creek and Palliser River. Maps: 82J11, 82J6.

Unnamed (10050)
Double summit 8 mi WSW of Mt. Abruzzi between branches of White River (218844–SE point). A long ridge line extends S and includes 3 distinct points exceeding 9000'.

Russell Peak (10050)
5 mi W of Mt. Abruzzi; the S culmination of a long ridge with snowfields and alpine lakes; W of White River; 6 mi S. of Mt. Shatch.

Mt. Shatch (9460)
3 mi W of Sylvan Pass in S angle of Joffre Creek and Palliser River; at N end of a sub-range W of main White River. Between this summit and Russell Peak is a substantial area of glaciation and several high points exceeding 9000'.

Mt. Joffre (11316)
SE of Mt. Mangin; SW of Mt. Petain; at headwaters of White River; 50 mi S of Banff. The highest peak between the International Boundary and Mt. Assiniboine. The Petain Glacier on the E supplies the farthest sources of Elk River.

F. A. Aug 1919, by J. W. A. Hickson, *E. Feuz, Jr.* **N Glacier.** From camp on Hidden Lake, proceed up Foch Creek to a level about 500' above camp; thence gradually ascending toward the peak; 3 hr to timberline and ¾ hr more to edge of Mangin Glacier. Rope at about 9500', the route over the glacier gradually bearing to the left to the rocks. A steep wall is ascended to a snow saddle in the NE arete whence the summit is reached without difficulty. Ascent from camp 7¼ hr; descent to glacier 2¼; total time from camp 12¾ hr (CAJ *11*–19).

2 — NE Ridge. July 1952, Mr. and Mrs. G. A. Cunningham, J. More. From Elk Lake via Petain Glacier to NE ridge (loose rock) to subsidiary N summit. Thence over ridge to main summit without difficulty, except that ice-cap requires crampons. Total time from camp 13 hr (CAJ *48*–184).

3 — Winter Ascent, March 1970. E. Grassman, J. Jones, A. Simpson. Approach across Upper Kananaskis Lake through forest to camp at Aster Lake. Thence up Mangin Glacier on skis to bergschrund. Steps kicked straight up the headwall to summit (CAJ *53*–72).

Mt. Nivelle (10680)

SW of Mt. Castelnau; SE of Mt. Joffre; between Upper Elk Lake and White River.

F. A. Aug 1928 by J. W. A. Hickson, *E. Feuz, Jr.* **SW Slope.** From Sylvan Pass down White River and up gulch of creek from Nivelle Glacier to camp (5800'). To roping place on SW scree shoulder (9400' — 4½ hr). Thence over narrow ledges covered with gravel and up a steep couloir on the SW side of the mountain, circumventing several prominent ridge-towers. The top of the couloir brings one under a subsidiary point which is turned by a traverse on its left to a short, steep chimney leading to the narrow summit. Ascent 7 hr, descent 5 hr (AAJ *1*–3; CAJ *17*–32).

2 — NW Ridge. July 1964, Miss S. J. Evans, R. Matthew, P. Nielsen. P. Wis. From camp at Upper Elk Lake via Petain Creek and Glacier, turning S toward the col between Joffre and Nivelle. The long NW ridge was ascended on very bad rock, the final part being firmer. Route one is preferable (CAJ *48*–185).

Unnamed (*De Gaulle*) (9750)

Between Mts. Nivelle and McCuaig; the E shoulder of Mt. Nivelle.

F. A. July 1964 by R. C. Hind and ACC party. **S Ridge,** via Nivelle Creek, meadows at timberline being crossed to the lateral moraine of Elk Glacier, which is followed to the N fork of the glacier. Thence around the foot of the cliffs to level ice. The W side of the S ridge is gained and the ridge followed to the summit. Descent to the glacier from the NW ridge. 8–9 hr.

Mt. McCuaig (9460)

E of Mt. Nivelle; SE of Mt. Castelnau, W of Nivelle Creek.

F. A. July 1952 by Mr. & Mrs. G. A. Cunningham, J. More. Following ascent of Mt. Castelnau (which see), the summit of Mt. McCuaig is gained via the W saddle in 3 hr. Descent E of Mt. Castelnau; 5 hr to camp (CAJ 36–83).

2 — SE Ridge July 1964, parties of ACC. Follow E side of Nivelle Creek for slightly over one mi, then cross to W. A break in the lower cliff provides access up the first steep section (500'). At this point the main creek turns E, and a small subsidiary stream is followed up the right side of steep grass and scrub trees. The next cliff band is turned by ascending a 15' wall. The route goes straight on up, turning the next cliff around the right side and reaching the SE ridge at 8000' and following it to the summit (CAJ 48–185).

Mt. Castelnau (9850)

One mi SE of Mt. Petain; NE of Mt. Nivelle; SW of Upper Elk Lake; head of Castelnau Glacier (Elk River).

F. A. 1952 by Mr. & Mrs. G. A. Cunningham, J. More. From camp below Petain Glacier ascend glacier and up easy N face. Ascent from camp 5 hr. Descent by S face crossing to saddle W of Mt. McCuaig (which see) (CAJ 36–83).

2 — NE Ridge. July 1971, E. F. Boss, J. D. Fitzgerald, L. Putnam, A. Wexler. From camp below Petain Glacier at top of headwall via glacier to NE ridge. Thence up slabs and scree, turning at times onto N face — 3¼ hr up (App 39–114).

3 — W Ridge. July 1964, several parties of ACC. From Petain Glacier to a point almost due N of the mountain, the route turning S toward the Castelnau-Ney col (9350'). When near the col, the W face and ridge were ascended to the summit. Most parties have descended across the Castelnau Glacier, McCuaig-De Gaulle col (8350') and down the SE ridge of Mt. McCuaig (CAJ 48–185).

Unnamed *(Ney)* (10040)

N of Mt. Nivelle W of Mt. Castelnau. Rotten rock on SW (CAJ 48–187).

Mt. Aosta (9820)

S of Ilk Lakes; 2 mi E of Mt. McCuaig. A 6 mi ridge extends SE terminating in **Riverside Mtn** (9050) 5 mi E of Mt. Abruzzi. This ridge is uniformly smooth on the SW but crenelated with small steep valleys on the NE. Between the termini are 9 high points substantially in excess of 9000'.

F. A. July 1964 by R. Neave and ACC party. From Upper Elk Lake camp the Nivelle Creek trail is followed for 300', then its SE fork to its head in a col, whence the SW ridge and S face of the objective are used for the ascent to the summit. The upper part of the ridge is narrow (CAJ 48–193).

Mt. Fox (9752)

W buttress of Elk Pass; 2 mi E of Mt. Foch.
F. A. 1916 by the Boundary Commission.

Mt. Foch (10430)

4 mi W of Elk Pass; 2 mi NE of Mt. Petain; S of upper Kananaskis Lake.

F. A. July 1930 by Miss K. Gardiner, *W. Feuz.* **W Ridge.** From summit of Mt. Sarrail the SE ridge was descended to Foch Glacier and Snowfield, reaching the NW side of the objective peak, ascended thence by steep snow to its W ridge (rotten rock). Ascent from Mt. Sarrail, 4⅓ hr, descent 2½ hr (CAJ *19*–66).

2 — NE Ridge and **traverse.** June 1957. F. Crickard, R. Higgins. From camp near Upper Kananaskis Lake gain NE ridge by long but easy slabs to low NE summit. Traverse rotten ridge (exposed but easy). Pass final gendarmes on W face. 8 hr up. Descent by W ridge. Directions thoroughly confused in CAJ *41*–60.

3—S Ridge. July 1964 by D. W. Beers, T. Goodwin, W. R. Joyce, W. L. Louis, R. Neave, E. G. Petrie, W. T. Sharp. From camp near Upper Elk Lake via E side of Petain Cirque to crest of ridge via easy slopes. Attained 10000' high point in 5 hr. Party prevented from traverse to main summit by severe drop. Descended to alplands of Petain Cirque and crossed to base of W ridge. Then up snow and rock — easy

Mt Sarrail

Mt Foch

Mt Fox

Kananaskis Lakes

View to West

E. Cooper

going. A scree pile except for short rotten cliffs near top — 2 hr up. Descent 4¼ hr. Total time from camp — 14 hr (CAJ 48–184).

Elkan, lesser point (9050) at end of S ridge of Mt. Foch, and E of Petain Cirque ascended in 1964 by large party from ACC camp vias basin to NE and ridge; no rope.

Mt. Sarrail (10410)

Adjoins Mt. Foch on N; S of upper Kananaskis Lake.

F. A. July 1930 by Miss K. Gardiner, *W. Feuz.* From camp at Hidden Lake to Sarrail Glacier and snowfield leading to middle of NW side of mountain, whence the W ridge is reached by traversing. This is followed over snow to the top. Ascent 5 hr. The ascent was combined wiih that of Mt. Foch (which see) (CAJ *19*–65).

Unnamed (10250)

On the W ridge of Mt. Foch; 2 mi NNE of Mt. Petain.

F. A. July 1951 by R. C. Hind, L. Kneeling, M. K. MacGougan. From Foch Creek by easy scree slopes and little ledges (CAJ 35–90).

Mt. Marlborough (9750)

The N ridge of Mt. Petain at head of Foch Creek with ridge extending N towards Aster Lake.

Mt. Petain (10440)

On Divide NE of Mt. Joffre; N of Petain Glacier.

F. A. July 1930 by Miss K. Gardiner, G. Harrison, *W. Feuz.* **W. Face.** From camp below Aster Lake and up snow of Mangin Glacier to foot of W face — 4 hr. Thence up snow couloir and a rock face to base of towers. Traverse 500', thence ascending broken rock to S ridge and summit. Ascent 6¾ hr (CAJ *19*–70).

2 — NE Ridge. July 1964, P. D. Baird, J. A. Bennet, D. Durdin, W. S. Frantz, W. R. Joyce, M. A. Meredith, F. Noel, *P. Fuhrmann.* From camp by Upper Elk Lake the Petain tongue is circled behind NE shoulder to the N side of the mountain to a snow and ice couloir above which a traverse to right leads to a steep snowfield and the bottom of the NE ridge, which is followed over good rock to the summit. 5 hr from glacier. Descent by the NW ridge, avoiding steep part by traverse onto N face, 1½ hr down to glacier (CAJ *48–195*, marked photo).

Mt. Mangin (10030)

On Divide one mi NW of Mt. Joffre; SE of Mt. Cordonnier; head of Mangin Glacier.

F. A. Aug 1928 by J. W. A. Hickson, *E. Feuz, Jr.* **W Face** — From camp (7400′) at head of Joffre Creek, 250′ below Sylvan Pass, immediately W of Mt. Joffre. A huge couloir on the W side of the peak presents no difficulty. Rope used above 9500′ in order to pass an exposed chimney, 150′ from the top, above a narrow ledge below which the rock is undercut. Thence easy going to spacious summit. Ascent 4½ hr, descent 3¼ hr (AAJ *1–2*; CAJ *17–30*).

Mt. Cordonnier (9910)

E of Joffre Creek; S of Mt. Warrior; one mi N of Mt. Mangin.

F. A. July 1930 by Miss K. Gardiner, *W. Feuz*. From camp below Aster Lake via Mangin Glacier to depression between Mts. Cordonnier and Mangin, thence up S ridge to summit. 5 hr combined with Warrior Mtn (which see) (CAJ *19–67*).

Warrior Mtn (9750)

N of Mt. Cordonnier; head of Aster Creek.

F. A. July 1930 by Miss K. Gardiner, *W. Feuz*. From summit of Mt. Cordonnier (which see) descend its NE arete, connecting with the S ridge of Mt. Warrior. Ascent 2¼ hr (CAJ *19–67*).

Mt. Northover (9840)

SW of Mt. Lyautey; N of Warrior Mtn; W of Aster Lake.

F. A. July 1957 by P. J. B. Duffy, S. A. Heiberg, R. C. Hind, P. Rainier, Miss I. Spreat. From camp in Foch Creek via the S ridge, one knife-edge at 40° and a 50° slab being the only difficulties (AAJ *11–96*).

Unnamed (9720)

E of Mt. Northover; S of Mt. Lyautey.

F. A. June 1957 by Miss E. Burton, G. Feistman, B. A. Fraser, Miss J. E. Shaxon.

Mt. Lyautey (10110)

SW angle between Foch Creek and upper Kanaskis River; NE of Mt. Northover; head of Lyautey Glacier.

F. A. July 1930 by Miss K. Gardiner, W. *Feuz*. From camp below Aster Lake traverse S side of mountain to W side and gain S ridge over steep shelves of rock and scree. Rotten rock forces traverse on the face. Ascent 5 hr; descent 4¼ hr (CAJ *19*–67).

Onslow Mtn (9150)

S of Defender Mtn; NE angle between Joffre Creek and Palliser River.

F. A. 1957 by S. A. Heiberg D. K. Morrison.

From camp below Aster Lake to the Warrior-Northover col, which is crossed to the B.C. side to a gravel flat with a small lake.Thence over easy 9000' W shoulder of Mt. Northover and follow the watershed for 2 mi. The ridge divides, one turning NW to Defender; the other SW to the E ridge of Onslow — 3 hr from camp. A scramble of 500' leads to the main buttress. Start in obvious chimney, followed by other chimneys and short traverse to a steep exposed 20' wall with small holds. The E ridge is gained and followed, with traverse on the N face, to the summit (CAJ *41*–68).

Defender Mtn (9150)

3 mi S of S Kanaskis Pass; S of Mt. Worthington.

Mt. Worthington (9640)

W shoulder is **Mt. McHarg,** also climbed by Boundary Commission. One mi SW of S Kanaskis Pass.

HARRISON GROUP

This widespread but marginally glaciated group, lying entirely W of the Divide is best approached from the upper Columbia or Elk Rivers. It is an area of lesser mountaineering interest although its highest peak, Mt. Harrison, exceeds 11000', being the most southerly peak of the range to attain such height. The area is separated from the Tornado Group to the E by Elk River.

The Harrison Group could be considered in part as the SW wing of the Joffre Group, connecting with peaks near Mt. Marconi, across the pass at the head of Forsyth Creek and the Connor Lakes. Several peaks rise in the terminal arc of White River, N of Whiteswan Lake. A long S wing of this group continues into the angle of the Bull and Elk rivers. The high points range S from Mt. Hadiken and are discussed below.

The White River Road leaves Highway 95 3 mi S of Canal Flats Ranger Station and reaches the White River via the N loop of Lussier River, and Whiteswan Lake. Crossing the White just E of the Whiteswan Lake, it turns both up (E) and down (N) the White River. It follows the E side of the White downstream to join with the Kootenay and upstream to the head of the North White. A branch road to the head of the East White connects to a road running S the length of the Bull River. A road goes up the Middle White as far as, and into Rock Canyon Creek. A trail continues up the Middle White, connecting at its headwaters with the Joffre Creek Trail. A side trail up Maiyuk Creek leads over to Connor Lakes at the head of Forsyth Creek.

S of Mt. Mike and surrounding the head of Quinn Creek are several summits of the Quinn and Van Nostrand Ranges exceeding 9500'. However, none appear to offer serious challenge. A B.C. Forest Service road on the W side of Elk River runs 26 mi from Round Prairie to N of Weary Creek. This road gives access to various trails and primitive roads. In 1972 a logging company was working in Bingay Creek with 3½ mi of road up from Elk River. In Crossing Creek a road extends

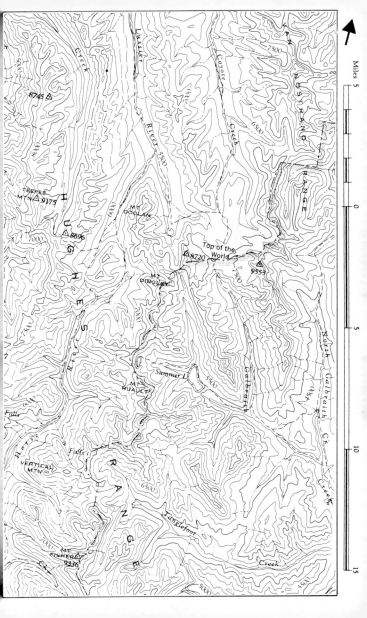

4 mi continuing as a trail over to Bull River, crossing some scenic alpine areas N of Mt. Hadiken. In Boivin Creek a primitive road goes 9 mi on the S side of Mt. Hadiken. Between Phillips Pk. and Mt. Vanbuskirk a primitive road runs 6 mi up the Weigert Creek. There is a road in Brule Creek for 3 mi on the N side continuing as a trail over Hornaday Pass 10 mi to Bull River. In Telford and Cummings Creeks an old logging road runs for close to 12 mi but is not maintained beyond the junction. Maps: 82J3 and 82J6. (Sketch map, CAJ 48–103.)

Mt. Nicholas (9260)
10 mi SSE of Whiteswan Lake; at W head of Blackfoot Creek; E of upper Coyote Creek.

Mt. Mike (10829)
5 mi SSW of Mt. Harrison at E head of Blackfoot Creek; lakes in valley to E (CAJ 48–107).
F. A. Aug 1969 by M. H. Benn, T. Sorensen, T. Swaddle. Via trail up Blackfoot Creek to camp in E tributary below SW ridge at 8000'. Ascend SW ridge over slabs. 4¾ hr from camp (CAJ 55–44).

Mt. Harrison (11020)
13 mi ESE of Whiteswan Lake; 6 mi SW of Bull-White divide; immediately S of head of last W tributary of Bull River.
F. A. Aug 1964 by W. Himmelsback, R. Hutchinson, J. Hutton, D. MacLaurin, B. Moss, P. Sherman. From camp at 6500' in valley to NE of summit through bush to saddle (9000') in NW ridge, crossing over scree to a further ridge, also crossed, leading to broad slope of debris below SW face. On the S side a stream from summit snow is ascended to the peak. 7 hr from camp (CAJ 48–104).
2 — W Ridge, July 1972. D. Forest, R. Matthews, L. Michaud, M. Simpson. From campsite at 7650' Route One was followed to the base of the first prominence on the W ridge. This was climbed on the S face by good ledges (some scree) returning to the ridge at 9450'. The ridge was followed to its highest point, then down 275' to a col. The second point

W of simmit was thence gained via the NW face. Thence alternately climbing and traversing, the W ridge was followed to the 10900' outlier. ¼ hr from there over final corniced ridge to main summit. 5½ hr from camp. Descent via same route to col W of 10900' then down snow couloir (1200') to avalanche debris and back to camp in 2¾ hr.

Mt. Folk (10130)

2 mi N of Mt. Harrison; on a ridge with 2 other summits of similar elevation.

F. A. Aug 1964 by W. Himmelsbach, R. Hutchinson, J. Hutton, D. MacLaurin, B. Moss, P. Sherman. By easy traverse SSW from Unnamed 10040' along intervening ridge (CAJ 48–104).

Unnamed (10040)

One mi N of Mt. Folk; 5 mi W of Munroe Lake.

F. A. Aug 1964 by Sherman party (see Folk) From camp as for Mt. Harrison, by easy scrambling in snow gully running SE from peak. Two of three summits were gained. 5 hr up.(CAJ 48–104).

Unnamed (10410)

Between Mt. Harrison and Smith Peak.

F. A. Aug 1964 by W. Himmelsbach, R. Hutchinson, J. Hutton, D. MacLaurin, B. Moss, P. Sherman. By way of the 9500' saddle E of Mt. Harrison and W arete of objective; 5 hr from camp.

Smith Peak (10260)

3 mi NE of Mt. Harrison; 6 mi SW of Mt. Peck (CAJ 48–108).

Mt. Peck (9583)

2 mi E of Munroe Lake (Bull-White divide) at S head of Lowe Creek (Elk River).

Mt. Hadiken (9470)

8 mi E of Mt. Harrison; N of Boivin Creek (old logging road from Elkford runs 9 mi up this stream)

Mt. Hornickel (9801)
E — W double summit one mi SE of Mt. Forsyth; 3 mi SSW of Connor Lake.

Mt. Forsyth (9820)
2 mi SW of lower Connor Lake, at head of Klookuh Creek.

O'Neil Peak (9230)
Double summit 2 mi W of lower Connor Lake; 9 mi S of Mt. Abruzzi.

Phillips Pk (9580)
5 mi S of Mt. Hadiken; 11 mi E of Mt. Mike, 5 mi N of Hornaday Pass.

Mt. Vanbuskirk (9250)
3 mi S of Phillips Pk; 3 closely spaced equal altitude summits at head of Weigert Creek (old logging road for 6 mi).
F. A. June 1972 Miss J. Brownell, J. Killam, *A. Larson* From camp on upper Weigert Creek circle to S side. Ascent via S cirque to W peak. 7½ hr up.

Mt. Terrion (9590)
7 mi S of Phillips Pk at head of Nordstrom Creek (old logging road for 4 mi on N side). 3 mi to WSW is **Mt. Frayn** of equal altitude but more accessible from Bull River.

Mt. Washburn (9970)
In forks of Telford and Cummings Creeks, at heads of both. One mi to N is **Mt. Gydosic** (9180′) 20 mi N of Fernie. The southernmost significant glaciers in the Canadian Rockies occur on the N slopes of this mountain at 49° 45′ 50″ N.

Mt. Dorman (9280)
10 mi N of Whiteswan Lake; 3 mi E of north-flowing (main) White River.

Franklin Peaks (9490)
7 mi N of Mt. Dorman; W of head of N White River.

ROYAL GROUP

This is a notable group, particularly its southern wing. It includes the Divide peaks from Palliser Pass N to White Man Pass. Most of the peaks are minor summits compared to the S wing, which lies entirely on the British Columbia side. All W drainage is to the Palliser River (or its N fork, Albert Creek) flowing S from Palliser Pass, which separates this group from the N ridges of the Joffre Group, lying to the E of the river. Its towers, precipitous walls, and glaciers, make it a landmark from all sides. Mt. King George is the outstanding summit.

According to Sir George Simpson, White Man Pass was crossed in 1841 by a party of emigrants, from the East, under the leadership of the Indian guide, Bras Croche (CAJ 28–213). In 1845, Father DeSmet ascended the Columbia and crossed the main range by this route, errecting his "Cross of Peace" on the water-shed.

Original approaches to this group were from the N, via Spray River and Palliser Pass. This is no longer used due to the very poor condition of trails. From the sawmill at Canal Flats a road goes N up the Kootenay River. The Albert River is 34¾ mi from the sawmill, and has a branch road continuing several miles further to an old camp whence approach was made in 1966 by crossing the ridges to the ESE and attaining the lake at the head of Queen Mary Creek. The main road continues E up Palliser River to Joffre Creek. At 7¼ mi from the Albert fork the road crosses a small creek down which the Palliser River is reached in ¼ mi. Ford the Palliser to the N bank and take the good game trail on the E bank of Queen Mary Creek. Easy going to the lake in 7 mi. Fynn Creek joins the Palliser about 6 mi upstream from Queen Mary Creek. This provides good access to the S peaks of the group. Ford Palliser River and follow game trails on E side of Fynn Creek 4 mi to headwall. Pass walls and cliff bands on the right to camp at foot of E lateral moraine of King George Glacier. **See intros to Joffre and Assiniboine Groups** Maps 82J11; 82J12

Mt. Princess Mary (10120)

S peak of group; one mi SE of Mt. King George at head of Fynn Creek (CAJ *11*–45).

F. A. 1928 by Miss C. Crosby, Miss H. Crosby, C. A. Willard, *R. Aemmer*. **SE Ridge,** from a bivouac at foot of S arete of Mt. Prince George, via couloir to the SE ridge, which is followed over firm rock to the summit. Ascent 6 hr.

2 — E Face. Aug 1970, I. Hamilton, W. Hurst (Kootenay Mountaineering Club).From KMC camp at foot of E lateral moraine of King George Glacier follow near direct line up east to summit. Ascent 2⅓ hr (CAJ *54*–82).

3 — E Face — SE Ridge Aug 1970, S. &. B. Port.From top of chute below Princess Mary-King George Col (see route 2, Mt. King George) make ascending traverse to foot of SE ridge.Follow ridge to summit except for one traverse onto E face beginning just below and ending just above vertical section (CAJ *54*–82).

Mt. King George (11226)

W of Palliser River; 7 mi S of Palliser Pass; 45 mi S of Banff. SW ridge has numerous high points exceeding 9000' along a 2 mi crest.

F. A. Aug 1919 by V. A. Fynn, *R. Aemmer*. **E Face** From bivouac above gorge on S side of Royal Valley ascend to flats E of Mt. Prince George without difficulty — 2½ hr. Traverse scree to S ridge of Mt. Prince George. Cross to King George Glacier and ascend into cirque between Mts. King George and Prince Albert — 4½ hr. Cross large bergschrund (often difficult) with steep ice above, leading to a firm but steep rock rib, just N of the hanging glacier on the E face of Mt. King George. The upper portion of rib was brittle and an ice ridge led to the main N arete — 2¼ hr. Thence the summit reached in 2 hr over fairly difficult rock and snow. Ascent from bivouac 11 hr; descent 7 hr (CAJ *11*–28).

2 — SE Ridge Aug 1970, G. Brown, J. Carter, W. Hurst. From camp at foot of E lateral moraine ascend King George Glacier to S of two rock chutes below Princess Mary-King George Col. Climb to top of left chute (chockstone), then traverse across top of 2nd chute to foot of SE ridge. Climb

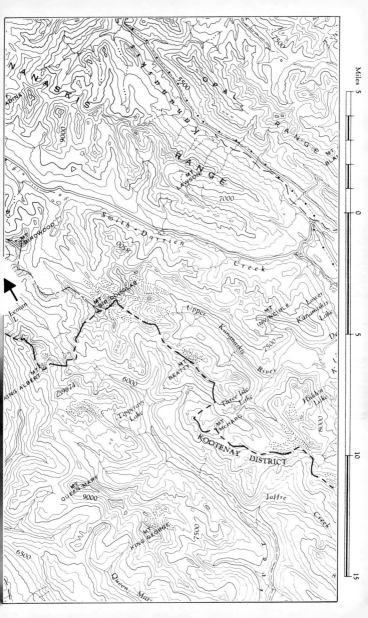

to top of SE ridge; some good pitches near top but rope not used. Then walk short distance on arete before traversing down on W side to level near bottom of notch. Summit attained over SW facing snow slope ending in easy rock and snow. On descent 2 rappels near top of SW ridge and another over chockstone in chute of bottom. Ascent 5½ hr. Descent 4½ hr (CAJ 54–80).

3 —W Ridge Aug 1970, D. Hurrell, R. Mill. From same camp as Route 2 ascend to head of valley W of Mt. Princess Mary. Climb narrow rock rib to left of hanging glacier to reach W arete of Mt. King George. Follow arete for 200 yards, thence traverse diagonally (sometimes steep) SW facing snow slope above hanging glacier until reaching final part of Route 2. (CAJ 54–80).

Mt. Prince George (9450)

E of Mt. King George; one mi ESE of Mt. Prince Albert. A scree slope on the S; accessible from King George Glacier (CAJ 11–45).

Mt. Prince Albert (10530)

Double summit one mi NE of Mt. King George; between Mts. Prince Edward and Prince George (CAJ 11–45).

F. A. 1928 BY Miss C. Crosby, Miss M. Crosby, Miss H. Pillsbury, C. A. Willard, *R. Aemmer* (N summit only). **SW Face:** From King George Glacier skirting SW slopes of lower S peak, and striking the S ridge of the higher N peak above the intervening saddle, the final 400′ requiring ½ hr. Ascent 4½ hr.

2—SE Ridge. Aug 1970, I. Hamilton, R. Mill, H. Ridge. From King George Glacier ascend SE ridge to S summit. Continue on to N summit and descend by original route. Ascent from camp at foot E lateral moraine 4 hr (1st ascent of S summit) (CAJ 54–82).

Mt. Prince Edward (10500)

Between Mts. Prince Henry and Prince Albert; probably the best climb after Mt. King George. Accessible from Royal Valley, up NE face to gap between it and Mt. Prince Henry,

Princess Mary

Mt King George

Mt Prince Albert

Mt Prince Edward

Mt Prince George

ROYAL GROUP FROM THE EAST

G. Boles

Palliser River

whence either peak can be gained by traversing to their W aretes.

F. A. Aug 1929 by Miss K. Gardiner, *W. Feuz.* **SW Ridge.** From camp on SW side of the mountain, up the W side, 4 hr to a depression on the SW arete, which was followed to the top, departing from the ridge at intervals to avoid unscalable bluffs. Ascent 5¾ hr; total time 12½ hr (CAJ *18*–30).

2—E & S Faces. Aug 1966, G. Brown, W. Hurst. From lake at head of Queen Mary Creek ascend cliff bands and scree slope to col between Prince Edward and Prince Henry — 4½ hr. Traverse to centre of E face, ascend steep couloir, thence zigzag to NE and SE ridges and final exposed pitch on S face to summit. Ascent 8½ hr; descent 4 hr (CAJ *50*–69).

Mt. Prince Henry (10587)

Between Mts. Prince John and Prince Edward (which see) at E head of Queen Mary Creek (AJ *42*–71).

F. A. Aug 1929 by Miss K. Gardiner, *W. Feuz.* **E Ridge.** From camp on Royal Creek, via rock rib between objective peak and Mt. Prince Edward to the SE ridge, 5 hr — thence to summit, 3 hr, the arete being very sharp in places. Ascent 8 hr; descent 5¼ hr (CAJ *18*–29).

Mt. Prince John (10620)

The SE and more massive but lower summit of Mt. Queen Mary; readily accessible from summit of the latter (CAJ *11*–45).

Mt. Queen Mary (10650)

The N peak of the Royal Group (see also Mt. Prince John) (CAJ 11–34).

F. A. July 1922 by C. F. Hogeboom, F. N. Waterman, *R. Aemmer* **W Face** — From Palliser Pass cross high pass (8850′) E of Mt. Back to Tipperary Glacier. Cross head of glacier and ridge NW of Mt. Cradock to head of Royal Valley. Descent slightly and then cross ridge S of Lockwood Peak to bivouac in valley NW of objective. Ascend to NW ridge overlooking valley W of Queen Mary (lake). Ascent was made largely on W face avoiding rock chutes between buttresses to reach NW ridge below gendarme and final cliff band. 9

hr from bivouac (CAJ *13*–102). This is an involved approach and no longer practical. Best approach is via Queen Mary Lake, SW of Mt Prince Henry (private cabin).

Some day after we have mastered the winds, the waves, the tides, and gravity, we will harness for God the energies of Love: and then, for the second time in the History of the World, . . . Man will have discovered Fire!

P. T. DeChardin

BRITISH MILITARY GROUP

This group occupies about 8 mi of the Divide between South Kananaskis and Palliser Passes, and extends a N wing into the angle between Spray Rivers and Smuts Creek. The E boundary is Smith-Dorrien Creek. The principal peaks occur in a compact cluster some 3 mi E of Palliser Pass, culminating in Mt. Sir Douglas.

The group is drained by Spray River on the N, by Kananaskis River on the E, and Palliser River on the W. Palliser Pass connects the sources of Spray and Palliser Rivers. The group is reached by the primitive road to the head of Spray Lake whence a trail leads S up Spray River (after 2 mi a branch leads right (W) to White Man Pass), for 15 mi to Palliser Pass connecting to trail and road system **described under Joffre Group.**

The smaller peaks on the N and E fringes of the group offer excellent rock climbing with many possible new routes while the peaks near Mt. Sir Douglas are of a more varied mountaineering nature.

The first peaks climbed in this group fell to the Boundary Commission in 1916. Between that time and 1922, when the ACC held a summer camp at Palliser Pass, many of the major summits were climbed and the group explored. Since that time the group has been visited mostly by parties looking for first ascents. In the last couple of years many local climbers have become interested in this area.

Access is easier via approaches on the E where a good fire road runs from Canmore along the E side of Spray Lake, up Smuts Creek and down Smith-Dorrien Creek to lower Kananaskis Lake. The Haig Glacier, which abuts the principal summits, can be reached from the S via trail in upper Kananaskis River. For a better approach to Haig Glacier, drive Spray fire road to lumber camp at Mud Lake. Drive over dam and follow lumber road staying to the right at each fork, to point even with the W end of upper Burstall Lake (in wet weather road may be impassable). Drop down through trees to gravel flats W of Lakes. Follow creek through woods to foot of glacier and up glacier to Robertson-Douglas Col. Haig Glacier is below other side of the col and can be reached by descending over loose shale. The col is just over 4 mi from Burstall Lakes and good going.

To Palliser Pass: cross gravel flats W of Burstall Lakes to an excellent trail leading up into the valley between Mt. Birdwood and long N ridge of Mt. Sir Douglas. Trail is on S side of creek. Steep climb at first to beautiful alpine valley. SW through valley, then up over alpine meadows to a W spur blocking view of Douglas. Drop down through meadows to SW to creek coming from glaciers on NW side of Sir Douglas (not shown on map). Follow creek to valley; there may be some bushwhacking before getting to Spray River. 2½ mi from here S to Palliser Pass. Maps 82J11, 82J14.

Mt. Putnik (9650)
One mi E of South Kananaskis Pass; in NW angle between Three Isle Creek and upper Kananaskis River.

Mt. Beatty (9841)
Between N and S Kananaskis Passes; a long sinuous ridge with E outlier (9250′).

F. A. 1916 by the Boundary Commission.

Aug 1919 J. W. A. Hickson, A. C. Stead, *E. Feuz, Jr.* From camp at the head of LeRoy Creek under W side of the mountain, 3 hr to N ridge which is then followed to summit; interesting climbing, rope advisable (CAJ *11*–17).

Mt. Indefatigable (8750)
SE peak of Battleship sub-group; W of the Lower Kananaskis Lake and N of Upper.

Mt. Invincible (8950)
One mi SE of Mt. Warspite; 3 mi SW of outlet of lower Kananaskis Lake

F. A. June 1957 by F. Crickard, R. Higgins, *H. Gmoser* From camp at Upper Kananaskis Lake an easy climb via W slope and S ridge.

Mt. Warspite (9350)
Between Mts. Black, Prince and Invincible; between head of Kananaskis River and lower Smith-Dorrien Creek.

Mt. Black Prince (9620)

One mi NW of Mt. Warspite; between Turbine Canyon and Smith-Dorrien Creek. Long ridge to N has several points of interest.

F. A. 1956 by B. Fraser, J. Gorrill, M. Hicks. From camp on Smith-Dorien Creek ascend cirque NE of objective. NE ridge attained to slabs and shale. No particular difficulty. 6 hr up. Descent by same route.

Mt. Maude (9980)

2 mi S of Mt. Robertson; N buttress of North Kananaskis Pass.

F. A. Aug 1922 by G. R. Adams, E. W. Crawford, M. D. Geddes, W. Gillespie, Misses M. P. and N. D. B. Hendrie, Miss J. B. Wilcox, *R. Aemmer*. From North Kananaskis Pass up scree and rocky watercourse (steep and smooth); thence E, gaining altitude to SE arete half-way between summit and col separating peak from E ridge. Broken poorly-defined E arete to summit. Ascent 7 hr Descent by arete and snow on Haig Glacier side to E col, thence down scree to Maude Lake; 5 hr (CAJ *13*–117).

Mt. Le Roy (9750)

2 mi E of Palliser Pass at head of Palliser River. Three high points 1½ mi S of Mt. Sir Douglas.

Mt. Williams (8950)

W outlier of Mt. Sir Douglas; E buttress of Palliser Pass.
F. A. 1922 en route to Mt. Sir Douglas.

Mt. Monro (10145)

One mi S of Mt. Sir Douglas; 3 mi E of Palliser Pass (AJ *33*–204, picture).

Mt. Sir Douglas (11174)

2 mi ENE of Palliser Pass. The highest peak between Palliser and North Kananaskis Passes. Attempt in 1919 on SW ridge by V. A. Fynn, *R. Aemmer* (AJ *33*–204, picture).

F. A. Aug 1919 by J. W. A. Hickson, *E. Feuz, Jr.* **W Ridge.** From camp one mi N of Palliser Pass, cross the valley to the

E and reach the NW side of the mountain, where two parallel glaciers descend to 7500' and 7000'. Ascend the W (lower) glacier to the W arete — 5 hr from camp. The arete is rotten with steep pinnacles, passed on S to ascend a big couloir up the SW face. From the top of the couloir traverse left and ascend a short couloir to loose rocks below the first summit — 7½ hr from camp. The E summit (100' higher) is quickly reached over a sharp rock ridge (CAJ *11*–14 — marked picture). Descent to foot of glacier 2¾ hr, total from camp 12 hr. Variant approach to W arete via SE glacier in 1922 (CAJ *13*–124, picture).

2 — NW Face. July 1971 G. Boles, D. Forest, G. Scruggs. From camp in meadows (7500') S of Mt. Birdwood. S over meadows to ridge running W from long NE ridge of Mt. Sir Douglas. Climb over ridge, then down a gully to moraines leading to twin glaciers N of the mountain. Ascend W fringe of higher (E) glacier to W base of face. Climb a snow ramp leading up in to centre of face crossing one deep chute. Then straight up for 500'. Party angled left over steep snow under a protecting rock overhang to the NE ridge. Heavily corniced ridge followed to the main summit in 7 hr. Party climbed face completely on snow; crampons used (early in summer). Descent over W summit, then W ridge to Col then down W of two N glaciers.

3 — N Ridge. Traverse Aug 1931, O. Stegmaier, *H. Wittich.* From camp E of Spray River at waterfall from glaciers on NW side of mountain, ascend W of glacier to rocks at foot of lower W summit. Chimney and crack to saddle between this and main peak, 4½ hr. Thence over knife-edge of ridge southward ¾ mi to peak. Ascent 9 hr. Descent over W ridge to Palliser Pass and camp, 4 hr. (CAJ *20*–164).

4 — E Ridge. Traverse June 1970, A. Cole, D. Lampard, C. Locke. Approach via Burstall Lakes, Creek and Glacier attain steep E ridge at col between Sir Douglas and Robertson. No serious difficulties although party bivouacked on W ridge below summit (CAJ *54*–80).

Mt. Robertson (10480)
    One mi N of Mt. Munro; E of Mt. Sir Douglas (CAJ *12*–50; *13*–7 attempts).

MT SIR DOUGLAS

South Ridge

North Ridge

G. Boles

East Arête

F. A. Aug 1928 by J. W. A. Hickson, *E. Feuz, Jr.* From camp (7250') near Turbine Canyon via Maude Brook to Haig Glacier, which is ascended to Sir Douglas-Robertson col, 4 hr. The SW ridge soon becomes extremely narrow and is followed nearly to the ACC cairn. A descent is then made over steep slabs for 100' to a ledge from which the summit cliffs are traversed for 300'. The pointed summit is attained after the passage of 20' of precipitous rotten rock. Ascent 6¼ hr; descent to col, 2¼ hr; to camp 2¾ hr (AAJ *1–5*; CAJ *17–35*).

Mt. French (10610)

Between Mt. Robertson and Mt. Smith-Dorrien at head of upper Kananaskis River; 4 mi E of Palliser Pass.

F. A. Aug 1921 by H. S. Hall, Jr. M. Morton, Jr., *E. Feuz, Jr.* From camp on Maude Brook at spring above Turbine Canyon. Through woods to Haig Glacier which is crossed to neve and the French-Jellicoe Saddle reached at lowest point, 2 hr. Follow SE arete over easy but rotten rock to low S peak, 1¾ hr. The ridge narrows for 120', following which a short scramble leads to central and highest point. Ascent from camp, 4¾ hr (App *15–324*; CAJ *12–38*).

Mt. Jellicoe (10165)

SE of Mt. Robertson, head of upper Kananaskis River.

F. A. 1916 by the Boundary Commission.

Aug 1922 E. W. Crawford, M. D. Geddes, W. Gillespie, Misses M. P. and N. D. B. Hendrie. From Kananaskis River (Turbine Canyon) cross Haig Glacier to SW face. Long snow slope leads to steep scree and rock outcrop (fossils), from which the SE arete is reached. Broken rock and two short chimneys lead to narrow ridge and double summit. Ascent 4¾ hr (CAJ *13–117*).

Mt. Smith-Dorrien (10350)

One mi E. of Mt. French; at head of upper Kananaskis River.

F. A. 1933 by Mr. & Mrs. Fraser, *E. Feuz, Jr.* From camp on upper Kananaskis River (Turbine Canyon) ascend small glacier E of Mt. Jellicoe to col between Mts. French and Smith-Dorrien. Thence over steep rocks of W arete to summit. Ascent 6 hr; descent 5 hr.

Unnamed (10470)
One mi N of Mt. French; NW of Mt. Smith-Dorrien; E of head of French Creek.

Mt. Murray (9920)
One mi N of Mt. Smith-Dorrien; in S angle between French and Smith-Dorrien Creeks.
F. A. Aug 1972 by C. Findley, P. Findley, M. Gould, P. Poole, J. Noakes, *B. Schiesser*. Easy ascent from French Creek up meadows and scree to summit. 2½ hr from peak to NE.

Unnamed (10450)
One mi N of Mt. French.
F. A. Aug 1972 by G. Boehnisch, C. Findley, P. Findley, M. Gould, J. Noakes. Up French Creek 5 mi to base of glacier. Then turn E and up bowl towards the ridge (10150) between French and objective. Easy rock and scree to summit. 7 hr from Mud Lake.

Unnamed (*Cegnfs*) (9210)
Last peak on ridge N of Mt. French; SE of French Creek.
F. A. Aug 1972 by C. Findley, P. Findley, M. Gould, J. Noakes, *B. Schiesser*. Easy ascent from French Creek. Up one mi past last road, then up (S) through easy timber and meadows. Scree and easy rock to summit. 4 hr to summit.

Unnamed (*Piggy Plus*) (9050)
1½ mi N of Mt. Robertson.
F. A. July 1972 by M. Brown, I. Carruthers, D. Cobb, T. Colwell, B. Seyforth, *B. Schiesser*. Ascend logging road S of upper Burstall Lake and continue up valley to attain the N ridge. Follow ridge to summit. 4½ hrs to summit. Descent via S ridge required difficult down climbing. Easy descent to E from the saddle.
2 — S Ridge 1972, I. Carruthers, C. Findley, P. Findley, M. Gould, C. Locke, L. Locke, J. Noakes. Ascend S ridge; F5 climbing, ½ way up ridge a narrow 150′ chimney was climbed. Descend by N ridge ½ way to base of mountain, then down E face to high valley, followed to Burstall Lakes.

Unnamed (*Whistling Rock Ridge*) (9610)

N of the 2 high points on the ridge; 1½ mi N from Sir Douglas

F. A. July 1972 by C. Findley, P. Findley, M. Gould, J. Noakes, P. Poole, M. Rosenbaum, S. Sabey, *B. Schiesser*. The ridge was attained on the N end. Ridge followed to final buttress. Here traverse on E side for 200′ to top of large pillar. Ascend directly up the first gully for 80′ and then left (S) and onto easy climbing to summit ridge. 8 hr to summit (large group.)

Mt. Burstall (9050)

5 mi NE of Palliser Pass; between Burstall and French Creeks; 2 mi SW of Mud Lake. A long high ridge extending S to join Mt. Robertson has other high points of comparable elevation.

F. A. July 1972 by M. Brown, I. Carruthers, C. Cobb, B. Seyforth, *B. Schiesser*. Ascend logging roads to W. Attain N ridge by climbing S side of major gully which leads to it from W face. 3 rope lengths of climbing to the ridge. Easy climbing from here to summit. 5 hr to summit. Descent via S ridge: 2 rappels and down climbing. Later descent by E ridge found better.

Mt. Birdwood (10160)

2 mi SE of Mt. Smuts; 3½ mi NE of Spray Pass; head of Birdwood Creek (CAJ *12*–41). In this vicinity are a number of minor peaks with good rock offering interesting varied climbing (CAJ 54–80).

F. A. July 1922 by C. F. Hogeboom, F. N. Waterman, *R. Aemmer*. From camp E of N end of Leman Lake, follow draw on E side of alley to top of ridge 8500 — 2 hr. Cross to, then climb 900′ talus slope to rock at base of SW face. Follow ledge to right (S) for 300′ to nose, passed to first chimney. Chimney widens to a 300′ gully (rotten rock) thence up left to a steep narrow chimney, last 30′ of which widens out with steep smooth walls. Top of chimney vacated to left. Thence open climbing to top of small buttress. From here a ridge (rotten rock) leads to main mountain, dropping slightly. Climb up face to long diagonal gully to the left which comes out on ridge, then short scramble over rotten rock to summit. 7½ hr from camp (CAJ *13*–110, picture).

2 — **E Ridge.** July 1972 by M. Brown, I. Carruthers, D. Cobb, T. Colwell, B. Demming, B. Seyforth, *B. Schiesser*. From Burstall Lakes up short scree slope to attain E ridge. Climb excellent limestone for 1400'. Ridge gets steeper and smoother for 200' (6 pegs placed) and for 15', 5.7. The ridge continues for 500' with good rock then merges into the NE face. Climb a series of gullys working E to the summit ridge. 13 hr with large party. Since done in 8 hr.

Pigs Tail (9260)
Lower E point of Mt. Birdwood.

F. A. 1971 by C. Locke, L. Locke, J. Tanner. **NE Face.** Prominent gully in centre of face climbed to ½ way point, from here traverse left to right edge of slab. Edge of slab followed to ridge then to summit. Easy descent by W ridge to col. F6.

Unnamed (9100)
One mi NE of Mt. Birdwood; NW of Burstall Lakes

F. A. 1970, C. Locke, L. McKay. **SE Face.** Generally keep between two obvious cracks in the face, then final ridge to summit. Descent to col to SW then to valley. 3¾ hr up, ½ down (CAJ *54*–80).

Mt. Smuts (9640)
2 mi NW of Mt. Birdwood; between Spray River and Smuts Creek.

F. A. 1926 by H. S. Crosby, Miss M. Crosby, Miss M. Kennard, C. A. Willard, *R. Aemmer*. From camp at NE angle between Birdwood Creek and Spray River, over scree and firm rock. Ascent 7 hr.

Mt. Shark (9140)
3 mi SSE of upper end of Spray Lake; at NW end of Spray Mtns; 2 mi NW of Mt. Smuts.

Lockwood Peak (9450)
3 mi SW of Palliser Pass; 3 mi N of Mt. Queen Mary.

Mt. Cradock (9950)

1½ mi SE of Mt. Back; at head of Tipperary Creek.

Unnamed (*Tipperary*) (9710)

½ mi NW of Mt. Cradock; W outlier of same.

F. A. 1919 by Mr. & Mrs. C. B. Eddy, Mr. & Mrs. V. A. Fynn, *R. Aemmer.* From camp near Belgium Lake via Tipperary Glacier to SE ridge. Descent via NW ridge. Easy.

Mt. Back (9874)

One mi S of Mt. King Albert; 2 mi SW of Palliser Pass between King Albert and Palliser Rivers (CAJ *13*–250).

F. A. 1916 by the Boundary Commission, via SE ridge from Palliser Pass.

Mt. King Albert (9780)

½ mi W of Mt. Queen Elizabeth; 2 mi W of Palliser Pass on the Divide.

F. A. Aug 1922 by G. A. Gambs, K. G. McClelland, T. B. Moffat, H. E. Sampson, D. R. Sharpe, *Ern. Feuz.* From camp at Palliser Pass via N col and arete to break in arete. 500′ below summit — 2¼ hr. Traverse short distance W over 40′ of difficult rock, after which the summit is easily reached. Ascent from camp 4½ hr (CAJ *13*–93).

Mt. Queen Elizabeth (9349)

E of Mt. King Albert; W buttress of Palliser Pass.

F. A. 1916 by the Boundary Commission.

Mt. Leval (9050)

NW buttress of Spray Pass; 2 mi E of White Man Mtn.

F. A. July 1972 by C. Findley, P. Findley, M. Gould, J. Noakes, C. Locke. Ascend NW from Leman Lake up S face of peak.

White Man Mtn (9768)

2 mi S of White Man Pass at E head of Cross River; on the Divide.

Mt. Vavasour (9250)

W of Spray River; 2 mi NW of Spray Pass; 2 mi ESE of White Man Pass (CAJ *13*–258).

Mt. Warre (9050)
2 mi E of White Man Pass; in S angle between White Man Creek and Spray River (CAJ *13*–258).

Mt. Soderholm (9682)
6 mi S of White Man Pass; 3 mi NE of Miller Pass, S of Cross River.

Tangle Peak (9143)
11 mi WSW of King Albert; W of Albert River; E angle between Cross and Kootenay Rivers; 3 mi SW of Miller Pass.

II CORINTHIANS-11
26, 27
In journeyings often, in perils from floods, in perils in the wilderness, in perils from false brethren; in labor and hardships, in many sleepless nights, in hunger and thirst, in fastings often, in cold and nakedness.

KANANASKIS GROUPS

Here are included those ranges lying E of the Divide and generally reached from the Kananaskis (Coleman) road, which offers many well maintained campsites. These peaks are E of Smith-Dorrien Creek and Spray Lakes, N of Elbow River and S of those included in the Environs of Banff. Being on the drier side of the Divide, there is little glaciation of importance, although certain routes require snow and ice techniques.

All mountains are destined to pass through several stages . . . . . inaccessible . . . . . the most dangerous point in the Alps . . . . . . a good hard climb, but nothing out of the way . . . . . a perfectly straight-forward bit of work . . . . . an easy day for a lady . . . . .

Leslie Stephen

FISHER RANGE

There are not too many peaks of any real mountaineering significance in this range, but there are some short rock faces excellent for training in the early season. This range has some fascinating scenery for hikers or climbers who prefer easier rock scrambling. Excellent views can be enjoyed into the higher ranges to the W and the plains to the E.

These peaks are N of Little Elbow River and border on the plains. A road along Jumpingpound Creek provides access to numerous trails leading up the valleys draining E into the plains. This road connects via Ford Creek with the Little Elbow road, which in turn runs along the SE border of these groups to join the Sheep River road. Trail connects across Elpoca Pass with Kananaskis road.

A trail crosses the N extremity of this range one mi S of Barrier Lake, but provides no access to points of mountaineering interest. An old trail in Evans-Thomas Creek (2 mi N of Limestone Mtn) traverses the height of land into Little Elbow drainage providing good access from the W to the higher summits of this range.

A road branches N off the Elbow River road at Canyon Creek, following Canyon Creek, it turns W and passes the ice caves to the S of Moose Mtn. Many people have been visiting the caves in recent years. The road has deteriorated much, so access is on foot for last few miles. Maps 82J14; 82J15.

Mt. McDougall (8945)
E of Evans-Thomas Creek, S of head of Wasootch Creek; 6 mi N of Fisher Pk. Highest point appears to be one mi NW of main massif. This is the N high point of the range. 3 mi E of summit, at end of ridge with many points exceeding 8500', lies **Mt. Bryant.**

F. A. 1952 by ACC party. No difficulties.

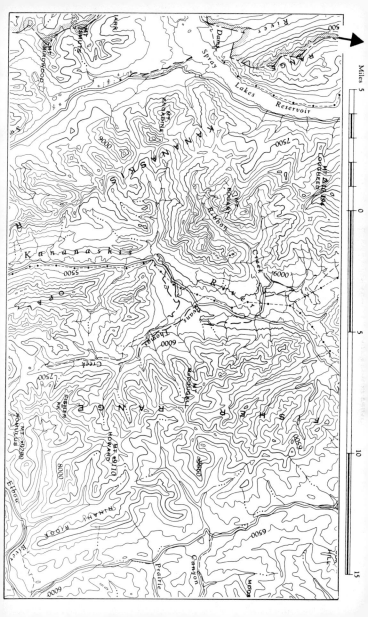

Unnamed (9220)

At W head of Canyon Creek; 3½ mi N of Fisher Pk (386367).

Mt. Howard (9110)

3 mi NE of Fisher Pk; at head of Canyon Creek. NE of this peak is **Compression Ridge,** along S bank of Canyon Creek.

Fisher Peak (10015)

Between forks of Evans-Thomas Creek; 5 mi SE of The Wedge.

F. A. in June 1950 by J. F. Tarrant party. **NW ridge.** Approach by trail in Evans-Thomas Creek to bivouac at 8200'. Thence moderate climbing with interesting pitches (CAJ 35–48).

Unnamed (9580)

One mi S of Fisher Pk; at W of head of Shoulder Creek.

Mt. Romulus (9290)

2 mi SE of Fisher Pk, N of Little Elbow River.

No information on first ascent.

Sept 1966, B. Fraser, E. Kinsey, R. Matthews, R. Peters, J. Tarrant. From forestry road on Little Elbow River, the river was waded at a point slightly E of the base of S ridge which was followed to the summit crossing en route one long stretch of slabs on which there was one short section of thin holds. No difficulty was encountered — 3½ hr. A large cairn was found on the summit from which the cairn on the summit of **Mt. Remus** (8820') one mi ENE was clearly visible.

KANANASKIS RANGE

This is the second line of peaks, being separated from the Opal Range to the E by the Kananaskis River and bounded on the W by Smith-Dorrien Creek. Very little climbing was done in this area prior to the forestry roads and at time of printing this group offers opportunity for many new routes.

The best approaches to the range are via the fire road on the W or the Kananaskis Road on the E. The Kananaskis River is in most places too deep to ford, but a road leading to the Snowridge Ski Area near The Fortress gives access to the peaks in that vicinity.

A trail up Ribbon Creek gives access towards Mt. Bogart, branching at the forks. A poorly defined trail (washed out in long stretches) leads to Sparrowhawk and Lougheed. The trail along the S fork of Ribbon Creek is a good one, leading by a spectacular waterfall to an alpine lake — 6800' S of Mt. Bogart. Low passes W of here lead to the W side of the range. Map 82J14.

Mt. Lorette (8160)

7 mi NNE of Mt. Kidd; the first high point on W of Kananaskis River after entering the mountains. S across the road from this peak, 3 hr up Wasootch Creek on the W is the spectacular Wasootch Tower. This has been climbed by several parties.

F. A. May 1952 R. C. Hind, B. Richardson, L. Keeling, J. Manry, J. Dodds, C. McAllister. S ridge is popular (including an interesting finger traverse). The S ridge is approached by crossing the Kananaskis River on the Ribbon Creek road, then following a crude road N along the power line (CAJ 36–144).

Mt. Lougheed (10190)

7 mi SE of Three Sisters; 3 mi E of Lower Spray Lake. Ridge extending for 2 mi has 3 points exceeding 10000'; NE face is impressive. The name **Wind Mtn** is now applied to a minor point one mi N of the middle summit. The name

(see under Rundle Peaks) **Windtower** is applied to a subsidiary summit (8850) one mi NW of the massif.

NW Peak. F. A. 1889 by W. S. Drewry, A. St. Cyr (T. E. Wilson, in a list sent to Mrs. Schaffer, claimed to have made the climb two days earlier). From Upper Spray Lake at W base of peak; 500′ of short cliffs below summit.

SE summit 1951, R. C. Hind and party, from Ribbon Creek via SSE ridge. This is an extremely pleasant rock climb following the S ridge. Two steps on the ridge are bypassed by traversing out to the right, onto the SE face. Believed to be the second ascent, but the first ascent of the SSE ridge. Descent via SW ridge, then snow slopes. (CAJ 36–145)

Traverse S – N, 1967, D. Gardner, N. Liske.

Traverse N – S, 1970, J. Atkinson, G. Boles, A. Cole, D. Forest. Approach was made from fire road E of Spray Lakes via creek bed to S ridge of N peak. Pleasant going to peak in 4½ hr. Less than 2 hr along ridge to point 10190. ½ hr to lesser third summit. SE summit attained by shelves to right (S) of gully to SW ridge. 2 hr from final col to summit. 15 hr from Spray Lake to Ribbon Creek (CAJ 54–83).

Mt. Sparrowhawk (10240)

2 mi S of Mt. Lougheed; W of Ribbon Creek. Impressive faces on N and NE towards Mt. Lougheed (234459).

F. A. 1947 by R. C. Hind, L. Parker, Mr. & Mrs. H. H. Rans. From camp at forks of Ribbon Creek via the ESE ridge. Near summit an overhang and cliffs required traverse to the S ridge (CAJ 35–48).

Mt. Bogart (10315)

4 mi SSE of Mt. Lougheed; 5 mi E of Spray Lake (236412).

F. A. 1930 by Miss K. Gardiner, W. *Feuz.* From fly-camp S fork of Ribbon Creek, via S side of mountain up shelving rock and scree slopes to summit rock bands, ascending a crack to the SE ridge along which the top is reached. Ascent 4¾ hr; descent 2½ hr (CAJ 19–71).

Unnamed (9450)

One mi NE of Mt. Bogart (on 82J14 the name Bogart is on this point).

Mt Birkwood

Mt Engadine

Mt Sir Douglas

The Fortress

Mt Bogart

G. Boles

NORTH FACE OF MT SPARROWHAWK

F. A. June 1957 by F. W. Crickard, R. Higgins, *H. Gmoser*. By trail to forks of Ribbon Creek. Thence to large avalanche slide and cirque below S face. Ascend this, bearing to right until the SE ridge can be attained and followed to the top. Chimneys and exposed slabs to the ridge 300′ below the summit which is thence attained without difficulty. Descent by SW ridge to depression above col E of Mt. Bogart, the col being reached by rappel (CAJ *41*–58).

2 — NE Ridge June 1957 J. Kato, D. K. Morrison. Base of NE ridge approached via trail in Ribbon Creek and climbed throughout. 3 hr to gendarme. Summit attained in 5⅓ hr. Descent via E face with rappel; to avalanche bowl — 1½ hr; trail ½ hr; road 1¼ hr.

Mt. Kidd (9705)

3 mi ESE of Mt. Bogart; 4 mi NW of The Wedge. One mi to SW is a subsidiary summit exceeding 9500′.

F. A. June 1947 by R. C. Hind, J. F. Tarrant. From camp at forks of Ribbon Creek, reaching NNW ridge at a large window by way of a small glacier below the peak. Difficult steep and loose rock (400′) to large plateau from which ridge is followed to summit, steep steps being turned on left (N). Easy descent by W ridge and NW face (CAJ *31*–237).

2 — NNE Buttress. June 1962, G. W. Boles, G. Gude, B. Greenwood. The ridge is seen in its entirety from the ranger station at Ribbon Creek. 1000′ of rock climbing. Lack of time prevented continuance to the main summit, and descent was made to S fork of Ribbon Creek. (CAJ *46*–99, marked photo). In July 1964, T. B. Mason, Miss I. Steinbach gained the tip of the buttress in 3½ hr and reached the subsidiary peak mainly on the N side of the ridge. A series of pinnacles lead to an overhang, bypassed by chimneys and traverses. The N side of the ridge was then followed to the main summit. 14 hr up. Descent on NW (CAJ *48*–151).

Mt. Buller (9200)

Above E shore of Spray Lake; W of S Ribbon Creek.

F. A. June 1956, B. Fraser, M. Hicks, J. Gorrill. From Spray fire road NW of peak, open slopes and scree were followed to the col SW of peak, thence over talus, slabs and a short ridge to the summit. No difficulty. The following day T. Messner, W. Rost traversed the peak by climbing the first ascent route, descending the NE side. In 1971, B. Struck, D. Forest, G. W. Boles reached the col from the S with approach by an excellent trail in Buller Creek. The party retraced their steps to the col then continued SW to climb an 8500′ subsidiary peak ½ mi SW of col. Descent was made over S slopes to Buller Creek trail.

Mt. Engadine (9750)

2 mi NW of Mt. Galatea; overlooking mouth of Smuts Creek.

F. A. June 1956, B. Fraser, J. Gorrill, M. Hicks. No particular difficulty. Ascent via WNW ridge throughout except for overhanging bands which party bypassed by traversing out on W face. 6 hr. Descent was made partly down the NNW ridge, then party down-climbed bands and scree-covered ledges (2 short rappels) to cirque N of mountain. This was descended to Buller Creek.

2 — NNW Ridge. 1971, B. Struck, D. Forest, G. Boles. Almost the same as the descent in Route One. A large overhang forced party off the ridge near the final summit pyramid. They traversed to the WNW ridge which was followed to the summit. 6¾ hr from Buller Creek including stops. Descent was made down the SW ridge for 400′, party then traversed to an old avalanche bed on the W face which was followed to tree line in ½ hr.

The Tower (10230)

One mi ESE of Mt. Engadine; terminal forks of Galatea Creek.

F. A. June 1957 by F. W. Crickard, R. Higgins, *H. Gmoser.* By way of Galatea Creek to second tributary from S, where the main stream is crossed to meadows NE of the peak. The key to the climb is to gain the N ridge. The E face is steep, with plentiful holds in loose rock. A 90′ vertical slab of sound rock required one piton. Above the rock bands a talus and snow-covered slope was traversed left to the col, whence the N ridge was followed to the summit without further use of rope. Descent by scree of S ridge, traversing W and S faces to regain the creek (CAJ *41*–57, photo).

Mt. Galatea (10450)

5 mi SE of Spray Lake, highest point of Kananaskis Range.

F. A. June 1930 by Miss K. Gardiner, *W. Feuz.* From Smith-Dorrien Creek, by way of the tributary from the S side of the mountain. Via the S face on hard snow to main E ridge, thence to summit. Ascent 6¾ hr (CAJ *19*–63).

Unnamed (9850)

One mi SE of Mt. Galatea towards The Fortress; 2 mi N of Mt Chester.

F. A. June 1972 by G. Scruggs, P. Roxborough, G. Boles, D. Forest. From Mud Lake via Chester Lake to a high valley between objective peak and The Fortress. Party climbed on snow, then broken rock to main S ridge which was followed to S summit. Then along ridge, one short rappel, to main summit. Descent down E side from summit.

The Fortress (9850)

4 mi SW of mouth of Galatea Creek; 3 mi NW of Mt. Inflexible.

F. A. 1957 by H. Gmoser, L. Grillmair. Ford Kananaskis River S of Mt. Kidd and ascend valley E of peak. Climb headwall to col S of summit, thence to W slopes and over easy scree and slabs to summit. Descent via SW ridge.

Mt. Chester (10020)

4 mi NW of Mt. Inflexible; E of pass between Smuts and Smith-Dorrien Creeks.

Unnamed (9950)

2 mi N of Mt. Inflexible; surrounding head of creek draining S; a complex horseshoe ridge with a subsidiary summit (9300) on the end of the long SSW ridge.

Mt. Inflexible (9850)

Double summit between head of Smith-Dorrien Creek and

Mt Galatea

The Fortress

Mt Chester

G. Boles

Kananaskis River

WEST FROM THE WEDGE

Kanaskis River; 4 mi E of Mud Lake. A subsidiary summit one mi to SW reaches over 9500.

F. A. 1956 by B. Greenwood, R. Lofthouse.

E face. Grade III. Ascent 4 hr.

Mt. Lawson (9170)

One mi SE of Mt. Inflexible; between Smith-Dorrien Creek and Kanaskis River.

Mt. Kent (8650)

4 mi S of Mt. Inflexible at S end of long ridge towards Kanaskis Lakes.

The ascent to the height of land from the East is through a wide, gently sloping valley, and the immediate watershed is formed by a narrow ridge . . . .

J. Palliser (of Kanaskis Pass)

OPAL RANGE

This small cluster of peaks extends parallel to and E of the Kananaskis River and is drained to the N by Evans-Thomas Creek, to the E and S by the Elbow River.

The peaks on the W of the group are remindful of the Sawback Range; sharp, jagged, slabby, grey limestone resulting from erosion of near vertical rock. This may one day be the most popular rock climbing area in the Rockies as it possesses easy access and excellent rock, but it has been neglected to date by climbers with only two or three ascents being made on most of the peaks.

Access is best from the Kananaskis Road on the W or by roads leading up the Little Elbow and Elbow Rivers from the E. The latter (not recommended all the way for late model cars) following the Elbow River, passes S of the range to join the Kananaskis Road 2½ mi N of Highwood Pass. A trail also leads into the group from the N via Evans-Thomas Creek. Maps 82J10W, 82J14E, 82J15.

The Wedge (8750)

4 mi SE of Mt. Kidd; N of Rocky Creek.

No information on first ascent. The mountain can be attained from N up open slopes to NE ridge, which is followed to summit without difficulty.

2 — W Face. Ascend Rocky Creek S of the summit. Thence via a prominent gully to a rib which is followed straight up. About 150′ below the summit ridge traverse right into a shallow groove to gain the S ridge. Climbing exposed but not difficult. Cross "au cheval" on S ridge to main summit pyramid, thence shale scramble to summit. Descend shale, before the "au cheval" descend left (S) to a piton, rappel to a ramp, descend ramp to another piton, rappel to easier ground, then traverse staying high (N) to point of start.

3 — N Ridge. May 1969 B. Martin, D. Forest. One hard pitch on this; a party had climbed the upper part of this ridge in the early 1950's.

Unnamed (9840)

2 and 2½ mi N of Mt. Packenham along the ridge E of Rocky Creek and W of the head of Evans-Thomas Creek are 2 summits (The N being double) of equal altitude. They appear to offer challenge comparable to the balance of this group.

Mt. Evans-Thomas (10160)

Highest peak of Opal Range; one mi N of Mt. Packenham. The name is incorrectly applied on 82J14 to a point 1½ mi E.

F. A. July 1954 by Miss J. Farman, M. S. Hicks, W. Lemmon, G. Ross, Miss I. Spreat, J. F. Tarrant. Up Grizzly Creek to col N of Mt. Packenham, whence the crest of the very sharp S ridge is followed for a considerable distance. Small towers bypassed on the W side, but a large tower forces descent on W face for 120′. A short wide gully leads to base of final peak. An exceedingly long and sharp ridge leads to a lower summit of approximately the same height, 3/5 mi to the N, as yet unclimbed (CAJ 68–66).

2 — NW Ridge. July 1972 P. Roxborough, J. Mellor. Up creek from Kananaskis Road, one mi N of Grizzly Creek. Party stayed high above creek to base of mountain. Then 800′ up grass slopes to meadow then more grass slopes to loose NW ridge. This was followed, heavily corniced in places, to summit mass, then a scramble to summit. (Partial cairn found) 7 hr. On descent the party glissaded a steep 2000′ snow gully to head of creek. 2½ hr summit to road.

Unnamed (9870)

Almost 2 mi NE of Mt. Packenham; S of head of Evans-Thomas Creek, in headwaters forks of Little Elbow River (Shown on 82J14 as Evans-Thomas).

Mt. Packenham (9850)

N of Mt. Hood; between Little Elbow and Kananaskis Rivers. Name erroneously applied on 82J11.

F. A. July 1954 by M. Dixon, N. Gish, S. G. Pearson, P. Rainier. From the Kananaskis Highway to col — 7350′ — W of objective. Thence along its NW ridge for a short distance, traversing onto the N portion of the W face. NW ridge followed to the summit. Descent via snow gully to SW (CAJ 68–65).

2 — N Ridge. June 1972. J. Pomeroy, M. Simpson, D. Forest, G. W. Boles. From the highway up grass slopes, traverse around hump to col as in Route One, then up grass and shale ridge to base of peak. Traverse N under NW Buttress; then turn up a series of gullies and cracks, some good rock, to subsidiary peak 8850; (downclimbed and a rappel to col, which appears to be the point where Route One starts up NW ridge). Follow NW ridge a short way, then traverse up left across NW face to N ridge, good rock to summit. D. Forest descended a notch and climbed a slightly higher summit, 300' to the E. Descend to col, then snow gullies down NW side to head of creek.

Mt. Hood (9525)

½ mi S of Mt. Packenham; N of Mt. Brock; 4 mi N of Mt. Wintour.

F. A. May 1953 J. Dodds, W. Lemmon & party. Via the N side not following N ridge from the col between Mt. Hood and Mt. Packenham. Traverse made on face to avoid step.

Mt. Brock (9520)

One mi S of Mt. Hood.

F. A. July 1954 by P. J. B. Duffy, K. Ingold. Via the SW face; 1000' of rock climbing. 3½ hr from the Kananaskis road (CAJ 38–86).

2 — S Ridge. June 1956, Miss J. Hewitt, W. Lemmon, R. Lofthouse. From Kananaskis road up King Creek to Brock-Blane saddle. Thence via S ridge.

Mt. Blane (9820)

One mi SSE of Mt. Brock; E of S fork of King Creek.

F. A. Sept 1955 by P. J. B. Duffy, G. Johnson, D. Kennedy, F. Koch. From the Kananaskis road at King Creek, follow the canyon to meadows and rocks below the col N of Mt. Blane — 4 hr. When 100' below the col a traverse to right is made to a saddle, whence the W face of the mountain is reached. A narrow ledge leads right to a safe 200' chimney, above which the face is crossed to an obvious 400' chimney, in which overhangs require safety pitons. Exposed but easy

Mt Blane

G. Boles

Route 3

Mt Brock

Blane 1 & 3

Evans Thomas
Packenham

VIEW UP N FORK of KING CREEK

Mt Kidd

Opal Ridge

King Cr

climbing for 200′ to summit (Koch was killed by a falling rock during the ascent) (CAJ 39–88).

2 — **SW Ridge.** 1957, P. Schotten, *H. Kahl.* Approach by grass slopes from King Creek to a snow patch directly below the prominent window on the W face. The first cliff band is broken, the second is climbed by an obvious large gully, then easier climbing over walls and scree leads to a point below and to the right of the window. From here a series of gullies and crack systems lead up to the right between the window and buttresses farther right. Very steep near the top. Above the buttresses steep walls and cracks lead to a subsidiary peak. The notch is crossed, then scramble to the top. The party found a gully near the summit and descended on snow to the bottom, E of the SE buttresses. A later party bivouacked just below the summit on the N ridge, then descended N ridge.

3 — **NW Ridge.** 1962, G. Prinz, H. Jungnitch, Miss L. Schmidt. Via King Creek to open grass slopes, then intermittent short rock walls and scree slopes to the N col. The ridge presented no difficulty, but proved interesting on good rock.

Unnamed (9580)
    ½ mi SSE along ridge from Mt. Blane toward Mt. Burney. This is not the impressive and unclimbed S gendarme (*Blade*) of Mt. Blane, but a separate summit.

Mt. Burney (9625)
    One mi SE of Mt. Blane.
    F. A. Aug 1956 by R. Lofthouse, alone. Via W face from King Creek. Easy climbing. Ascent 3½ hr.

Mt. Jerram (9830)
    One mi SE of Mt. Burney; 2 mi NW of Tombstone Mtn.
    F. A. June 1957 by D. K. Morrison, J. F. Tarrant. From Kananaskis road up King Creek canyon and S fork below Mts. Blane and Burney until objective is in sight. Ascend wide avalanche gully for 1000′ to W ridge. Thence 500′ up to where ridge merges into face. The W face is climbed direct (high-angled walls of considerable exposure) to summit ridge, which is broken by a 100′ gap before the highest point is gained. 6¼ hr from the road (CAJ *41*–65).

Mt. Wintour (8850)

1½ mi W of Mt. Jerram; in S angle of King Creek and Kananaskis River. The N ridge has been climbed quite often to its high point; very easy but spectacular, excellent for introducing beginners.

F. A. main summit; Sept 1968, G. Boles, E. Peyer. Follow N ridge, then descend to saddle at base of main summit block. Traverse right, up short wall between a gendarme and main tower, then traverse on ledges, up first corner, then up right to W ridge. Follow ridge, first on good rock, then loose rock to summit. 6½ hr. Descent by W ridge to col, then gully to the left (S) then W down water course, one 120′ rappel and one short rappel along the way (CAJ 52–71).

Elpoca Mtn (9959)

2 mi S of Tombstone Mtn; NE of Pocaterra Creek; at head of Elbow River. A long jagged crest almost one mi above 9500′.

F. A. 1960 G. D. Elliott, H. Kirby, P. S. Scribens. Hike in past Elbow Lake from Kananaskis road. After passing W of the Lake continue N downstream along Elbow River for ½ mi. Cut through trees to NW, then mount a scree slope leading to a large gully. Climb ⅓ up gully, then traverse up slabs on the right to the ridge. Then follow ridge N to a large turret, which was climbed direct, then more ridge to summit. Party noted spectacular pinnacles on N ridge. 2½ hr, scree to summit. Descent by the same route.

Tombstone Mtn (9950)

5 mi E of outlet of Lower Kananaskis Lake; 3 mi SE of Mt. Blane. Name is placed on lower S summit on 82J11.

Mt. Glasgow (9630)

One mi N of Mt. Cornwall; in SW angle between Elbow and Little Elbow Rivers.

F. A. May 1949 by A. Choquette, alone.

Mt. Cornwall (9750)

Between Mt. Glasgow and Banded Peak; in center of group between Elbow and Little Elbow Rivers.

F. A. May 1949 by A. Choquette, alone, on skis.

Banded Peak (9626)
Between sources of Elbow River; 2 mi SE of Mt. Cornwall.

JOSUE 9
3-5

> But they dwelt in Gabaon, took for themselves provisions, laying old sacks upon their asses, and wine bottles rent and sewed up again, and very old shoes, which for a show of age were clouted with patches, and old garments upon them: the loaves also, which they carried for provisions by the way, were hard, and broken into pieces.

ASSINIBOINE GROUPS

This is a famous area owing to its accessibility and splendid scenery. 23 mi SW of Banff, Mt. Assiniboine is the seventh elevation of the Canadian Rocky mountains, rising in a striking pyramid high above its neighbors and visible from vast distances on every side. Mt. Assiniboine is the highest summit S of the Bow River, its name meaning "stone-boiler", from the tribe's practice of cooking by means of hot stones dropped in a vessel of water. The passes of the Divide are White Man, Wonder, Assiniboine, Fatigue, and Simpson. In 1841, Sir George Simpson crossed the pass which bears his name, travelling W on the first overland journey around the world (CAJ 28–210). Trail distance from Banff to the Assiniboine area is considerably in excess of the airline figure given above.

Access to the groups from the British Columbia side is varied:

Simpson River trail commences a short distance N of its junction with the Vermilion River. Opposite the junction and beside the highway is a large rock monument, the best landmark. A short distance N is an access road across the Vermilion which goes ½ mi from the river and ends in a gravel pit. This is a good parking spot and connects with the trail. The trail goes the full length of Simpson River and into Mount Assiniboine Park. There is also a branch trail up Surprise Creek into the Park. As far as Surprise Creek the trail stays N of the river, but from then on crosses many times "which is OK on horseback but not so good on foot."

Daer Creek trail is reached by a Park protection road which leaves the main highway about half-way between McLeod Meadows and Kootenay Crossing and is not normally open to the public. Key from Superintendent of Kootenay Park at Radium.

In **Cross River** a mining access road now goes to the main forks. A good horse trail extends the length of the Mitchell and into Assiniboine Park. The "Settlers" Road, which joins the main highway about 10 mi E of Radium, gives access to the Cross. Logging bridge across the Kootenay River at Year-

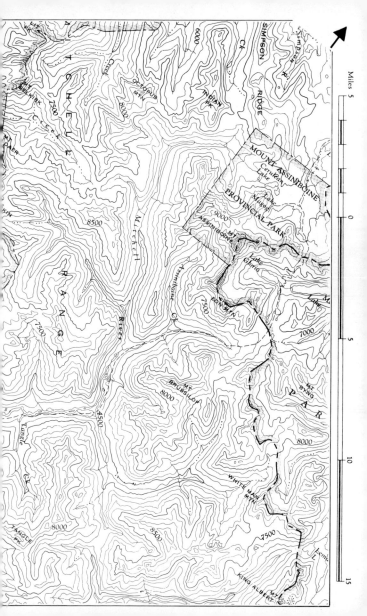

ling Creek to the E side. Cross River road leaves the main logging road at the top of the bench on the E side. The logging road above gives access directly beyond this point; a mining exploration road continues along the S side as far as Joffre Creek. The main horse trail went along the N side of the creek but there is now a connecting trail to the end of the road. Queen Mary, Joffre and Tipperary Creeks have horse trails. The Kootenay River road from Canal Flats also provides access to the Palliser road.

A logging road extends up the **Albert River** to the main forks of this stream and also up the W Fork almost to the divide between it and the Cross River.

Spray Pass trail is very poor.

In mountaineering, as in many other things, to despise is criminal, to relax is dangerous; and it is to those who do not expect an accident that it will come . . .

J. Outram

BLUE RANGE

This small group includes only 6 mi of the Divide, from White Man Pass to Marvel Pass. None of the more attractive summits occur on the Divide. The range is of little mountaineering interest, being overshadowed by more spectacular groups to both N and S.

Access is best from the upper end of Spray Lake (road) via trail in Bryant Creek to ranger station. Thence via Marvel Lake trail to Marvel Pass. This trail is in good shape to the upper end of Marvel Lake but poor after trail branches up to Wonder Pass. Access can also be made to the SE of these peaks by trail from Spray Lakes up Spray River and White Man Creek. On the British Columbia side, these trails deteriorate to impassable. Access from the W via trail in Mitchell River is good but limited in valleys closest to the mountains herein described. Map 82J13; 82J14.

Mt. Currie (9210)
2 mi N of White Man Pass; between White Man and Currie Creeks, 2 mi NE of Red Man Mtn.
F. A. 1916 by the Boundary Commission.

Red Man Mt. (9530)
NW buttress of White Man Pass. Subsidiary summit 9250' one mi to NW.
F. A. 1916 by the Boundary Commission.

Mt. Brussilof (9860)
S of Mt. Alcantara; 5 mi W of White Man Pass.
F. A. Aug 1929 by Miss K. Gardiner, *W. Feuz*. From camp on Aurora Creek, skirting Mt. Alcantara on E to the Alcantara-Brussilof col, whence the N arete of the objective peak affords good rock climbing — 2 hr to the summit. Ascent 5 hr; descent 4 hr. Pass difficulties on NW face (AJ *42*–70; CAJ *18*–29).

Mt. Alcantara (9850)
One mi N of Mt. Brussilof; 3 mi SSW of Marvel Pass.

F. A. Aug 1929 by Miss K. Gardiner, *W. Feuz*. From camp on upper Aurora Creek, one mi below Marvel Pass, to the Alcantara-Brussilof col — 3½ hr; whence the S arete is followed over good rock to the summit. Ascent 5 hr; descent 3½ hr (AJ *42*–70; CAJ *18*–28).

Unnamed (9350)
Double summit on Divide; 2 mi NE of Mt. Alcantara; 2 mi S of Marvel Pass.

Mt. Aurora (9150)
SE buttress of Marvel Pass; W shoulder is on Divide and was ascended by Boundary Commission in 1916. Main summit is one mi E of Divide.

Mt. Byng (9650)
NW of Mt. Currie; 2 mi E of Marvel Pass.
F. A. 1934 by H. S. Crosby, *R. Aemmer*. From Marvel Pass by way of the NW ridge.

Mt. Morrison (9050)
W of Spray River between Mt. Turner and Currie Creek. This is a complicated ridge system with several points exceeding 9000′.
F. A. June 1955 by D. K. Morrison, *alone*. From end of road at Spray Lake, the Palliser Pass trail was followed for 1½ hr, then through bush to SE ridge. Thence without difficulty to the summit in 6 hr (CAJ *39*–83).

Mt. Turner (9230)
2 mi N of Mt. Morrison; 4 mi SE of Bryant Creek Ranger Station.

ASSINIBOINE PARK GROUP

This is the most famous climbing area of the Southern Rockies and includes a number of interesting lakes, many of which have subterranean drainage. A lodge open to the public is situated at the NE end of Lake Magog, though the long-standing AAC cabins near this spot are now removed. The area, while a center of high angle and alpine climbing for half a century, is also popular with hikers and campers. The principal peaks are situated along a reentrant curve of the Divide, between Marvel and Wonder Passes.

Access is best to the main Assiniboine Group generally via the poorly maintained road to the head of Spray Lake. From this point one day of backpacking up Bryant Creek over good trails leads to Magog Lake. The distance is somewhat over 12 mi by either Assiniboine Pass (lower) or Wonder Pass (more scenic), the trails diverging at the Bryant Creek Ranger Station and meeting again near Strom's Lodge.

From the N, approach can also be made via Brewster Creek and Allenby Pass or Healy Creek and Valley of the Rocks. These approaches are much longer than those via Bryant Creek but are extremely scenic and hence often taken in preference. Trails in all cases are clearly marked, though used for horse travel. The Alpine Club of Canada maintains an **alpine hut** at 8700' above the Lake Magog headwall. The hut sleeps 12 and is situated below Mt. Strom. White gas for stoves should be carried, and clean dish towels.

The most commonly used approach in the winter is from Sunshine Village via Citadel Pass, Golden Valley and Valley of the Rocks; 22 mi. Map 82J13.

Mt. Gloria (9540)

NE of Mt. Eon; W buttress of Marvel Pass.

F. A. 1929 by Miss C. Baldwin, Miss E. Bigelow, F. X. Bigelow, H. Bigelow, H. Bigelow, Jr., Mrs. H. B. Bigelow, Miss S. Detty, Miss G. Duffy, R. Hallowell, H. Howe, Miss C. Saltonstall, R. Saltonstall, R. Walcott, *C. Coyteaux*. From camp at SW end of Marvel Lake, via Marvel Pass, whence talus and broken rock are traversed to easy couloirs and ledges leading to snowsaddle between objective and subsidiary peak to S. Thence 800′ of steep but easy rock to summit. Rope not used. Ascent 4 hr.

2 — **W Ridge** July 1966, ACC party of 8 from Wonder Pass via E Assiniboine cirque to glacier. No difficulties.

Eon Mtn (10860)

One mi SE of Mt. Aye; one mi SW of Mt. Gloria; 2 mi W of Marvel Pass.

F. A. July 1921 by W. E. Stone (CAJ *12*–14). **SE Ridge** — From Assiniboine camp cross Wonder and Marvel Passes to bivouac below E face of Mt. Gloria. Cross the col — 8650′ — S of Mt. Gloria and work S gaining the first broad ledge of Mt. Eon at 7800′ passing around SE ridge to base of wide S face of the mountain. At the E end there is yellow-capped outlying tower. Ascend easy slopes and ledges for about 800′ followed by steep ledges and couloirs for 500′. Then ledges with broken faces to SE arete at 9500′. Follow arete closely on S side to snow band at 10300′; steep snow to broken ledges and short couloirs of unstable rock to a final wide, steep, irregular chimney, opening to the summit (CAJ *12*–86).

Mt. Aye (10640)

S of Lunette Peak; NW of Mt. Eon.

F. A. Aug 1934 by H. S. Crosby, *R. Aemmer.* From camp between Mt. Gloria and Marvel Pass, around S side of Mt. Eon — 2 hr, to a point on Eon Creek (largely underground) S of Aye-Eon Col. The col is easily reached over scree, after which the rock of the SE face is ascended to the long, sharp summit ridge. Ascent from col 6½ hr (AAJ *2*–331).

2 — **S Face** 1935, E. C. Brooks, Miss P. Prescott, Miss M. Schnellbacher, R. Whitney. From Aurora Creek up Eon Creek, with snow to Aye-Eon col; thence left to ledge below a band of yellow cliffs — 3½ hr. Follow cliff around to left until past a buttress, when the nearest chimney is ascended. 1¼ hr of good rock climbing to scree leading to first summit, whence the highest point is attained after a short descent on rotten rock. Ascent 9 hr.

Lunete Peak (*Lost Peak*) (11150)

High point on S arete of Mt. Assiniboine; N of Mt. Aye.

F. A. Sept 1901 by J. Outram, *C Bohren, C. Häsler*. From Lake Magog via Wedgewood-Assinboine and Sturdee-Assiniboine cols to the Assiniboine SW arete as in Route One for Mt. Assiniboine. From this point ascend loose rocks to the foot of the wall at 10750', the base of which is traversed for a short distance to the right (S) where a narrow 15' chimney with firm holds permits an ascent. A narrow ridge running up from the W can now be reached over steep ledges and followed to the top. This summit was ascended by Outram's party in thick mist in mistake for Mt. Assiniboine(App *10*–47).

Mt. Assiniboine (11870)

Headwaters of Spray, Cross, and Simpson Rivers; highest peak between International Boundary and CPR (AJ *18*–397; App *9*–196; *29*–105; CAJ *2*, 1, 10; Outram–38). The mountain was named in 1885 by G. M. Dawson of the Dominion Geological Survey, who saw it from afar. Its base was reached in 1893 by R. L. Barrett and T. E. Wilson. Attempts to ascend the mountain were made in 1899 by H. G. Bryant and L. J. Steele, by the NW arete; in 1900 by E. & W. Walling, *C. Clarke, E. Feuz, H. Zurfluh*; and in 1901 by H. G. Bryant, W. D. Wilcox, *E. Feuz*, who attained 10850' on the SW side. **All routes subject to avalanche.** F. A. Sept 1901 by J. Outram, *C. Bohren, C. Hasler*. **SW face.** From camp on Lake Magog, up slopes and craggy wall to the N glacier. Cross to Assiniboine-Strom col — 9350' — Outram's 1st pass. Descend slightly on far side to glacier and cross to Assiniboine-Sturdee col — Outram's 2nd pass — 9950' — at base of W arete. At this level traverse ledges across SW face to S ridge at 9500'. From this point ascend scree ledges to the foot of a 70' cliff at about 10750'. A short distance to W a broad snow couloir, trending upward toward the Assiniboine-Lunette depression, is crossed to a point where the cliff recedes into the SW face. The face is ascended diagonally over steep ledges and escarpments, interspersed with snow and ice. The S arete is reached at a point 300' below the summit which is then gained by means of easy snow. Ascent from Lake

Magog, 10 hr; from 9500' on SW arete, 5½ hr. Descent via N face (App *10*–48; AJ *20*–545 CAJ *1*–90).

2 NW Face July 1910 T. G. Longstaff, *R. Aemmer*. To Assiniboine-Sturdee col at base of SW arete, see Route One. Traverse up steep snow toward the middle of the face to avoid ice-couloirs. Constant ice climbing except for two vertical 15' bands of rock. The final cliff is almost devoid of handholds for the first 12' and the rocks are usually icy. 60' above, steep snow leads to summit. 9 hr from Lake Magog; descent by N arete, 11 hr. (CAJ 3–174). **Descent** July 1952 by G. Hattersley-Smith, A. C. Lembeck, E. Petrig, approximately by this route. The W arete was followed most of the way, rappelling three steps, two of 60', and one of 90'. In the last third of descent, snow and ice chutes of the SW face led to the Assiniboine-Sturdee col. Summit to col 8¼ hr (AJ 58–534).

3 — N Face. July 1967, Y. Chouinard, J. Faint, C. Jones. Approach as for Route One to snow couloir descending on right of shoulder ⅓ of distance up N face. Bivouac on shoulder. Route passes red rock by distinct but narrow ice gully. Thence slightly right to final rocks. Danger from loose and falling rock. Mostly on ice. Summit by noon. IV, F7 (AAJ *16*–57, plate 60, marked).

4 — N Ridge. 1903, W. Douglas, *C. Häsler, C. Kaufmann*. The N glacier is reached from Lake Magog, the general line of ascent being the narrow arete. Ascend via NW face, gradually working onto arete and following it to summit. Two almost perpendicular cliffs cross and divide the arete into distinct sections, the rock walls affording good climbing. The ridge above the second cliff also offers climbing, but the face is generally easier. Ice may require considerable effort. To lower rocky N summit, 5½ hr; main summit ⅔ hr more. Variations of this route are the most popular on this scenic climb. Descent to wall of Wedgwood Peak, 5 hr (App *12*–233; AJ *33*–207).

5 — E Face. Sept 1969, W. Davidson, A. Simpson. Approach through bush from Wonder Pass trail to head of Lake Gloria; thence up rotten and broken glacier to most prominent rib. Average rock quality. Some severe pitches, few objective hazards. Party bivouacked once, IV, F7 (AAJ *17*–148).

Mt Assiniboine

Mt Magog

Mt Sturdee

Mt Strom

Route 4

FROM NORTHEAST

Magog Lake

G. Boles

Winter Ascent — (Route 4) Dec 1967, D. Gardiner, E. Grassman, C. Scott.

Winter Traverse — Feb 1971, Y. Kraulis, S. King, P. Morrow. Up by N Ridge, down SE (Route One). Possibly done earlier.

Mt. Sturdee (10350′)

W of Mt. Assiniboine at head of Assiniboine Creek; 2 mi SW of Lake Magog.

F. A. Aug 1920 by W. W. Foster, E. L. T. Taylor, Mr. & Mrs. P. S. Thompson. **E Ridge.** From Lake Magog to Assiniboine-Sturdee col, see Route 1 for Mt. Assiniboine, reached by ascending on the S side. Then up snow and rock of N face above the bluff to depression between two pinnacles of the ridge—one hr from col; thence 100′ of snow on N face and a short steep pitch to the ridge at foot of peak, scree and a second short pitch leading to summit (CAJ *12*–56,176).

2 — W Ridge 1920, a party of the ACC, the route being on good rock with short difficult stretches.

3 — Traverse 1920 ACC party led by A. H. MacCarthy, ascending by the N arete and descending by Route 1.

4 — NE Face 1934 Miss G. Engelhard, *V. Kutschera*. Usual route was followed up Assiniboine Glacier to Assiniboine-Sturdee col. The NE face was ascended by the steep icewall which terminated at the depression below the final rocks. Ascent 8 hr, descent by E arete.

The Marshal (10465)

NW of Mt. Sturdee; E of Mitchell River.

F. A. Aug 1919 by V.A. Fynn, *R. Aemmer*. From Sunburst Valley and Cerulean Lake, via head of Wedgwood Creek (CAJ *11*–47).

2 — E Slope — 1920, Party of ACC, *Ern Feuz*. From Lake Magog via the Strom-Marshal col and the E slope.

3 — W Face — 1935, W. H. Cleveland, F. McCulloch, Miss P. Prescott, Miss M. Schnellbacher, R. Whitney, G. Woodsworth. From Mitchell River by NW ridge and W face.

Mt. Watson (9750)

S angle between Wedgwood Creek and Mitchell River.

F. A. 1935 by R. J. Cuthbertson, Miss L. Gest, Miss G. Johnson, Miss J. Spieden, Miss H. J. Zillmer, R. T. Zillmer. From camp near Wedgwood Lake down trail on W side of Mitchell River, with difficult crossing at point where creek enters from SW face of Mt. Watson. Follow up this creek and ascend scree slopes of face. Mitchell River to summit, 3½ hr (AAJ 4–493).

Centurion Peak (9150)
SW of Mt. Sturdee; S of The Marshal; between Mitchell River and Assiniboine Creek.
F. A. 1920 by members of ACC.

Mt. Strom (9920)
One mi NW of Mt. Assiniboine; one mi N of Mt. Sturdee. This is the S summit of Wedgwood Peak, also known locally as Norwegian Peak.

Wedgwood Peak (*Katherine*) (9940)
NNW of Mt. Assiniboine, SW of Lake Magog.
F. A. July 1910 by T. G. Longstaff, Miss K. Longstaff, *R. Aemmer*. The Wedgwood-Assiniboine col is reached as in Route One for Mt. Assiniboine, the SE arete thence being followed over several minor summits to the highest point (the peak was traversed from W to E) (App 24–255).
2 — SE Face. 1954. T. Church, C. Meyer, Miss J. Townsend, *H. Gmoser*. From Lake Magog N of waterfall; reaching ridge S of Goats Tower. Thence to summit. 7 hr up. Good rock above scree.

Sunburst Peak (*Goats Tower*) (9250)
One mi N of Wedgwood Peak (which see), terminating the long N spur of Mt. Assiniboine; W. of Lake Magog.
F. A. July 1910 by T. G. Longstaff, Miss K. Longstaff, *R. Aemmer*. Via the steep rocks of the SE face (CAJ 3–175).
2 — NE Face-Ridge Aug 1953, F. Dopf, *H. Gmoser*. Begin midway in W Face, 100′ left of lowest point. Ascend 100′ to "old" piton. Traverse on grassy ledges 100′ right, then up 2 pitches following slight crack depression in face; the top ½

of second pitch is a flaring chimney. Traverse from top of chimney 10' right (to avoid overhang) then up sheer wall for 20' (5.2). Wall ends on ledge, then continues mixed 4th class to 1st large terrace, to meet NE ridge. Continue 400' up ridge past 2 more terraces. Avoid rotten inside corner which drains into main couloir separating faces. Stay on ridge. 1800' total, good rock. Variation — July 1966 III F5 (CAJ 37–109).

3 — NW Ridge 1941, P. Bergsland, B. Raeder. Approach from direction of Wedgwood Lake to third crest from N (*Raeder Point*).

Mt. Magog (10150)

NE of Mt. Assiniboine; W of Terrapin Mtn.

F. A. July 1920 by A. J. Gilmour, A. H. MacCarthy, A. W. Wakefield, F. N. Waterman. From Assiniboine camp over scree and rock slides direct to Naiset Point and thence over Naiset to Naiset-Terrapin col. Up steep ice couloir on N face of Terrapin, over ice and rock to cliff and slabs above, whence scree slopes on N face are ascended to summit of Mt. Terrapin (which see). Descend scree to Terrapin-Magog col; then up narrowing ledges for about 100' to bottom of steep 80' crack in yellow rock — "Golden Stairs", which is ascended to broken slabs and the summit ice-cap reached easily by the NE shoulder. Ascent and return 13½ hr (CAJ *12*–64).

2 — E Face and traverse. This route had, a few days earlier, been followed in part by L. H. Lindsay, A. H. MacCarthy, E. O. Wheeler, who ascended via Wonder Pass direct to the Naiset-Terrapin col. From the top of last difficult crack skirt summit on NW and descend steep rock of W arete to Magog-Assiniboine col (CAJ *12*–53).

Sept 1934, Miss G. Engelhard, V. *Kutschera*. Via Terrapin Glacier and col up the steep E face and to the right of the "Golden Stairs". The wall is almost 200' high, with small holds. Route One for remainder of traverse. Total time 13 hr (CAJ *22*–210).

The mountain is most easily climbed from the snowfield (NE) below Mt. Assiniboine; the Wheeler descent of 1920. The usual route is from Lake Magog to the Terrapin-Magog col and thence by either the E arete or the NE face.

Terrapin Mtn (9660)

E of Mt. Magog; one mi SW of Mt. Towers.

F. A. 1915 by H. O. Frind, L. Jeffers, *C. Kain.* From Wonder Pass traverse W on a level with the pass to col on the NE side, from which an easy ridge leads to the summit. Descent may be made via the glacier to Lake Magog. No summit cairn was made because of snow.

The mountain was traversed in 1920 by L. H. Lindsay, A. H. MacCarthy, E. O. Wheeler, en route to Mt. Magog (which see). It is ascended readily from Lake Magog (CAJ *12*–53).

Naiset Point (9050)

N arete of Mt. Terrapin; SE of Lake Magog.

F. A. 1920 by N. Allen, H. E. Bulyea, Miss M. Gold, D. J. McGeary, Miss J. Stewart, E. L. Taylor, C. G. Wates. From Assiniboine Camp via scree and rock above Gog Lake.

2 — E Buttress. 1954, *H. Gmoser* party. A prominent buttress (between 2 couloirs of E face). From crest of buttress over easy slopes and snow to summit. Descent towards Towers and Gog Lake.

3 — W Face. 1931, O. Stegmaier, *H. Wittich.* From Lake Magog. Ascend direct through W wall to lower W summit, then traversing to N ridge, climbing latter over all needles and pinnacles to summit. Ascent 4 hr, descent by ridge leading toward Mt. Terrapin — one hr (CAJ *20*–164).

The Towers (9337)

NE of Mt. Terrapin; W buttress of Wonder Pass. E point higher.

F. A. 1916 by the Boundary Commission.

2 — E Face. Sept 1934, Miss G. Engelhard, *V. Kutschera.* From Wonder Pass over shale to base of peak. The E face was ascended first up two chimneys and thence along the jagged ridge leading to easy final scree slopes. The rock is exceedingly rotten and great care is necessary on the narrow ridge. Descent made by W ridge over broken cliffs and scree (CAJ *22*–210).

3 — W-E Traverse. 1954, Miss E. Meyer, *H. Gmoser.* Except for the first tower (ascended from col between #1 and

#2 with descent the same way) the route stays close to the ridge. No great difficulties. 9 hr round trip from Gog Lake.

Wonder Peak (9350)
E buttress of Wonder Pass; S of Mt. Cautley; actual summit lies E of Divide.
First ascent 1913 by the Boundary Commission.

Mt. Cautley (9380)
N of Wonder Peak; SE of Assiniboine Pass.
F. A. 1916 by the Boundary Commission.
Gibraltar Rock (9418) culminates NE shoulder, precipitous E face — but gentle approach from SW.
Cascade Rock (9250) is SE buttress of Assiniboine Pass and 3½ mi NNW of Mt. Cautley; severe NE face.

Benedictio Instrumentorum ad Montes Conscendendes

Oremus:
Benedic, quaesumus, Domine, hos funes, baculos, rastros, aliaque hic praesentia instrumenta; ut, quicumque iis usi fuerint, inter ardua et montis abrupta, inter glacies, nives et tempestates ab onmi casu et periculo praeserventur.

Achille Ratti

MITCHELL RANGE

This is a diffuse assortment of peaks, entirely in the Kootenay drainage, and largely W of the Assiniboine Park. These peaks are bounded on the W by the Vermilion River and on the E by the Cross River and its NW fork, Mitchell River. On the N is Simpson River.

Access along the N is via good trail in Simpson River leaving the highway 28½ mi S of Vermilion Pass and continuing via Surprise Creek and Ferro Pass into the vicinity of Lake Magog. A branch of the Simpson trail 3½ mi from the road (cabin) ascends Lachine Creek to Park Boundary. Along the W is a road on the E bank of the lower Vermilion and Kootenay Rivers. The road and companion trail system up the Cross and Mitchell Rivers is described above. NPS maintains a trail up Pitts Creek, to the Park Boundary at the height of land. In Daer Creek (3 mi SE of Vermilion Crossing) a trail leads across the height of land — 10 mi — to join the Mitchell River trail at a point 4 mi W of Mt. Aye. Condition of trails outside the parks is questionable as no regular maintainance is done. Map 82J13.

Mt. Docking (9362)
3 mi SW of junction of Assiniboine Creek and Mitchell River; 6 mi W of Mt. Brussilof, at SE of range. "Uninspiring."

Mt. Harkin (9780)
At head of W fork of Mitchell River; N of Pitts Creek; 2 mi SSE of Mt. Daer, with high ridge between.

Mt. Daer (9710)
6 mi E of Vermilion-Kootenay junction. Fire lookout (road) on lower W slope. Sharp ridges and good E face. Subsidiary point on 4 mi long E ridge reaches 9477'.

Mt. Selkirk (9640)
NNW across Daer Creek from Mt. Daer; at SE of massif with Split Peak. A severely crenelated ridge line with steep faces extends 2½ mi NNW parallel to lower Vermilion River.

Split Peak (9610)

Double summit 5 mi E of Kootenay Crossing; SE angle between Simpson and Vermilion Rivers.

F. A. June 1961, W summit only, by J. S. Gardner, R. J. Hopf, P. B. Spear, I. Stirling. From Kootenay Crossing up Vermilion River to stream on S side of objective to timberline bivouac. Thence ascend snow couloir between peaks to waterfall. Slabs of E peak ascended until the higher W peak is in view, thence traverse back to couloir and summit. E peak appeared more severe (CAJ 45–137).

Octopus Mtn (9620)

3 mi SW of Indian Peak, at W head of Mitchell River. 2 mi furthur S with more interesting N face is **Mt. Sam** (9450).

Indian Peak (9817)

SW of Nestor Peak; W of Ferro Pass. Faces on NE impressive.

F. A. 1912 by R. D. McCaw and party during survey for the Banff-Windermere road. Easy from SW.

Nestor Peak (9750)

NE of Ferro Pass; 3 mi NW of Cerulean Lake. Icefield SE of summits is source of Mitchell River. A long ridge running NE then SE for 3 mi terminates in **Nub Peak** (9016) directly N of Sunburst Valley, climbed in 1913 by the Boundary Commission.

Simpson Ridge (*Edmonton*) (9430)

NE angle between Simpson River and Surprise Creek; at NW of massif with Nestor Peak.

F. A. July 1920 by H. C. Bulyea, Miss M. Gold, C. G. Wates. From camp in Golden Valley, descend Simpson River one hr, thence to cirque S of NE buttress. Snow slopes and rock to buttress between two cirques NE of ridge. 400' tower of good rock leads to crest of N arete. Thence unstable rock with poor belays to level summit ridge — 8 hr, with highest point at SE end — 2½ hr. Descend to Edmonton-Nestor col and down to Simpson River — 3½ hr (CAJ 12–73).

SUNDANCE RANGE

Bordering at its N on the Banff area section, this is a poorly defined group including those peaks W of the Spray River (fire road) and those residual Divide peaks N of Assiniboine Park. Access is good via Bryant or Brewster Creek trails to Allenby Pass. From Sunshine Village trails also lead along and below the Divide over Citadel Pass and via Fatigue Pass. The peaks E of the Divide in general have not offered real challenge and have remained largely untouched. Map 82J13, 82J14.

Cone Mtn (9550)
In N angle of Bryant and Turbulent Creeks; 3 mi E of Marvel Lake outlet.

Mt. Mercer (9750)
4 mi E of Assiniboine Pass at head of Mercer Creek; a double summit, the W being sharper.

Mt. Allenby (9820)
4 mi E of Assiniboine Pass; in NE angle between Allenby and Mercer Creeks; one mi N of Mt. Mercer. W of the main summit a sharp outlier reaches 9500'. E of the main summit and separated by a deep col is a subsidiary point in excess of 9600'.

Mt. Turbulent (9350)
3 mi E of Mt. Mercer; forming the crest between Turbulent Creek and Spray River.

Unnamed (9970)
2 mi E of Allenby Pass; N of Mt. Allenby; a long ridge with glacier to NW at head of Brewster Creek.

Unnamed (9840)
E buttress of Allenby Pass.

Og Mtn (9430)

W buttress of Allenby Pass. The Divide and Park Boundary pass over the W shoulder which lies N of Og Pass (trail).

Unnamed (9440)

2 mi NW along the Divide from Og Mtn; SE of Nasswald Peak. SE of Nasswald Lakes, NE of Divide is companion summit of equal height.

Nasswald Peak (9985)

SE buttress of Fatigue Pass.

F. A. 1913 by the members of Boundary Commission, *C.Kain*, (for whose birthplace the peak is named). **Golden Mtn** is the lower W summit one mi along the Divide towards Fatigue Pass.

Fatigue Mtn (9707)

Head of Fatigue Creek; between Citadel and Fatigue Passes.

F. A. 1889 by W. S. Drewry.

Go carefully, lads, be careful; a single moment's enough to make one dead for the whole of one's life.

J. Pecosta

PEAKS IN THE ENVIRONS OF BANFF

These are mostly one-day or weekend climbs generally done from a car left on the roadside. Some require bivouac, some are several hours hiking before actual climbing can be done. For the most part the peaks herein described are of lesser altitude, but the routes done in recent years are of a higher standard than is generally possible for climbs in more remote areas. All the peaks described here are on the Alberta slope and belong to the bare limestone mountains principally of Devonian or Cambrian Age (AAJ 17–84).

I failed to realize that one book was as full of grotesque blunders and inaccuracies as the other . . .

A. Crowley (on guidebooks)

Another point is that it is at least twice as hard to find two competent companions as it is one.

A. Crowley (on climbers)

FAIRHOLME RANGE

These are the first peaks seen as one approaches the Rockies from the East. This group is bounded on the N by Lake Min-newanka, on the SW by the Bow River and on the E by the plains. Largely snow free in summer, they are characterized by impressive faces and are quite popular early and late in the season. A greater volume of climbing per lateral mile of cliff is done here than in any other part of these ranges and the descriptions that follow are thus likely to become obsolete more rapidly than elsewhere.

In August 1841, George Simpson, the energetic Governor-in-chief of the Hudson's Bay Company, in his journey around the world entered these mountains through the Devils Gap, enroute from Edmonton to the pass now bearing his name. "Marching for nine hours through dense woods. This valley, which was from two to three miles in width, contained four beautiful lakes, communicating with each other by small streams, and the fourth of the series, which was about fifteen miles by three, we named after Peechee".

Access to the western peaks can be from Two Jack Lake or via the trail up Carrot Creek which runs from a point on the Trans-Canada one mi W of the Park Entrance to the S shore of Lake Minnewanka 4840′ and out to the Ghost Lakes. The old highway, largely along the N side of the Bow River, provides ready access to the S faces of most of the well frequented climbs. Map 8203

Mt. Inglismaldie (9725)

Forms the S shore of Lake Minnewanka.

F. A. June 1933 by Misses H. Foster, J. Packer, M. C. Wylie, Messrs. Betts, Dickson, Innes, DeCouteur, J. Miskow, Sadler, Vallance, *L. Grassi*. From Lake Minnewanka, landing at little bay at the foot of the second draw W of severe buttress (known as Gibraltar). Ascent via NW face. Through woods, up a stream bed filled with boulders. This is followed by small cliffs, a chimney and long scree slopes, which are traversed

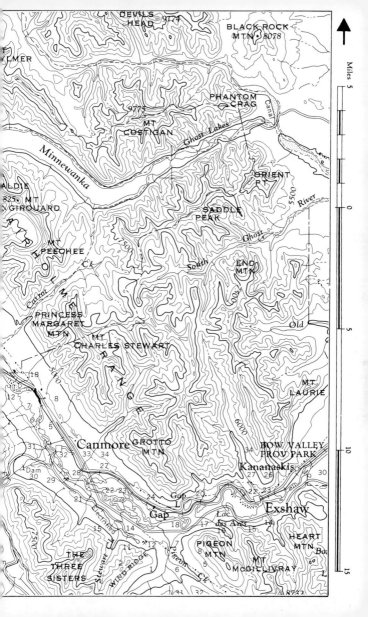

to a narrow ledge from which an overhanging cliff rises for 60'. Breaks are found through this and a second wall of equal height, bringing one to the summit ridge. Thence ¾ hr to top (CAJ 22–212).

2 — SW Ridge 1938, E. E. Bishop, D. R. Crosby from Anthracite by way of the SW ridge in 5 hr. Thence to Mt. Girouard.

Mt. Girouard (9825)

SE of Mt. Inglismaldie; between the latter and Mt. Peechee.

F. A. 1938 by E. E. Bishop, D. R. Crosby. From summit of Mt. Inglismaldie by the intervening col and ridge. In 1968 the Peechee-Inglismaldie massif was traversed — see Peechee.

Mt. Peechee (9625)

Double summits S of Lake Minnewanka; next SE of Mt. Girouard; N of Carrot Creek.

F. A. 1929 by L. Grassi, alone. From Lake Minnewanka by way of the steep N slopes.

2 — NE Face. Traverse. June 1968, D. Gardner, C. Locke, C. Scott. Approach up Carrot Creek, thence W to below middle of NE Face. Class 4 up face to summit. Traverse was made NW to bivouac on Mt. Girouard. Thence to Mt. Inglismaddie and descent to Lake Minnewanka.

3 — SW Ridge. To SW summit, 1929, Miss M. D. Fleming, Miss M. Macleod, F. Neave. From camp on N tributary (dry) of Carrot Creek via creekbed, going to right to pass cliff (waterfall) and scree slopes to upper cliff band. S arete was followed on W side to summit. 8 hr up.

Saddle Peak (9288)

4 mi E of Lake Minnewanka; between N and S forks of Ghost River.

Orient Point (8650)

Eastmost point of prominence N of the Bow River; between the forks of Ghost River; 3 mi. ENE of Saddle Peak; SE of Ghost Lakes.

Mt. Charles Stewart (9215)

4 mi NNE of Canmore; in E angle between Carrot Creek and Bow River. **Princess Margaret Mtn** is the W shoulder. The cirque facing NE on the N side of this massif has excellent walls.

F. A. 1947 by R. C. Hind, Mr. & Mrs. H. H. Rans, J. F. Tarrant. From near park entrance up through the short canyon SW of the mountain, the main branch being followed over slabby rocks and scree to the ridge at a point about ¾ mi SE of the objective, 3½ hr from highway. The narrow, rotten ridge is easily followed to the summit — 1½ hr, a minor obstacle forcing descent of a short step before gaining the highest point. Descent can be made easily down the wide scree gully which rejoins the ascent route above the upper canyon. If snow conditions are good it is possible to glissade this gully from the summit ridge in ¼ hr.

Unnamed (9270)

Around the head of the South Ghost River is a mile-wide, N facing, double cirque (dry) which is marked by high points, one at the NW and other at the E.

Grotto Mtn (8880)

4 mi E of Canmore; 3 mi NW of Lac des Arcs; at S end of range.

This mountain has been ascended many times from earliest days of white exploration. It is easily done by a variety of routes on the side facing the highway. In May 1955 B. A. Fraser, R. C. Hind and Miss I. Spreat made a new route involving good rock climbing on the NW ridge. 4½ hr from the highway to the summit (CAJ 38–67). In Dec 1955 D. Morrison and J. Tarrant approached the SE ridge from Gap Lake. Minor difficulties were encountered on steep rock. 3½ hr up (CAJ 39–87).

Mt. Fable (8865)

4½ mi NW of Exshaw; 4 mi W of Yamnuska. Good rock on S.

F. A. May 1947 R. C. Hind, L. Parker, J. F. Tarrant. **NE**

Ridge From camp on creek E of peak, ascend a stream to the N of peak until easy scree slopes can be followed up to the left to the NE ridge. Ridge climbed for several hundred feet affording difficult climbing, including 2 short but severe cracks. A small plateau reached, then easy going over scree, slabs and snow to the summit. Descent was made down the N face swinging left to a long snow couloir leading to head of creek on the N side of the peak. (CAJ *31*–237)

2 — S Ridge. June 1964 D. Gardner, C. Locke, G. Walsh From Exshaw follow old road and then horse trail for one hr up Exshaw Creek. Then left (W) up side valley to base of ridge (stay in bottom on avalanche snow). 3 hr to base of climb. A choice of slabs is available for the first half of the climb. If the lowest is used some difficulty will be found in switching to a higher one later on. The second to the last slab provides a classic route with six pitches of continuous 45° F3 climbing on excellent water-grooved limestone. At the point where the lower slabs steepen to 60° and the upper ones end, climb left into an obvious gulley system. Climb to the highest reasonable horizontal ledge then right up a thin 100′ crack (F4-several pitons). This leads back to the SW ridge just below the summit. Descent via the scree col to the W, thence down shale slopes to the approach gully. 12 hr round trip.

End Mtn (7940)
6 mi N of Yamnuska, S of South Ghost River. Good cliffs of rock comparable to those peaks described below.

CMC Valley
In 1969, the late Archie Simpson insisted there was great climbing potential from the valley W of Yamnuska and that the Calgary Mountain Club should rebuild an old log cabin in the area. The cabin, left by a logging operation, was in terrible condition, but with a little money and a lot of work it was restored and has become a haven for rock climbers in this beautiful little unnamed valley which drains E to Old Fort Creek on the N or back side of the Yamnuska.
Since the cabin has been open, close to thirty routes, not

more than ½ hr from the cabin, have been pioneered on the limestone cliffs N of the valley. From the very easy to a super bolt diretissima, routes for beginner to expert offer pleasure to the rock climber.

It is nearly impossible to list in detail all of the routes, so below are 23 climbs and their grades, with a sketch to show where they are located. There is a book in the cabin describing most of the routes in detail.

The area is approached by the access road to Yamnuska off highway #1A. From a quarry at the end of the road a trail leads NE through the woods, climbing slowly to the open slopes E of Yamnuska. The ridge E of Yamnuska is crossed (stay off Indian land E of fence), then a good trail descends to the cabin, roughly 2 mi from the quarry. The cabin sleeps 12 people and is open to all. The CMC asks only that the valley and cabin are left clean and garbage carried out when leaving. Key to hut and additional data from CMC, Box 1421, Calgary, Alberta.

BILBO BUTTRESS

1.	Magnetic Floss	F7	Grade 1	
		J. White & J. Martin		Oct 1971
2.	Electric Apples	F6–7	Grade 1	
		J. White & J. Martin		June 1971
3.	Vegetable	F6	A2	
4.	Blackened Rat	F5		
		S. Stahl, S. Slymon & J. Martin		April 1971
5.	Cat Knackerer	F7, A1 or F9		
		S. Slymon & B. Greenwood		May 1971
6.	Knackered Cat	F6		
		F. Williamson, J. Keunzel, B. Greenwood		
7.	Peanut Point	F5	J. Martin, G. Pilkington	
8.	Devil's Banquet	F7	G. Pilkington, S. Slymon	
9.	Crowley's Corner	F8		
		J. White & P. Zrengrowski		May 1971
10.	Devil's Desert			
11.	Lacquered Crow	F6	Grade 1	
		J. Jones, B. Schneider, C. Smith		Oct 1970

12. Dogleg Corner	F8	R. Breeze, J. Horne
13. Dirty Dago	F8	
	J. Jones & G. Homer	April 1971

THE RUNES

14. Chingle	F8	Grade 11
	J. Jones & B. Greenwood	Oct 1971
15. Weed	F6	
	J. Jones & S. Sylmon	March 1971
16. Double Direct	F 7–8	Grade 1
	J. Martin & J. White	May 1971

FRODO BUTTRESS

17. Indecision	F8	Grade 1
	J. Jones & C. Smith	Nov 1970
18. Luminous Pigeon	F7	Grade 1
	J. Jones & B. Schneider	Oct 1970
19. The Illiad	F8	Grade 11
	R. Wood & G. Homer	Nov 1970
20. Parasite	F8	
	D. Jones & B. Haggerstone	May 1972

WACONDA BUTTRESS

21. Waracrasquechimsla	F8, A2	Grade III
	M. Galbraith & B. McKeith	
22. Iron Suspender	F8, A4	1971
	G. Homer & W. Davidson	
23. Mayflower	F7	
	G. Homer, J. Jones &	
	P. Morrow	April 1971

Mt. John Laurie (*Yamnuska*) (7890)
A limestone uplift on the E edge of the Rocky Mountains. N of the Calgary-Banff highway, 50 mi W of Calgary and 30 mi E of Banff, its E face plainly visible. A short gravel road on the old highway one mi E of the connecting road between old and new highways allows cars to be driven to the foot of the slope leading to the face, which is then one hr distant. It is popular with local climbers, particularly in spring and fall when, because of its position, it is often in good condition when other peaks are not. (CAJ 49–127), Yamnuskanalysis).

The climbing is generally very steep, often vertical or over

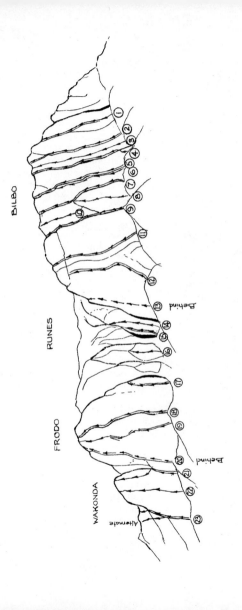

hanging, a characteristic of limestone. The face is over a mile in width and reaches a maximum height of 1200'. A variety of routes have been put up over the full length of the face, ranging in length from 200' to over 1000'. Caution is advised on account of loose rocks, but this is becoming less of a problem on the more popular routes. The possibilities of additional routes still remain, and to date there has been little use of artificial aids. Essential pitons are often in place, but it is advisable to carry a small supply on most routes.

The routes are listed from S to N, left to right.

King's Chimney, 1964 B. King, D. Vockeroth. Start as for Unnamed, traversing left after the first pitch to reach the chimney. Follow this to the top and traverse left to finish. I, F4.

Unnamed A prominent diagonal line to the top of the face. 1961, J. Steen, *B. Greenwood*. Same standard as Calgary route, but shorter. Height of climb 600' (CAJ 45–124). I,5.4.

Missionaries Crack. 1964. B. Greenwood, D. Vockeroth. From top of first pitch of Unnamed traverse right to a chimney; climb this and the steep wall on left above, then left to where the crack can be easily reached. II, F8

Belfry. 1957, *R. Thompson, B. Greenwood*.

In a prominent break W of Calgary route. A prominent corner marked at the top by an easy angled slab. Start right of the corner and follow an easy gully system to the foot of the corner. Strenuous climbing; small overhangs continually block the way and must be taken direct. More difficult but shorter than Direttissima route. No pitons used (CAJ 45–124) 11, F7.

Necromancer. 1971, C. Homer, J. Jones.

W of Mum's Tears. ½ way up, a large ledge exists to the Calgary. 5.8, A, 1000'.

Mums Tears. 1968, C. Locke, D. Vockeroth. W of Calgary.

Calgary. 1952, H. Gmoser, L. Grillmair. A long diagonal line starting directly below the summit and ending some distance W of it. First section fairly easy, but becomes blocked by a large overhang, requiring traverse to right. Vertical climbing thence required two pitons. I, F5 (CAJ 27–110).

CMC Wall. 1972, W. Davidson, U Kallen. A severe artificial climb between Calgary and Direttissima. VI, 5.8, A4.

Direttissima, 1957, H. Gmoser, L. Grillmair, H. Kahl.

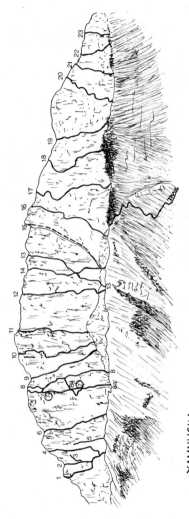

YAMNUSKA

1. King's Chimney
2. Unnamed
3. The Toe
4. Missionaries Crack
5. The Tongue
6. Belfry
7. Necromancer
8. Mums Tears
8A. Mums Tears Alt
9. Calgary
10. CMC Wall
11. Direttissima
12. Balrog
13. Chockstone Corner
14. Bottleneck
15. Grillmair
16. Kahl Wall
17. Forbidden Corner
18. Red Shirt
19. The Bowl
20. Corkscrew
21. Freakout
22. Pangolin
23. Gollem Grooves

Starting from a large ledge after easy scrambling, follow a series of inside corners ending a few feet E of the summit (CAJ *41*–52, marked photo). III, F7.

Balrog. B. Greenwood, J. Moss, R. Nicholas IV, 5.9.

Chockstone Corner. 1963, H. Kahl, R. Lofthouse. Climb starts midway between Direttissima and Grillmair routes 150'past the left edge of the large scree bowl, and W of a buttress. Ascend a chimney and over a slab to a large ledge. Continue to right, climb a crack behind a large pinnacle, gain a belt of slabs and climb the wall to right, gaining the exit chimneys. 20 pitons left in place (CAJ 47–116; marked photo). III, F7. Alternate start. F8, A2. Climb the corner to right of buttress to gain the detached pinnacle. The steep crack to the left of this start has been climbed; I Hayes, G. Homer. 5.9

Bottleneck. A. Cole, R. Lofthouse. Start as for Chockstone Corner, but follow independent line above the pinnacle.

Grillmair Chimneys. 1952, Miss I. Spreat, H. Gmoser, L. Grillmair. A broken section directly above the scree bowl. By the corner formed against the steep wall on left (preferable), or by a series of gullies and chimneys to right (CAJ 37–109). I, 5.4

Kahl Wall 1971 T. Auger, D. Vockeroth 8½ pitches 5 — 6 hr Follows big corner right (N) of Grillmair Chimneys III, 5.7, A2, 900'.

Forbidden Corner, 1965, L. MacKay, D. Vockeroth. An inside corner for 300' followed by easier climbing to left, then a series of zigzag traverses to top of the face. III, F8

Red Shirt. 1962, B. Greenwood, H. Kahl, R. Lofthouse. (U1AA 5) From left side of the bowl climbing slight left for 300'. Descend slightly and traverse left 100'. Climb out above end of traverse (CAJ *46*–97). II, F6.

The Bowl. 1965, L. MacKay, D. Vockeroth. From right of the bowl by a sloping ramp for two rope lengths, climb wall above to a steep chimney, above which go left and climb out in the middle of the bowl. III, A2.

Corkscrew. 1967, H.Fuhrer, B. Greenwood, D.Vockeroth. 5.8, A3.

Freak Out. 1971, B. Davidson, J. Horne. To the left of Pangolin. 5.9; 300'.

Pangolin. 1965, B. Greenwood, R. Lofthouse, D. Vockeroth. From a very slight outcrop of rock by a series of cracks until it is possible to traverse left below the exit chimney. II, F7, A2; or 5.9.

Gollem Grooves. 1962, B. Greenwood, R. Lofthouse. By a wide groove for 150'. Traverse right and climb over loose rock to a large ledge. Usual finish is by traverse to right from above the ledge, although the crack above has been climbed direct to the top. (CAJ 45–99). I, F7

Goat Mtn (7850)

The actual summit is 4 mi NNE of Exshaw, but the cliff lines are ½ mi E of the Top *(Goat Buttress)* and one mi SSE *(Goat Slabs).* This area is SW of the Yamnuska and the cliff faces are considerably higher. A line near the N edge of Goat Buttress was climbed in 1961 by B. Greenwood, R. Lofthouse, J. Steen (CAJ 45–119) and little has been done since then. Goat Slabs, however, has been the scene of two routes, with the potential of a great many more (CAJ 55–83.)

1. *Dream of an Electric Sheep* 5.8, IV B. McKeith & B. Greenwood 1971.
2. *Chocolate Frog* 5.7, III B. McKeith & Miss J. Sterner 1971.

SAWBACK RANGE

These are the peaks N of the Bow River from Banff W to the mouth of Baker Creek. Access to the peaks bounding the W of Forty Mile Creek is best via Edith Pass trail which is approached from the Vermilion Lakes road, 3 mi W of Banff. Cars may be left here and trail followed (N of the main highway) 2½ mi to Edith Pass. Thence trail descends to Forty Mile Creek and an approach to Mts. Louis and Edith. At height of pass branch left to N base of Mt. Edith; then drop down over talus to base of Mt. Louis. Access is also possible via trail from Mt. Norquay parking lot #3, but is longer than via Edith Pass; 2-3 hr to base of Mt. Louis by either route.

A number of high points in the area N of Cascade Mtn were occupied by various parties of Dominion surveyors between the years 1887 and 1953. These are partially reported in CAJ *18* – 50 by one of the greater names in surveying, M. P. Bridgland.

Cascade Mtn (9836)

4 mi N of Banff; NW of junction of Cascade and Bow Rivers; E of Forty Mile Creek. Dr. Hector triangulated this summit on August 15, 1858, obtaining an elevation of 4521' above the valley (CAJ *1*–58; *22*–161).

F. A. 1887 by L. B. Stewart, T. E. Wilson. From Banff ascend valley to Forty Mile Creek for 2 mi whence the long SW arete may be gained and the summit reached without difficulty. Mt. Assiniboine is visible.

A. H. MacCarthy reported SE arete a good climb with firm rock.

E Face. Aug 1934, J. Miskow, *L. Grassi*. S of the waterfall. Ascent 8¼ hr, descent by S face (CAJ *22*–212).

There are many good rock climbs on the lower buttresses of the E face. The largest of these buttresses (to the right) gives the greatest scope for routes. Six routes were done in 1971 and 1972 mostly by L. MacKay and K. Baker. The severity is generally F 7 on excellent rock ranging from 1000' to

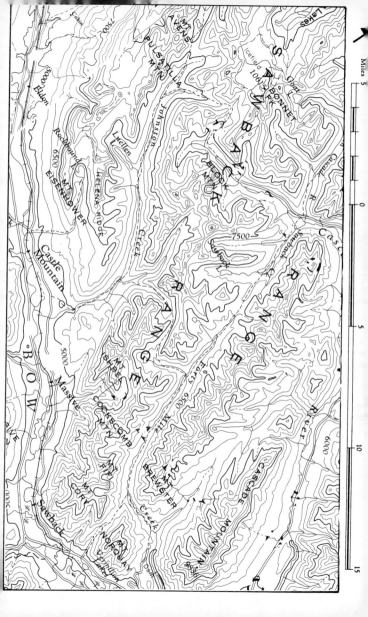

1500′ in height. Two routes have been done on the impressive cliffs N of the waterfall. They follow corner lines in the middle of the face. The line to the right is III, F7 and 15 pitches. The left line is somewhat harder. Descent from climbs on these buttresses is made by climbing shale and scree above the cliffs, then descending into the valley to the N.

Mt. Norquay (8276)

Adjoins Mt. Edith on E; N of Bow River; ski area on E slopes (CAJ 8–79, 135).

F. R. A. 1917 by N. W. Greenham. From NW corner of second Vermilion Lake, near motor road, ascend rocks to E ridge. A large gendarme is traversed to SW. Easy going on arete to final tower which is ascended by a short, wide chimney. Road to summit, 4 hr.

In 1941 the W (highest) summit was ascended via rocks of the S ridge in 3⅓ hr by E. Cromwell, Miss G. Engelhard. The same party later ascended the E peak by way of the E and NE slopes to the intervening col, thence following the N ridge. Summit cairn, but no record. No challenges (AAJ 4–493).

The ski lift is now the accepted starting point for the mountain.

Mt. Brewster (9380)

Between Cascade Mtn and Forty Mile Creek. On the ridge extending for 12 mi N are numerous points higher than Mt. Brewster (AAJ 4–308).

F. A. 1926 by H. W. Greenham, Miss D. Pilley. From camp at foot of Mt. Edith, crossing Edith Pass and down Forty Mile Creek to the SW slope of the Vermilion Range, of which Mt. Brewster is the S peak. No difficulties following line of least resistance. Descent via terraced E cliffs, the only obstacle being a 6′ fissure just before reaching upper meadows. Thence down easy turf to trail. 16 hr round trip.

Mt. Edith (8380)

In NW angle between Forty Mile Creek and Bow River. This mtn consists of three major summits, the highest being the northern (farthest from the road). The most popular climbs are on the S peak. The easiest approach to this popular climb is to branch off from the trail to Edith Pass on a side trail which mounts the S ridge, then skirts the W scree slopes. This can be followed to the Edith-Cory Col.

F. A. 1900 by J. N. Collie, P. Stevens. **W face to N peak.** Ascend valley W of Mt. Norquay (2 mi W of road to ski area) to Edith-Norquay Pass. From this point a natural bridge is visible crossing a gully halfway to the summit. Ascend scree slopes and steep rocks, keeping well to the right of the bridge to the col between the peaks of Mt. Edith. Cross col and ascend W side on steep but firm rocks to reach a large slab split off from the face. Ascend between this slab and the peak and an almost vertical 60' chimney leading to the summit (App 17–13; CAJ 2–1, 136)

2 — N Face to N Peak. 1961, G. W. Boles, B. Greenwood. The route is seen from Mt. Louis. From the point where the E face sweeps around into the gap between Mts. Louis and Edith, there is a stretch of good clean rock 1000' high, ending to the right in a section of scree-filled gullies that go up to the main peak. The ascent, including the final easy scramble over the ridge to the main peak, required 8 hr after leaving the scree. Descent by the W face and the Edith Pass trail (CAJ 45–125).

3 — NE Face. 1941, E. Cromwell, Miss G. Engelhard. The second (middle) summit was ascended by the NE face via a gully between second and third summits. Steep, loose scree. Gully leads to the ridge immediately below and to the NW of the summit — 4 hr. Cairn, but no record. Thence a traverse was made N to the third summit. Cairn, without record (AAJ 4–493).

4 — E Face. 1956, F. J. Garneau, *H. Gmoser*. A more direct route on the E face than the following, starting 150' further N and following a crack for 250' before traversing a long way upward along a wide ledge. This leads to the bottom of a chimney system intercepting the S ridge below the summit.

5 — E Face. May, 1953, F. Dopf, P. de la Salle, *H. Gmoser*. Via the E face, 600' N of the big gully that cuts through the

SE face. The first pitch leads up over a slab onto a small shelf. Thence follow a steep rib for 150', traversing 30' to right before following a small crack up for 40'. The big shoulder on the S ridge is gained and the ridge followed to the summit (AAJ 10–2, 158; CAJ 37–108).

6 — S Ridge. May 1951, M. Hicks, R. C. Hind, J. F. Tarrant. From road follow trail to open slope leading to base of S ridge. Smooth slabs lead to ridge and a prominent gully just E of the arete. This is ascended to its top just below the crest (cairn). Follow ridge over broken rock to summit. Ascent 4½ hr (CAJ 35–158). At base of S ridge is a spectacular 80' spike climbed in 1962 by B. Greenwood.

Mt. Cory (*Hole-in-the-Wall*) (9194)

Adjoins Mt. Edith on W; N of Bow River.

No data as to first ascent.

1939, Miss G. Engelhard, F. S. North. From old road at Mile 6 out of Banff via the S ridge. An easy ascent to a double summit, both points of equal height and with cairns. Ascent 4½ hr.

2 — SW Chimney. July 1960, J. R. MacKenzie, *H. Gmoser*. From the old highway when just W of the "hole" via base of the triangular 1000' face and the crack which breaks it from top to bottom. Solid rock. From the summit an easy walk in gully on SE leads back to highway in 2 hr. 4 hr on rock up. II, 5.4 (CAJ 44–52).

3 — SW Face. *Moss Crack.* Sept 1969 by J. Moss, D. Steenkamp. 300' right (SE) of Gmoser Crack to right of prominent inside corner. II, F6 (CAJ 53–72).

4 — SW Face. *Clockwork Orange.* 1971, C. Jones, G. Pilkington, G. Thompson. 150 yards right of main crack. Climb obvious crack for 2 leads. 3rd pitch requires aid in lower blank section. 3 more leads in crack, thence left (N) unroped to summit. III, 5.5. A1. A less distinct line (*Arboreal Delight*) between Moss Crack and Clockwork Orange was done in 1971 by G. Pilkington, W. Smith. 1000' III, 5.5.

Mt. Louis (8800)

The first tower N of Mt. Edith; W of Forty Mile Creek.

One hour from Mt. Norquay parking lot #3 by trail; approach also over Edith Pass.

F. A. July 1916 by A. H. MacCarthy, *C. Kain*. **SE Face.** Keep main couloir of E face to right, and at times stay as far left as SE ridge until easy ledge system skirting base of steep E cliffs is reached. Descend left in short chimney to S around corner on easy ledge to grassy platform on the S face. After steep 75' climb into the base of a steep gully above and to W, traverse left (W) over a rib, across a second gully and onto a rib beyond, working up to effect the traverse. Climb this rib over exposed but firm rock to broad platform 450' below the summit. A chimney 12' deep and rising at 75° leads to summit in ¾ hr, 3½ hr from base of rocks (CAJ 8–79). Parties subsequent to the 1916 ascent have varied the original route in many particulars on the SE side (AJ 32–68; App 17–18; CAJ 9–32). Descent in 2½ hr if familiar with route.

Variant. 1952, H. B. Burton, *W. Perren*. At the base of the final tower diverge to right (towards Banff) up a series of slabs and small faces (3 pitons), avoiding the deep, narrow chimney (AAJ 10–124).

2 — S Face. 1964, J. Fuller, L. Kor. Start directly above the Louis-Edith saddle. The first leads follow a large gully system, difficult in first lead. From the top of the gully a steep ramp was ascended to the left where holds on the face were thin. Above this, slabs and chimneys were followed to the summit. NCCS III, F8, A2 (AAJ 14–439).

3 — W Face. July 1962, F. Beckey, Mr. & Mrs. J. A. Rupley. This is the shortest route but has a forbidding lower wall of friable rock. From W col climb two pitches of steep, loose rock to a gully. Some piton work needed, and there is a bolt in place. Then climb a chimney forking right; traverse around a corner (right), and climb several hundred feet. Thence scramble to the summit. Descent by rappel (AAJ 13–2–499).

4 — N Face. Aug 1930, S. B. Hendricks, Miss P. Prescott, *E. Feuz, Jr.* Climb upwards to right (NW) from high point of E alpland. Descend slightly to cross the great couloir and continue N along base of vertical wall until near N face. Turn W and cross base of first platform to right (W) edge of N face. Ascend ribs, bearing gradually left until a difficult vertical wall

MT LOUIS

E Ridge

Mt Fifi

Kor

Kain

Gmoser

is reached. Traverse left above this into a broad couloir leading to highest point of first buttress. Descent 50' from this point and up narrow crack to top of the second buttress, from which summit can easily be reached. Ascent 5 hr (CAJ *19*–52).

5 — NE Face. June 1962, K. Hahn, G. Prinz. Ascend main couloir to narrows. Move right to E ridge. Stay on ridge to rejoin face. Ascend well defined gully separating E face from main mass of mtn. Loose rock. Follow gully-chimney to notch below summit. 5 hr (CAJ *47*–112, marked photo).

6 — E Ridge. (600'S of NE ridge, across huge chasm). 1969, G. Rowell, T. Auger. Follow E arete direct to summit, crossing Route 3 at base of vertical slabs of main face. Good rock. Follow dihedrals on steep 80° wall. F8, 10 hr RT from Banff; 4½ hr on rock (AAJ *17*–148).

Winter Ascent. March 1965. B. Greenwood, L. MacKay. Via S Face.

Mt. Fifi (8600)

Adjoins Mt. Louis on NW.

F. A. Sept 1921 by L. S. Crosby, J. W. A. Hickson, *E. Feuz, Jr.* From Forty Mile Creek, ascend into amphitheatre between Mt. Louis and Mt. Fifi work around to S of latter to couloir running deep into the mountain on S side; 3⅓ hr. Ascend couloir (falling stones and rotten rock near top) to narrow notch between N and S towers, ⅔ hr; both towers may be ascended over steep rock, one hr, the N being the higher by 50'. Rappel necessary for its descent (CAJ *12*–59).

2 — W Col. Aug 1930, S. B. Hendricks, Miss W. MacLaren, Miss P. Prescott. The recommended route follows goat tracks around the E face of the mountain, gaining the high W col by short scree slopes on the N side (CAJ *19*–150).

Mt. Finger (8350)

2 mi W of Mt. Louis; a spur of an unnamed peak (9040'). 11 mi NW of Banff on Lake Louise highway. W face 1000; E wall is 200' above a col. (CAJ *46*–88, marked photo and diagram).

F. A. in 1930's by L. Grassi and party. From high col on the E side, after approach from NW up a creek gully.

2 — W Ridge. 1956, K. Baker, *H. Gmoser*. 5 hr to top (CAJ *40*–84).

3 — SW Face. 1958, J. Board, Miss A. Morton. Via the SW ribs and ridge of S peak. Best rock climbing is on this route.

Variant. 1962, D. Brewer, *P. Fuhrmann*. SSW ridge, descending by rappels on Route 2, making first traverse.

Mt. Cockscomb (9110)

One mi N of Mt. Finger; SE of Mt. Ishbel.

Although higher than neighboring peaks to the SE, this summit offers less challenge and has not been climbed with regularity.

Mt. Ishbel (9540)

E of upper Johnston Creek and N of Banff-Lake Louise highway. Many points on the ridge, extending 6 mi to N, exceed 9000'.

F. A. Sept 1933 by Misses D. Day, J. Packer, V. Waters, Messrs. J. Farish, W. Innes, L. LeCouteur, J. Sterling, *L. Grassi*. From SW through underbrush and grass slopes to ledges and couloirs, affording 1½ hr of climbing to the ridge, whence the summit is attained in ⅓ hr. Descent by N slopes. Total time 12 hr (CAJ *22*–212).

2 — S Ridge. 1957, Dr. & Mrs. D. J. Fabian, P. Reid, A. G. Reynolds. From the highway the ridge is followed throughout 6 hr, with descent on E side into the SE valley to regain the road (CAJ *41*–70).

Variant. 1964, D. J. Forest, Miss K. Forest. The E ridge is ascended for half its length. Thence follow a distinct ledge on the E face about two rope lengths lower than the summit ridge. The ledge ends just below the top; thence to the crest and along it to the summit. Less exposed than Route 2.

3 — N Face. 1972, K. Baker, L. MacKay. Easy class 4 over good rock.

Unnamed (10040)

2 mi SE of Block Mtn; 2 mi W of Sawback Lake (Cascade

River); E of Johnston Creek; W of pass connecting head of Forty Mile Creek an Cascade River.

F. A. 1890 by W. S. Drewry, *T. E. Wilson*. From Johnston Creek tributary.

Block Mtn (9633)

4 mi S of Bonnet Peak; 5 mi E of Pulsatilla Mtn. Attractive lakes to SE. Accessible by Cascade River road and trail.

F. A. 1920 by Topographical Survey (Bridgland)

Protection Mtn (9140)

5 mi N of Baker Creek Bungalows; 8 mi E of Lake Louise.

Mt. Avens (9750)

One mi W of Pulsatilla Pass at head of Wildflower Creek.

Pulsatilla Mtn (9950)

4 mi N of Stuart Knob; 3 mi SE of Protection Mtn.

F. A. July 1930 by J. W. A. Hickson, *E. Feuz, Jr.* From camp S of Pulsatilla Pass via small glacier on E side of objective peak to rock wall at 8800'. The wall is ascended for 450' to the N ridge (9350). Descend loose rocks to the NW side and up glacier to summit rocks. Ascent 5¼ hr (CAJ *19*–46).

Variant. Aug 1969, W. L. Putnam, L. R. Wallace. From camp near Pulsatilla Pass via Pass and E side of lake to W of subsidiary summit one mi NE of objective. Ascend snow (S) to col thence scramble to N ridge and N glacier as in Route One 5 hr to summit.

Unnamed (9750)

4 mi NW of Mt. Eisenhower; 2 mi N of Luellen Lake. Presently an antenna site for Park radio system.

F. A. July 1949 by Miss C. Cromwell, Mr. & Mrs. E. Cromwell. From old highway via creek W of Stuart Knob. No difficulties (CAJ *33*–31).

Stuart Knob (9350)

3 mi NW of Mt. Eisenhower above Luellen Lake (Johnston Creek).

F. A. date, route and party unknown, probably by O. Montanus. Aug 1971 W. L. Putnam, A. Wexler from camp by Tower Lake via E side of Rockbound Lake, and E ridge. 5 hr RT. Class 4. T. E. Wilson and/or J. J. McArthur climbed N end of Castle Mtn ridge in 1888.

Helena Ridge (9390)
NE of Mt. Eisenhower Tower.
1941, E. Cromwell, Miss G. Engelhard.
From Castle Ranger Station via S bank of Castle Creek, up broken rock to summit. Small cairn with no record. Ascent 5½ hr (AAJ *4*–493).

Mt. Eisenhower (*Castle*) (9076)
Opposite Vermilion Pass, a challenging rock climb from every approach exept from NW. For change of name see CAJ *29*–305. The faces consist of two tiers of cliffs each approximately 1000′ in height and divided by a wide scree ledge— the Goat Plateau. The upper cliff contains several routes of medium or high standard, and shows possibility of very high standard routes. The lower cliff has not been seriously touched except as an approach to the Plateau, although routes have recently been done from Tower Lake. In 1967 the Calgary Mountain Club erected a six-man bivouac hut equipped with gasoline stove and mattresses, on the Plateau at third buttress W of SE end.

The Goat Plateau is generally reached via the trail to Rockbound Lake until just after it narrows and flattens out over the shoulder. Through the trees to the left (W) footpaths can be followed to the base of the tower. The lower cliff can be climbed (a) to the right of a big tower of rock, then diagonally across to the left. It was on this approach where a fatality occurred in 1962 when an unroped climber fell due to a loose handhold (CAJ *46*–103) or; (b) easier — from the tower of rock follow a good ledge several hundred feet left to its end then up a gully which leads back right to the plateau.

A second approach leads directly to the hut. Take the trail to the fire lookout which starts about 4 mi towards Lake Louise from Eisenhower Junction on the old highway. The trail is marked but easy to miss. From the fire lookout a sometimes ill-defined trail leads up the steep slope to a large gully. Enter gully over a rock shoulder (don't get into gully too low). The top of this gully is the regular water supply for the hut which is located on the edge of the cliff some distance to the right, toward Banff.

F. A. 1884 by A. P. Coleman. **NE Approach.** From Castle Ranger Station via good trail in the valley E and N of the mountain to Rockbound Lake from the head of which the only difficulty is a short cliff belt with loose rock easily passed to N of lake (Coleman–43; AJ 38–251).

2 — NE Face. Aug 1971, E. F. Boss, L. Putnam, W. L. Putnam, L. R. Wallace, A. Wexler. From camp at Tower Lake, lower cliff can be climbed by several 5.3 buttresses to Goat Plateau. Route starts 50 yds right (W) of watercourse ¼ mi W of notch separating SE Tower. In three leads gain crest of buttress to NW of watercourse. Route stays on or near crest of buttress. Numerous pitons. Five leads to an easier stretch of continuous climbing. Then one lead to top. Crux at third pitch. Loose rock. II, 5.6 (CAJ 55–85).

3 — SW Face. June 1961, D. Brewer, L. Irwin. (1200') directly to the summit. Approach as for SE tower, skirting below the cliffs from the foot of the tower, from the main peak. The route follows the general line of a slight ridge or buttress in the face, the lower part being just right of the obvious buttress at the foot of the ridge. Good rock throughout. (CAJ 45–122). (UIAA IV+)

In 1972, G. Homer, J. Jones, G. Rogan, R. Wood ascended W of Brewer Buttress 5.8, A1, Grade IV. A hard varied route of free climbing and aid over 13 pitches. Bolt required above mid-point of climb to reach a crack system higher up. Corner led out to the top.

4 — S Face. Central buttress. June 1963, F. Beckey, B. S. Marts. Route follows right corner of great central buttress (left of Route 3). Chimneys are climbed several pitches from the great transverse ledge; thence on a face directly to the top. The angle is high, and pitons are needed for safety on most pitches. Due to absence of cracks, some of the harder sections were climbed unroped because of lack of means to

135

Route T2

E. Cooper

SE Tower

Route T3

Goat Plateau

Mt Eisenhower from SW

Brewer Ridge

Route 4

Catch 22

Bass Buttress

Bivouac Hut

protect them. Rock is not sound except final three pitches (AAJ *14*–203).

5 — SW Face. 1968, P. Jackson, R. Hogan. Chimney to right of wall beyond Bass Buttress. Cairn at start of route. The route follows a large open chimney for half the distance to the summit. Then a face with options to the right; 5.6.

6 — Bass Buttress, 1968, B. Greenwood, J. Farrand. Directly above bivouac hut, right of gully. Ascend chimney 300′ to crest of steep arete (buttress) which is then followed throughout, bearing left onto W face at final pitch; 5.4.

7 — SW Face *(Catch 22)* above bivouac hut, 1971, B. Greenwood, J. Jones. Right (E) of two obvious breaks. Culminates in a difficult, sensational and exposed pitch, breaking left from cave at top of chimneys. Thence back to right and easier ground to top. F9, 12 leads, 1200′. (CAJ *55*–83).

8 — SW Ridge. 1967, G. Crocker, H. Gude. 8th Buttress N of skyline as seen from SE. Move NW on Goat Plateau from hut to base of buttress, one hr. Start to left of ridge up concave wall. Route is on or near crest of ridge and is similar in character to Brewer Buttress but one grade easier. Excellent rock. No pitons. Descent via gully to hut. 6 hr RT.

9 — NW Approach. 1949, Mr. & Mrs. E. Cromwell. The NW summit was reached from the old highway via a gully system near the NW edge of the face. Approach via trail to fire lookout branching left (N) below lower cliff. (CAJ *33*–29).

SE Tower (9030)

F. A. Aug 1926 by P. Cerutti, *L. Grassi.* Move right (N) on Goat Plateau until prominent couloir dividing Tower from mountain proper is reached. Ascend this to its crest and then climb upward on NW face to the tower on the S side of the couloir in the face. Summit gained near mid-point of NW face, 2½ hr from base (CAJ *18*–92; *19*–54.)

Variant Aug 1927, C. Newhall, F. Zwicky. As in Route One, save that the couloir descending between mountain proper and the tower was gained from the SW (CAJ *18*–93).

2 — SE Ridge. Aug 1926, J. W. A. Hickson, *E. Feuz.* Gain the top of the SE buttress by cracks in its S or N face and cross this to the base of the steep slopes of the tower. Climb to SE of the broad open couloir, keeping about midway between it and the S face until a broad gravelly platform is reached. Ascend, bearing N. 2½ hr base to summit. The first party on this route rappelled four times in descending (CAJ 16–52; 19–54).

Variant. Aug 1928, Miss E. Greer, F. Neave. As in Route 2 save for final pitches being to right (N) of couloir in upper part of Tower. 2½ hr up from Goat Plateau. (CAJ 18–93).

3 — W Face. July 1967, R. Lofthouse, E. Peyer. From couloir in center of face to rib at left, and severe overhang. Zig-zag upwards, traverse to right and into couloir again about halfway up. Up icy chimney, out to right and up edge of large flake. Thence up severe pitch and left up easier corner. III, F7 (AAJ 16–171).

4 — N Ridge. Aug 1971, E. F. Boss, L. R. Wallace. From camp near Tower Lake, ascend lower cliff line or by talus cone to N of col separating tower. At major chockstone (about halfway up) exit left (Tower side). Four leads on buttress N of open upper couloir (of Rte. one). Then cross to join Rte. One for final 3 leads. Numerous rappels on descent. III, F6 (CAJ 55–85).

5 — N Face. 1972, K. Baker, L. Mackay
Route begins 1/3 of way across face from left-hand (E) side. 5.7,A1.

Und willst du die schlafende Löwin nicht wecken / So wandré still durch die Strasse der Schrecken
And if you don't wish to waken the sleeping avalanche, then walk quietly along the road of fear.

J. C. F. Schiller

BALL RANGE

The airline distance between Simpson and Vermilion Passes is 14 mi, two minor passes, Ball and Redearth, occurring in the interval. Mt. Ball is the dominating peak. The whole E face of the massif presents a precipitous rock escarpment, hung with glaciers, which at Mt. Ball is nearly 4000' high. On the SW the group is bounded by Vermilion River and on the NE by Bow River. The Continental Divide passes over the principal summits.

This group is reached easily from various directions. On the SW the Hawk Creek trail (cabins at highway) ascends steeply from a point 13 mi S of Vermilion Pass, connecting through Ball Pass (6 mi) with trails in Banff Park. On the W an excellent trail leads up through the 1968 burn from a point on the highway 2 mi S of Vermilion Pass along the creek draining the glacier N of Stanley Peak. From the N the Twin Lakes trail leaves the highway from the picnic area just E of Eisenhower Junction reaching Twin Lakes in 4½ mi. At the lakes it meets the trails from Storm Mtn Lodge and from Gibbon Pass.

From the NE, access is via fire road in Redearth Creek and trail to Shadow Lake (9 mi from highway). At the end of the fire road the Pharaoh Creek trail branches off to SE reaching Redearth Pass (cabin below Egypt Lake) in 7½ mi. From Shadow Lake (cabin) the trail continues 3 mi to Ball Pass.

From the E a fire road (closed to normal vehicular traffic) leads up Healy Creek a distance of 10 mi to the lodges W of Lookout Mtn. Near the headwaters of Healy Creek the trail connects with others in the Kootenay drainage, SE towards Mt. Assiniboine and W, over Healy Pass to Pharaoh Creek.

Vermilion Pass, an old route of Cree war parties, was traversed by Dr. Hector, of the Palliser expedition, in 1858, his party then crossing from the Kootenay to Beaverfoot River and descending the latter to the Kicking Horse valley. Maps: 8204; 82N1

Storm Mtn (10372)

N of Mt. Ball; SE buttress of Vermilion Pass.

F. A. 1889 by W. S. Drewry, A. St. Cyr, *T. E. Wilson*. Via creek on S emptying into Vermilion River; camp at timberline; 7 hr to summit. Inferences in CAJ *1*–88 indicate that Whymper may have made an ascent from Vermilion Pass in 1901. However, recent revelations cast doubt on several of the mountaineering feats credited to Whymper in the Rockies.

2 — NE Ridge. June 1961, G. W. Boles, B. Greenwood. From Twin Lakes the NE ridge forms a broken wall and is reached by one of many gullies. A series of gullies to the left of the ridge is the easiest approach and the ridge is followed only for the last 300′. Descent by the B. C. slopes to the Radium Highway (CAJ *45*–119). Ridge W of, and paralleling the long NE ridge was climbed by B. Greenwood & D. Lofthouse in 1958. No particular difficulties.

Unnamed (10160)

2 mi N of Mt. Ball; NE of Stanley Peak at head of glacier draining to Shadow Lake. A double peak, its E and W summits nearly equal, with lesser points on ridge to E towards Gibbon Pass.

F. A. **W summit,** 1971. F. Campbell, S. King, Miss P. McBeth. Via Stanley Glacier trail to its end. Thence angle up toward summit on S side of NW ridge over much scree and rotten rock. Route not recommended. Descent straight down face to head of valley.

Stanley Peak (10351)

4 mi S of Vermilion Pass; just W of the portion of the Divide connecting Mt. Bell with Storm Mtn.

F. A. 1901 by E. Whymper and guides. (See Mt. Whymper). The easiest route is via the Stanley Glacier trail and the NW ridge.

2 — N Slopes. 1970. G. Boles, *R. Geber*. Approach as for Route 3 under N face to round buttress. Ascend rocks W of glacier; E of buttress continue on rock and scree-covered ledges to snow basin. Thence on right side over steepening snow to snow shoulder of buttress, on shoulder to snow face which leads to the final ridge to summit.

3 — N Face. July 1966. N. Ellena, *H. Kahl*. From Banff-Windermere highway to end of Stanley Glacier trail. Thence attain upper level of glacier. Via snow and ice of N face throughout. A long and tedious climb over steep snow, minimum protection. Descent via Route One. (Kahl's last climb) (CAJ *50*–36; App 37–491, marked photo).

Winter Ascent Feb 1969, E. Grassman, U. Kallen. Via Kahl Route (N Face).

Beatrice Peak (10250)

Midway on ridge W of Mt. Ball towards Stanley Peak.

F. A. Aug 1912 by J. P. Forde with party of 12 (3 ladies). Ascent from bivouac in valley S of Storm Mtn. Party progressed along ridge attempting Mt. Ball but ran out of time en route (CAJ 5–123).

Mt. Ball (10865)

2 mi N of Ball Pass and Isabelle Peak; S of Storm Mtn; W of Shadow Lake.

F. A. June 1904 by J. D. Patterson, *C. Kaufmann, H. Kaufmann*. **W Arete,** From camp 2 mi SW of Vermilion Pass. Ascend a draw toward SE past timberline, gaining a buttress NW of the peak; thence up steep scree slopes to a snowfield which is crossed to the W arete. Follow arete to a small snow col which is crossed to the mass of the mountain. Keep to rocks marking the W edge of the snowfield and ascend to a saddle 150' below the summit; then up snowslopes to heavily corniced peak. From camp 9½ hr descent 5 hr. (CAJ *1*–87).

2 — NW Glacier. 1935, F. H. LeCouteur, S. R. Vallance, *L. Grassi*. From warden's cabin up trail on Haffner Creek for one mi continuing through bush 6 mi to head of creek; thence up the cliffs and along the glacier to the W of the mountain, then to the right up the hanging glacier, some 300' of ice and snow necessitating 100' of step-cutting near the top. Thence left up the steep snowslope just below the ice-cap between two peaks; thence left to the saddle and over easy scree and snow to summit. Ascent 9 hr; descent 6¼ hr.

3 — NE Buttress. 1965. F. Beckey, G. Fuller. From upper

North Goodsir

Route 3

Stanley Glacier

G. Boles

Route 2

Stanley Pk

FROM COL TO THE NE

end of Shadow Lake climb rockslides to snow and icebasin leading to the prominent col below E buttress of the mountain. Parts of this basin are steep, and can be icy. Climb W to the buttress, following its many steps until it merges with the summit icefield. In some rock steps rock is excellent. Once on the ice, climb to the summit. IV.

4 — E Basin. June 1958, Miss B. Bolton, Miss T. Goddard, S. Heiberg, S. Klein, R. D. Lyon, E. Mason, R. McFarlane, Miss M. McKinney, K. Ricker, C. Smith, W. Tupper. From cabin below Shadow Lake around S of lake to moraine below E face. Ascend snow gully to col in S ridge. Thence to summit. II, RT 12 hr.

5 — E Buttress. (S of Route 3) 1969, D. Lampard, A. Cole, G. Boles. From bivouac at Ball Pass, descend to, and cross wooded valley to the N, climb scree and talus to top of E buttress, directly up snow run out, then steep very rotten face (falling rock) to a point below the black band. Traverse left (SW) to prominent ridge bordering E side of S glacier. Thence easy going on ridge to within 150' of top glacier. Then climb second gully to left on steep but stable rock and across glacier to summit. Rope used only on glacier (a handicap on bad rock). 6¼ hr up from Ball Pass; 3¼ hr down.

Isabelle Peak (9640)

S of Mt. Ball; W buttress of Ball Pass.

F. A. 1913 by Interprovincial Boundary Commission.

Copper Mtn (9170)

3 mi NW of Pilot Mtn; in W angle between Redearth Creek and Bow River.

F. A. 1885 by J. Macoun, W. T. Macoun.

Pilot Mtn (9690)

N of Mt. Brett; in S angle between Redearth Creek and Bow River.

F. A. 1885 by the Geological Survey.

July 1930, Miss H. I. Buck, A. J. Gilmour, N. B. Sanson, Miss H. Smith, F. N. Waterman, *L. Grassi*. From Massive Station by way of road on Redearth Creek; through forest to

W slopes and W arete. An icy chimney and a short bit of steep rock are encountered below the summit. Ascent 9 hr; descent 5 hr (CAJ *19*–151).

Mt. Brett (9790)

S of Pilot Mtn; NW of Mt. Bourgeau, between Healy and Redearth Creeks.

F. A. 1916 by A. H. Bent, C. F. Hogeboom, K. D. McClelland, J. Outram, E. G. Ritchie. From camp on Healy Creek via W slopes, 4 hr to base of narrow W arete. 1½ hr to summit. Rope unnecessary. It was then possible to return via long snow slopes where glissading allowed descent of 1000′.

Mt. Bourgeau (9615)

4 mi NE of Simpson Pass; 9 mi W of Banff.

F. A. 1890 by J. J. McArthur, *T. E. Wilson*. Easily ascended from camp in Healy Creek Valley.

Pharaoh Peaks (8895)

Three lesser summits along W side of Pharaoh Creek; E of Haiduk Lake.

Unnamed (9450)

One mi NNW of Haiduk Peak; SW of Haiduk Lake; a double summit, the E being 100′lower.

Easily approached from Ball Pass.

Haiduk Peak (9580)

Culminating point between Ball and Redearth Passes.

F. A. 1934 by A. H. Crosby, Mr. & Mrs. H. S. Crosby, Miss M. Crosby, *R. Aemmer*. From SW side of Haiduk Lake over easy rock of E slope (fine views of Mt. Ball). On descent the watershed ridge was followed for a short distance to N, thence down interesting rock and a steep snowfield draining to the lake.

The Monarch (9528)

2 mi SW of Simpson Pass; in angle between Verdant Creek and N branch of Simpson River.

F. A. 1913 by the Boundary Commission.

Ascended in 1916 from Healy Creek camp by parties of ACC. A good rock climb on the E side.

Mt. Shanks (9330)

NE of junction of Simpson and Vermilion Rivers; 3 mi S across Verdant Creek from The Monarch. This is the SE terminus and highest point of a lesser and parallel line of peaks on the B.C. side — **Hawk Ridge.**

Eagle Mtn (9250)

NW of Mt. Howard Douglas, above Healy Creek; 5 mi S of Sawback siding. Easily approached from S or W.

Mt. Howard Douglas (9250)

One mi SE of Eagle Mtn; 4½ mi N of Citadel Pass; W of Brewster Creek. N face coincides with E face of Eagle Mtn as cirque into tributary of Healy Creek. Easily approached from S or W.

No true mountaineer takes anything for granted in such a place, except the fact that everything is unreliable.

J. Outram

RUNDLE PEAKS

E of Brewster Creek and S of Bow River are a number of interesting climbs, some quite severe. Access is good from a variety of roads and trails or directly from the main highway. The fire road up Brewster Creek towards Allenby Pass offers access to the W of the Sundance Range. The fire road up Spray River gives access to the E. From Canmore the road up past the hydro installation leads to a trail in Goat Creek which connects with the Spray River road about 6 mi from Banff. This road is open to public traffic, though not well maintained, and continues on SW of The Three Sisters and S along the Spray Lakes to Bryant Creek. At the E end of this group a trail along the power line up Pigeon Creek from Dead Man Flat leads SE over to the Kananaskis River road at Ribbon Creek. Maps: 8203, 82J14.

Tunnel Mtn (5550)

A lesser point readily accessible SE of Banff and campground.

Gooseberry Route (E Face). Start from cone at base of face and climb a shallow chimney-gully system for 100'. Then move up another 100' to a tree. A broad ledge then leads left to the break in centre of face, which is then climbed. Fourth lead is over delicate friable quartz. Then up a flaring and overhanging chimney on good rock, traversing slightly left to reach a ledge. Move up and left for remaining 200'. Emerge 20' from foot trail.

2 — E Face (S of Gooseberry) 1972 L. MacKay, D. Vockeroth. Start from island of trees under left centre of face. Move up and diagonally left for 200' — mixed aid and free (3 bolts left in place). Above this area easier going over fourth class rock to last 40' bulge. Climb either of crack systems to top.

Sundance Ridge (9520)

E of Brewster Creek; W of Sulfur Mtn and Spray River.

This area is visited infrequently and does not appear to offer much mountaineering history or challenge.

F.A. Aug 1951 by M. Allen, R. C. Hind, J. F. Tarrant. From Sundance canyon up creek — 2 hr to camp. Follow creek into NE cirque, a scree slope leading to E ridge and summit. Ascent 4¼ hr (CAJ 35–158).

Mt. Rundle (9675)

A long ridge with seven distinct high points, SE from Banff to Canmore Gap. The highest point is the third SE from Banff. Robert T. Rundle, Methodist Missionary at Edmonton, passed through site of Banff in 1847 (where Sir George Simpson had preceded him in 1841). (CAJ 27–182).

F. A. 1888 by J. J. McArthur. From Spray Lake cross stream and ascend gully above bridge. Gully ends in scree slopes below tower on ridge. Traverse N below tower and attain ridge which is broken, but easily followed to summit. Rope not required. (AJ 18–99).

In 1907, G. Brewster, J. W. A. Hickson ascended (from Banff) second and third peaks.

East End of Rundle (EEOR) has become a popular high-angle area with several high standard routes in recent years.

First Buttress, NE Ridge. June 1972, C. Scott, D. Smith. Start 200′ left of arete and angle up left over easy ground for 200′. Climb chimney corner on right side of broad gully. Scramble and climb edging right towards arete. Climb steep inside corner on left side of arete to easier ground above (5.6). Edge right again and climb corner next to arete (difficult to start). Follow crack which angles right around arete and up easy ground and slabs to shallow notch. The tower above is climbed by a crack in the centre for 50′ until it is possible to traverse right under an overhang to easier ground (5.7). Continue angling up and right to easy ground to top; II, 5.7.

Balzac. May, 1972, M. Toft, U. Kallen. Start out on the right edge of the face to the right of the Guides' route and follow the edge for two-thirds of the climb to a ledge with a tree. From here cross the gully to the right, then climb the next gully (diminishing to a crack). The route is quite obvious from here, the last four pitches follow a rib to the top. Except for

EAST END OF MT RUNDLE

NE Ridge

A. Settari

Balzac

Guide Route

Quasar

Reprobate

aid being necessary to climb a 30′ wall 300′ fom the start, this climb includes 15 rope lengths of good fifth class climbing on very good rock. Just left of this line is a route by L. MacKay, D. Vockeroth, U. White which follows a right-leaning corner, mixed free and aid; III, 5.8, A2.

Guides' Route (First Buttress); 1970, A. Cole, C. Locke, L. MacKay. Emost buttress. Left face. Ascend gully system diagonally right towards middle of face to grassy ledge. Zig-zag to crack system 200′ right of prominent inside corner. Rockfall. F6.

Quasar; July 1972, Mrs. C. Calvert, B. McKeith. Start 150 yards around the buttress to the right of Reprobate. Ascend wall to corner with tree. Move left to easy gully (snow) and up to crest of pillar. Thence up a groove to overhang and twin cracks about halfway up face. Move left at crack (F5). Then ascend thin cracks, wall and chimney to shallow corners. Make tenuous traverse left to cave. Exit via crack in roof, crux (F9), thence easy going to top in 400′, 1500′; IV, 5.9.

Reprobate; 1971, B. Greenwood, G. Horne, R. Wood, O. Woolcock. Near the left (W) edge of the crag. Follow a chimney system. 3 leads to ledges. From the large ledge climb a short pitch to a smaller ledge. Climb 100′ then traverse left around a corner. Continue up slabs and ramps trending right. From a broken section climb a steep 10′ crack (aid) to a jam crack. Follow to the top. 6-7 hr. III, F7, A1, 1500′.

Second Buttress 5.7; 1968, L. MacKay, D. Vockeroth. Poorly described in CAJ 53–72. This route is on the NE face; all others are on the true E end.

Winter Ascent and **Traverse** Jan 1961, B. Greenwood, G. Boles. From power road above Canmore to crest at SE, 2½ hr. Good going on ridge to bivouac at base of main summit, 5 hr more. Descent from main summit to Spray Valley road. Complete traverse Dec 1964, D. Gardner, C. Locke (3 days) one bivouac W of 4th peak (from Banff) second bivouac W of main summit.

Goat Range

This is an isolated group W of the N end of Spray Lake, and E of the Spray River. The principal summit is 10250′,

3½ mi S of Spray Lake Dam. 2 mi N is a crest at 9640' and at the S end of the massif is **Mt. Nester** at 9760'. There is no record of ascents, but access is easy and the topography is generally similar to Mt. Rundle.

Chinaman Peak (8800)

2 mi SW of Canmore; SE buttress of Canmore Gap. Accessible from power road. An outlier of 9300' peak S of Canmore. NW of Three Sister.

F. A. via easy W cree slopes. A number of routes have been placed on this generally attractive rock, but accurate data has escaped the editors.

2 — E Face. June 1961 by G. Prinz, D. Raubach, W. Twelker, *B. Greenwood*. Approach along scree from gap above Canmore. The route basically follows the left-hand edge of the E face, the left skyline when approaching from Banff. Above lower slabs is crux. Where ridge joins upper wall move right for final pitches to top (CAJ *45*–121).

Variant. 1970, G. Colliver, R. Cuthbert, S. Herrero. After 4th pitch traverse (E) left to large blank wall. Ascend thin crack up middle of this wall, thence a long (170') lead on loose rock to summit. F7 (CAJ *54*–83).

Ships Prow. W of Three Sisters — very prominent knife-edge ridge. July 1965, L. McKay, C. Scott. From base of ridge follow fourth class cracks and chimneys for two or three pitches angling left on E side of ridge. From large terraces climb up traversing right above the prominent overhang. (5.7, — one A3 move), and continue straight up ridge. Moderate fourth and fifth class follows for several pitches, to base of final grey wall. A mixture of fine aid and free climbing (5.7, A2) angles up and left for a pitch to cracks which are followed to the top. III, 5.7, A3. Decend via shale slopes to the E.

Three Sisters (NE 8840; C 9085; SW 9634)

5 mi S of Canmore.

NE Peak. F. A. 1925, A. W. Drinnan, M. D. Geddes, T. B. Moffat, *L. Grassi.*

Central Peak. F. A. Aug 1921 by M. B. Morrow. From

Canmore via Three Sisters canyon and steep, difficult climbing to 2-3 saddle; thence to summit (CAJ *12*–182).

SW Peak. F. A. 1889 by J. J. McArthur. From camp at SW base (upper Spray Lake). The biggest point was occupied as a triangulation station.

2 — N Face. June 1968, R. Cuthbert, Miss A. Purdey. From camp at 6300' in Three Sisters Creek to saddle NW of summit. Thence via right buttress to middle of face. Trend left to NW ridge. Difficult lower part, with two overhangs. 13 hr to summit. Bivouac on descent to Spray Lakes. 5.3 (CAJ *52*–73).

Windtower (*Lougheed Tower*) (8850)

2 mi NW of Mt. Lougheed (202497)

F. A. date and party unknown, but easily reached from Spray Lakes and SW slopes.

SE Face. 1958 by P. Jenkinson, *H. Kahl*. Via prominent chimney.

3 — NE Ridge to NE summit, July 1965, Miss B. Corbeau, G. Crocker, H. Hahn. Follow old fireroad S towards base of NW ridge. 4 hr from highway to base of rocks below NW face. Climb followed right side of obvious gully. Descent by scree on E side from col to Mt. Lougheed. 10 hr round trip (CAJ *49* — 138).

4 — N Face. 1972 G. Homer, R. Wood. When viewing the N face from the valley below, a definite ridge cuts the very steep face into two sections. To the left of this ridge is a big inside corner, 200' to the right of which the route generally lies. 5.8, A2, 17 pitches.

Mt. McGillivray (8040)

S of Exshaw are three lesser summits. **Pigeon Mtn** (7855) to W and **Heart Mtn** to E offer interesting rock climbing. Some of these cliff lines were popular with the late Heinz Kahl, whose Lac des Arcs School of Climbing frequented some of them. Cliffs on NE face of Pigeon Mtn can be approached via the valley between Pigeon and McGillivray. Easy descent on ski slopes to SW.

BOW PEAKS

This very popular area is bounded on the NE and NW by the main line of the CPR and Trans-Canada highway, along Bow and Kicking Horse Rivers; on the SW by Ottertail River and the SE by Vermilion River. Airline distance between Vermilion and Kicking Horse Passes is 19 mi. The Divide peaks of the area bound the Ten Peak (Wenkchemna), Paradise and Lake Louise valleys. For good early descriptions see Stutfield-16.

On the Divide the average elevation exceeds 10000', Hungabee Mtn being the highest, though surpassed by Mt. Temple lying E. On the Divide, Mts. Deltaform, Lefroy and Victoria also exceed 11000', while on the W slope, Mts. Huber and Biddle are the highest peaks. An additional 27 named summits exceed 10000'. The peaks are generally accessible from Lake Louise, Moraine Lake, or Lake O'Hara, where permanent accomodations may be had. For a geological explanation of the dam at Moraine lake, see AAJ *1*–189. For geology of Consolation Lake area, see CAJ *28*–214.

A scenic loop, requiring 2 days and giving access to the Lake Louise, Paradise, Wenkchemna, Prospectors and Cataract valleys, may be made from Lake O'Hara by the passes: Abbot, E Mitre, Wastach, Wenkchemna, and Opabin.

A trend of climbing in this area is toward ever-increasing traverses, which began on Mt. Victoria in1903 and was later extended to Popes Peak in 1936. Traverses have been made from Moraine Lake in various combinations of the Ten Peaks. This culminated in the great traverse of 1965 made by Gardner and Locke from Moraine Lake to Lake Louise, covering 23 summits in 6 days: The Ten Peaks, Hungabee, Ringrose, Glacier Peak, Lefroy, Victoria, Collier and Popes Peak, omitting only the Glacier-Lefroy ridge (CAJ *49*–131).

Some of the better views are from the lower peaks which also offer less climbing challenge.

MORAINE LAKE AND EAST

Moraine Lake is the centre of some of the most varied and interesting climbing in the entire Canadian Rockies, including the subsidiary valleys of Consolation Lake and Paradise. The area contains climbs of every standard of difficulty, pure rock climbs, pure ice climbs, and long mixed alpine routes. There is no campsite at Moraine Lake but there are many at Consolation Lake, in Larch Valley on the way to Sentinel Pass, at Eiffel Lake in the meadows below Wenkehemna Pass, or at the head of Paradise Valley.

Climbing along the ridge of the Ten Peaks is generally easy, seldom more than a scramble. All the peaks from Mt. Fay to Mt. Allen can be reached within two hours from the Graham Cooper Hut, consequently in good weather, it makes a really pleasant day to climb several of the peaks in combination. Mt. Fay provides some of the best climbing, particularly on the ice of the N Face, up to a little over 1000′ in height, which allows a climber to pick any degree of steepness up to the vertical and perhaps even overhanging ice of the central line up the largest of these slopes. Map 82N8; 82N1

PASSES

Consolation — By trail from Moraine Lake, passing below the Tower of Babel and the E face of Mt. Babel. From Consolation Lakes the trail is indefinite, by moraine, scree, and snowslopes to the pass, 3 hr-1¾ mi to lower lake. From the Fay Hut (or the Graham Cooper Hut) traverse below Mts. Little & Fay on the S and via Middle Pass, cross the snowfield S of Bident Mtn to the pass.

Middle — From Consolation Pass cross the snowfield S of Bident Mtn. From the Fay or Graham Cooper Hut circumvent Mts Little & Fay.

Wenkchemna — By trail from Moraine Lake. Branching W from the lakeshore trail near the lodge, the trail climbs the wooded slope, forking close to timberline. The S fork, now level, leads to Eiffel Lake, 3½ mi, and the slopes E below the Pass. The trail below the Pass may be snow covered. An

154

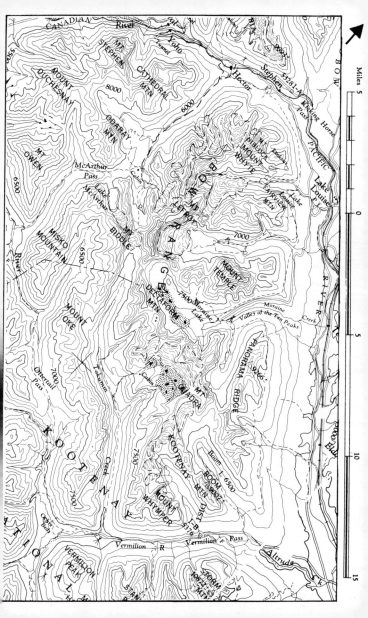

alternate trail following the lake shore and valley floor to Eiffel Lake is difficult to follow and not recommended. There is a long, steep scree slope S from the Pass to Tokumm Creek with no obvious trail. 7 hr from Moraine Lake to Lake O'Hara via Opabin Pass.

Wastach — Climb steep scree slopes above the Wenkchemna Pass trail from a point ¼ mi E of Eiffel Lake — 2 hr.

Sentinel — Take the N fork from the Wenkchemna Pass trail above the switchbacks. This trail leads through Larch Valley to Sentinel Pass. Larch Valley is about one hr from Moraine Lake, a second hr to the Pass. 3²/₅ mi from Moraine Lake to pass.

Mitre — From Paradise Creek, above the Giant Steps, by scree and snowslopes. Trails in this part of Paradise Valley are indistinct. On the Lake Louise (N) side this pass can be treacherous in late summer; crampons needed.

Saddleback — Good trail, a easy half-day circuit from Lake Louise or Paradise Valley.

MAJOR FEATURES accessible from Moraine Lake. Use only designated campsites.

Consolation Lakes — Good campsites situated below face of Mt. Babel. Good trail from Moraine Lake, ⅔ hr.

Moraine Lake — Commercial lodge, parking facilities, picnic ground, no camp facilities. Good lake side trail only along W shore.

Kaufmann Lake — On the S slope of the Ten Peaks below Mts Allen, Tuzo, & Deltaform. Old trail from Tokumm Creek.

Eiffel Lake — Good campsites in the Valley of the Ten Peaks below Mt Deltaform. The Wenkchemna Pass trail leads by Eiffel Lake. 1½ hrs.

Lake Annette — Good campsites in Paradise Valley below the N Face of Mt Temple. A good trail from the Paradise Creek trail. 1½ hr from the Moraine Lake road.

Larch Valley — Good campsites. The trail to Sentinel Pass leads through Larch Valley, one hr.

Paradise Valley — Good campsites towards the head of the valley. Paradise Creek crosses the Moraine Lake road 2 mi from the junction with the Lake Louise road. Good trail through the valley to Sentinel Pass.

Mt Perren

Mt Bowlen

Mt Little

E. Cooper

Mt Babel

Moraine Lake

View to South

Tower of Babel

Mt Quadra

Consolation Valley

Bident Mtn

HUTS

Graham Cooper Memorial — At head of the 3-4 couloir on the ridge of the Ten Peaks. Accommodates 8; bunks & mattresses, Coleman stove (bring fuel), some cooking and eating utensils. Erected by the Calgary Mountain Club for general use. Named for a member of the club fatally injured while climbing the 3-4 couloir to assist in construction.

Approach: Follow the lakeshore trail, take branch to W, N of creek from Wenkchemna Glacier for several hundred yards, then cut S to the terminal moraine of the glacier. Cross the moraine and:

1. Cross the scree slopes below Mt Bowlen to a spur descending from the Fay Glacier. Climb this and cross the glacier passing behind Mt Bowlen to the hut. This approach is least exposed to objective danger. 3 hr up. 5.6 in places.

2. The steep snow couloir seen from Moraine Lake. The hut can be seen from Moraine Lake on the rocks above and to the W of this couloir. 3½ hr.

3. By the steep rock buttress to the W of this couloir. (See peak 3½).

4. The 3-4 couloir. Follow the E bank of the Wenkchemna Glacier to a subsidiary moraine from cirque below peaks Five, Allen, & Tuzo. The 3-4 couloir leads SE from the cirque. The shorter, steeper 4-5 couloir is dangerous and should be avoided. The lower snow of 3-4 couloir is swept by stonefall from #4. Stay left and leave snow halfway up the scree to follow cliff bands on left side of couloir.

Fay — Located at 7850′, above Prospectors Valley (Tokumm Creek), reached via trail from Vermilion Pass Highway at Marble Canyon (indistinct). AAC hut, but in generally poor condition; 2 mi S of Mt Perren (#4) (AAJ *1*–45). Can be reached (at timberline) in one hr from the Graham Cooper Hut.

Mt Whymper (9330)

E-W double peak, ½ mi apart, W of Vermilion Pass; 2 mi SW of Boom Mtn.

F. A. 1901 by E. Whymper, *J. Bossoney, C. Kaufmann, C. Klucker, J. Pollinger*. From Vermilion Pass via E and S slopes to W ridge to summit.

Unnamed (9050)

1½ mi W of Mt Whymper; 3 mi SSE of Chimney Pk on ridge connecting with Mt Whymper.

F. A. Aug 1957, R. Jones, D. Morrison via SW ridge. Ascent made through gully to S ridge of subsidiary point — 9050′. Traverse of summit following curving crest N and NE, rounding E — facing cirque, to attain summit via SW ridge. Thence traverse to W ridge of Mt. Whymper which was ascended. RT 9 hr (CAJ *41*–66).

Boom Mtn (9050)

One mi SE of Boom Lake; 3½ mi ESE of Chimney Peak; NW of Vermilion Pass.

F. A. Dominion Survey, 1903, from Vermilion Pass via SE slopes.

2 — N Face. 1968, J. Farrand, R. Lofthouse. Rrom the E end of Boom Lake observe a deep gully. Climb rocks to the right (E) of this gully until face steepens. Traverse right, then left to top of quartzite band. Thence over easier slopes to summit. Aid was used in bad weather to ascend limestone overhangs. III, F7, A2 (AAJ *16*–411).

Chimney Peak (9850)

2 mi W of Boom Lake; 2 mi S of Mt. Quadra; much moraine to E.

F. A. July 1910 by T. G. Longstaff, E. O. Wheeler. **N Ridge** From Consolation Pass, round SE shoulder of Mt. Bident to moraine of glacier E from Middle Pass. Thence SW across glacier to col — 9500′, between Chimney Peak and Unnamed 10050 to N. Follow snow N ridge to 60′ chimney in middle of N cliff. Climb up 15′, then move W and continue to top of chimney by rocks on W. The N ridge is regained via a short gully to the E and followed to the summit. Ascent from moraine of Boom Glacier — 3 hr (App 7–129; CAJ *3*–75).

N col can also be reached from the Fay Hut via W slopes.

Unnamed (10050)

2 mi W of Boom Lake; one mi S of Mt. Quadra; N of Chimney Peak (CAJ *3*–55).

F. A. July 1904 by Miss G. E. Benham, *C. Kaufmann.* **N Ridge.** From Moraine Lake, via col W of Mt. Bowlen (3-4) SE across snowfields to Middle Pass. Thence follow the N ridge ½ mi to summit (AJ 22–333).

Variant: Follow description as for Chimney Peak. Cross Boom Lake Glacier. Thence to Middle Pass and route above.

Mt. Quadra (10410)

2½ mi SSE of Moraine Lake; 2½ mi NW of Boom Lake; SE of Mt. Fay; W of Bident Mtn (AJ 35–42; CAJ *12*–178; AAJ 5–152).

F. A. July 1910, by F. C. Bell, A. M. Gordon, J. W. A. Hickson, *E. Feuz, Jr., G. Feuz.* From Consolation Pass contour past S side of Bident Mtn crossing Boom Lake Glacier and snowfield to Middle Pass. Thence via ridge with roped scrambling. Three highest points attained in 6 hr from camp near Consolation Lake. Consolation Pass to summit, 3¼ hr (App *12*–235). From the main W summit it is possible to traverse the remaining three summits by going E along the arete. The two lower summits are difficult, and the E is more accessible from the Quadra-Bident Col. (W-E: 3½ hr) (CAJ 5–136). From the Quadra-Bident Col it is possible to descend the long S couloir to the Boom Lake Glacier and return to Consolation Pass.

2— NW Ridge. July 1934, Miss G. Engelhard, *Ern. Feuz.* From Fay Hut cross the S glacier basin, Moraines and snowfields, to Quadra-Fay col and the NW ridge of Quadra. Ascend steep and moderately firm rock to foot of final tower, 200′ below summit. Traverse easy ledges on W face to a couloir leading to the S ridge. Thence join Route One to the summit. Ascent from Fay Hut, 6 hr (CAJ 22–213.

Bident Mtn (10119)

2½ mi NW of Boom Lake; 3 mi SE of Moraine Lake; E of Mt. Quadra App *11*–128, good photos).

F. A. Aug 1903, C. S. Thompson, *H. Kaufmann.* **E Face.** From Moraine Lake follow trail to Consolation Lakes and Pass — 3 hr. From here, the NE ridge and the E face are visible. The rock wall, about ½ mi long, presents no difficulties except the black band, 400' above the pass. This band is climbed in the central portion of the face below an avalance chimney. Ascend snow below this chimney and rock on N edge. Thence a delightful scramble via E slopes to rib between couloirs below S peak. Skirt on SW to notch and main summit. 5 hr up. Descent via SW slopes, mostly glissade, to Boom Glacier (AJ 22–205).

2 — (*Bident Tower*) **SE ridge** Aug 1937, E. Cromwell, Miss G. Engelhard, F. S. North. From Consolation Pass traverse scree slopes and boulder fields to reach SE ridge. Ascend jagged arete, bypassing some pinnacles on the E face, to reach a prominent tower of the SE ridge of Mt. Bident, cut off by overhangs from the two main summits. Descend to Bident-Quadra Col, thence couloir to Boom Glacier.

3 — **NE shoulder and N face** July 1907, C. T. B. Beechcroft, D. R. Parkington. From Consolation Pass ascend W across the lower snowslopes to the shoulder of the NE ridge (9100') that forms the W margin of Consolation Pass. Cross the ridge to gain the snow on the N face, and ascend snow directly toward the summit, taking advantage of several rock islands. Regain the NE ridge about 200' below the summit. Thence ⅓ hr to the top. Ascent from Consolation Pass, 2 hr (AJ 24–236).

Mt. Bell (9550)

E of Consolation Pass; N of Boom Lake.

F. R. A. Aug 1965, G. Crocker, P. Gooding, T. Vockeroth. **NE Ridge** — Approach by trail to Taylor Lake, then towards Lake O'Brien until below ridge. Start in wide chimney SE of point of ridge. Two F3 pitches on good quartzite to top of steep section. Thence scrambling to summit. Descend via SE col into valley above O'Brien Lake. 12 hr RT from highway. Cairn found on summit.

Panorama Ridge (9266)

N of Consolation Pass; E of Consolation Lakes

TEN PEAKS
Mt. Fay (10612) (*Peak One*; *Heejee*)

Much confusion in early literature on application of this name. 2 mi SE of Moraine Lake; S of Mt. Babel; NW of Mt. Quadra; E of MT. Little (#2) (AAJ 5–122).

F. A. 1904, by Miss G. E. Benham, *C. Kaufmann*. From Moraine Lake via the 3-4 couloir. Ascend W side of couloir on rock and snow; cross col 9450' and traverse snowfield S around Mt. Little to foot of the peak whence SW snowslopes lead to top (AJ 22–334).

2 — SW Face. July, 1927, E. Cromwell, J. E. Fisher. From the Fay Hut via the S glacier. Cross to E lobe of ice and reach SW face where a well-defined snow couloir leads up to W of summit. The icy couloir is followed to higher slopes and the final arete. 9 hr from hut. (AAJ *1*–48; CAJ *25*–105; ski ascent).

3 — N Glacier July 1907, L. Q. Coleman, W. J. Haggith, G. R. Kinney, J. A. Reid, *G. Feuz*. From Moraine Lake via glacier SW of Mt. Babel, ascending close to rocks of latter, utilizing them where possible; then by left margin of the icefall. Care must be taken not to ascend the rocks of Mt. Babel too far as cliffs cut off access to upper snowfield. The upper neve is traversed to the W base of the peak near Mt. Little. The W ridge, loose rock, then leads to the summit snowfield. The lower part of the route is somewhat exposed to falling ice from the upper glacier, which, in recent years has become more difficult and dangerous. Ascent from Moraine Lake, 7½ hr (AJ *24*–234; App *11*–332).

Winter Ascent. Dec 1937, D. Crosby, R. C. Hind, E. R. Gibson.

4 — N Face, W Snow Couloir. July 1968, F. Roth, U. Kallen. Via 3-4 Couloir to the Fay Glacier, from the bergschrund 8 rope lengths on 40°-45° snow to top, 1⅓ hr from bergschrund.

5 — N Face, Centre Ice Bulge. Aug 1968, O. Berle, U. Kallen. From Cooper Hut to Fay Glacier, cross bergschrund and follow snow E of centre ice bulge between ice and rock, 50° near top. 9 rope lengths from bergschrund to top.

6 — Glacier & Ice Couloirs of N Face. 1970, Y. Chouinard, P. Carman, D. Eberl. Approach as in Route 3 to bivouac on moraine below glacier. Route essentially follows the easterly

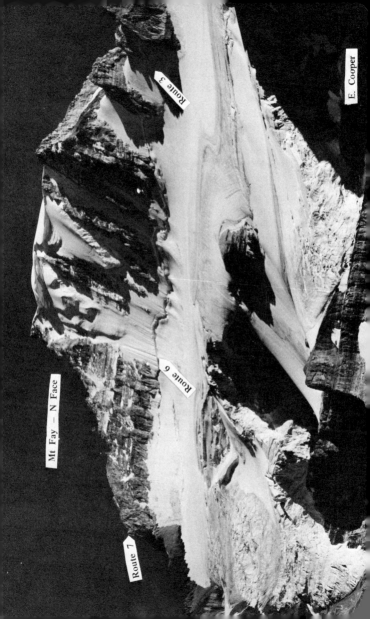

Mt Fay – N Face

Route 3

Route 6

Route 7

E. Cooper

of three ice walls descending from the crest. Eight leads were made on the ice, bearing around to the E near the top to avoid overly steep bulge at the crest. 6 hr. Descent via Cooper Hut (AAJ 17–297).

7 — **NE Ridge.** 1961, C. A. Fay, R. Kruszyna. From Moraine Lake follow Route 3 to the upper snowfield below Mt Fay. Cross snowfield toward the Fay-Babel Col and gain ridge by a couloir W of the col. Follow the crest around small towers and gendarmes (loose rock) to the summit snow.

Mt. Babel (10175)

1½ mi SE of Moraine Lake Lodge; N of Mt. Fay.

F. A. July 1910: A. R. Hart, E. O. Wheeler, L. C. Wilson, H. H. Worsfold. **Fay Glacier and S Ridge.** Circle NE of Moraine Lake and ascend moraines of Fay Glacier N of Mts. Fay and Little. The Fay Glacier is split, the upper snowfield terminating in a hanging glacier. To avoid danger of icefall, ascend the lower glacier staying close to rock buttress along NE margin, scrambling the rock buttress, when the base of the icefall is reached. At some point, cross onto the upper glacier (crampons useful) and ascend snow to the Babel-Fay col — 9480. Easy scrambling on S ridge to the summit, 700′ higher. The Fay-Babel col has also been reached from the Fay Hut, via Fay-Little col. Descent via same route (CAJ 3–73).

2 — **N Ridge and Face.** 1961, G. W. Boles, B. Greenwood. From Moraine Lake climb the scree past Babel Tower and follow the long easy N ridge to the steep upper part of Mt. Babel. The upper part is comprised of alternating rock walls and scree-covered ledges; considerable variation is possible; F3-4.

3 — **NE Face.** Aug 1970, B. Greenwood, J. Moss. A difficult and serious pure rock climb. The crux pitches are high on the face and retreat from this section is difficult. From the outlet of Consolation Lakes climb the scree slopes to the left (E) of two couloirs. The climb starts directly opposite the top of E couloir. Climb a ramp sloping left to a steep chimney, above which climb a short wall and go right over scree to the top of a buttress. Climb over loose rock to a shallow inside

corner; followed by a chimney with a ledge to the E above. Climb inside a deep chimney for 40' until forced to the outside, where a steep difficult crack is climbed. After a short chimney continue fourth class to a ledge. Climb a slab, first in the corner, then crossing to the left. Above the slab is a large ledge which appears to run the width of the face. A difficult wall puts one into the prominent upper line of the face, which is followed for 600' (good bivouac site in the middle of this section), to a ledge which runs 25' across the face to the W. Traverse to the right end of the ledge up to and across a steep wall to sloping ledges above. Climb a steep difficult wall to a good ledge. Go round the corner to the right to a small ledge. The next 150' constitute the crux of the climb, two pitches of difficult aid climbing. One additional lead completes the climb. 35 — 30 pitons, including 2 each. 2″, 2½″, 3″, and 1 — 14″ (CAJ 53–38; AAJ 17–79) V, F8, A4.

4 — E Face. 1963, B. Greenwood, L. Grillmair. From Consolation Lakes climb a rock buttress which descends almost to the level of the lakes. The crest of this was reached in two leads from a large ledge on its N side and some distance above the foot of the buttress. Follow the crest easily to where it ends against a steep wall of grey rock. Climb the grey wall, more or less direct, in about eight pitches, ending on scree slopes below and to the right of the summit III, F7.

Tower of Babel (7750)

½ mi E of Moraine Lake lodge, rising E and directly above the N end of Moraine Lake at the end of the long N ridge of Mt. Babel. Although the Babel Tower is a lesser summit, this striking obelisk of rock requires a place of importance because of its interest to rock climbers due to its easy accessibility and particularly good quartzite.

The front (N) of the Tower has several routes and variations and is a very popular short rock climb (3-5 hrs) of moderate difficulty — F6. The various routes are similar in character and difficulty, and for this reason 4 routes are described, all of which join above the "ski jump", an obvious feature of the face (CAJ 45–116).

The E face has many possibilities for short artificial climbs, the W face has been neglected and rightly so because of rock fall.

NE Corner 1957, B. Greenwood, D. Lofthouse, R. S. Thompson. Go under the E face beyond the scree of the separating gully to an amphitheatre not visible from Moraine Lake. Climb the right edge of this basin to a ledge; alternatively, this ledge can be reached by traversing ledges left from the separating gully. Leads follow the edge on good holds to a large broken area where easier climbing brings you out on the top of the "ski jump". Above this is the final steep wall with a good ledge below it. Climb a crack in the centre of the wall for 20', continuing by a rising traverse right then left to a ledge in the centre of the face. The climb may be finished from either end of the ledge. III, F6.

2 — N Face. (First complete climb of tower) 1959, G. Boles, B. Greenwood, A. Washington. Start at the small group of trees at the W side of the face. Climb up over ledges, then veer right of the overhangs. The second rope length ends at the base of a rotten gendarme or tower on the NW corner of the face. Climb 10' up gendarme, then make a long step onto main tower and continue for 3 rope lengths up and to the left to the middle of the face. A direct line slightly right is followed (2 rope-lengths) to the top of the "ski jump". Finish as in Route One.

3 — N Face. 1963 L. MacKay, H. B. Mutch. Start at the very lowest point of the face, climb up and to the left to a large ledge with a fir tree. The climb continues over excellent rock to a looser, more broken section which in two leads gains the large broken area. The final wall is climbed as in Route One.

4 — W Face & NW Corner 1960, K. Baker, J. Fairley, *P. Fuhrmann*. Climb scree on the W side of Tower to a good ledge. On this ledge party traversed left to a weakness, then climbed to next ledge, traversed and more of the same. Climb on the fringe of the W face at the NW corner to the top of the "ski jump" and join Route One.

Descent is very easy. Walk back over Tower to the scree slope on the W side, descend scree, ½ hr to Moraine Lake.

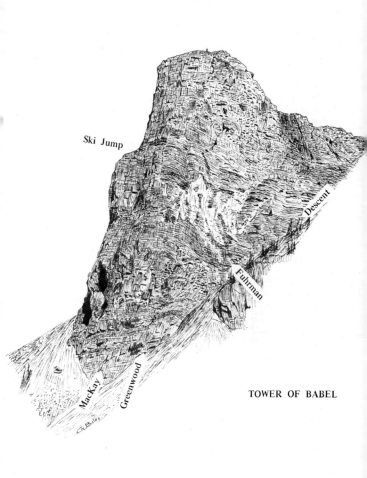

Ski Jump

Descent

Fuhrman

MacKay

Greenwood

G. Bailey

TOWER OF BABEL

Mt. Little (*Peak Two, Nom*) (10300)

2 mi S of Moraine Lake; one mi SW of Mt. Babel; W of Mt. Fay.

F. A. July 1901, G. T. Little, C. S. Thompson, G. M. Weed, C. Kaufmann. **W face.** From Moraine Lake ascend the long snow couloir to the 3-4 col. Ascend couloir staying on the left (E) side and using rocks along the side as well as the snow. From the col, head S past Mt. Bowlen crossing snowfields to W slope which is followed easily to summit. 9½ hr RT (App *10–92*).

2 — NW Ridge. July 1966, J. Lisoway, G. Boles. From Cooper Hut to Little-Bowlen Col, a short way across Fay Glacier to a prominent wind ridge which crosses glacier. This ridge gets sharper and steeper ending below the bergscrund on the NE Face of Mt. Little. The bergscrund was crossed, then on snow to the NW ridge, which is easily followed to summit; 2¼ hr from Hut. Descent via NW ridge to Little-Bowlen Col.

3 — SE Face. 1927, E. Cromwell, J. E. Fisher. From Fay Hut cross the S glacier direct to the rocky SE face of Mt. Little. Thence scrambling to the top. Ascent from Hut, 6 hr (AAJ *1–47*).

Ascent may be combined with Mt. Bowlen and Peak Four (see descriptions for both peaks). Both the SE face and the W slopes may also be reached from Consolation Pass via Middle Pass and the S snowfields.

Mt. Bowlen (10080) (*Peak Three, Yamnee*)

One mi S of head of Moraine Lake; N of Mt. Little (Peak 2); NE of Peak Four.

F. A. July 1901, G. T. Little, C. S. Thompson, G. M. Weed, H. Kaufmann. Approach from Moraine Lake via 3-4 couloir; following ascent of Mt. Little (which see) via easy scree slopes of S face. Readily done from Graham Cooper Hut on less than one hr. (AAJ *1–47*; App *10–92*).

2 — S Glacier. From Fay Hut the ascent may be combined with Mts. Little and Perren. See Mt. Little (AAJ *1–47*).

Unnamed (9520) (*Peak 3½*)

The rock buttress to the SW of the prominent ice couloir

as seen from Moraine Lake. Frequently mistaken for Peak 4, it is E of the Divide and only slightly higher than the Divide.

F. R. A. 1966, B. Greenwood, R. Hogan. The buttress was climbed as an approach to the Cooper Hut, but may well be considered as a complete climb. From the lower left corner climb up and across ledges to the SW until overlooking the bottom of a short couloir. Climb a steep pitch and along the left (E) side of the buttress to where steep grey rock forces a traverse left until easier rock leads to the crest of the ridge. Follow the ridge over to the hut. Variations possible. III, F6.

Mt. Perren (*Peak Four; Tonsa*) (10020)

1½ mi SSW of head of Moraine Lake; W of Mt. Bowlen; E of Peak Five (AAJ *1*–47; App *10*–92).

Various approaches have been made to this peak. It is easily accessible from the Graham Cooper Hut, the Fay Hut, and the 4–5 col. Some question exists as to the make-up of the first ascent party. All routes on the final peak have been on the SE or SW and presented no technical difficulties. See Mts. Little and Bowlen.

Peak Five (*Sapta*) (10010)

2 mi SW of Moraine Lake; SW of Mt. Perren; NE of Mt. Allen. The lowest of the Ten Peaks and so dominated by Peak 6 that it appears rather as a spur of the latter. From Moraine Lake it is often confused with Peak 4.

F. A. 1927, H. F. Ulrichs, et al. (see note below) The peak is readily ascended by a variety of easy routes.

S. Ridge. From Fay Hut ascend the S glacier moraines and snowfields to either the E face (steep snow with ice and easy rock) or the W face (snow, loose scree and rock scrambling). Both lead to the S ridge which is easily followed to the summit. Ulrichs then traversed E over Peaks 4 and 3.

Reasonable doubt may be expressed as to the first ascent of this mountain. G. T. Little included it in his list (A.C. Register, 1908). G. M. Weed, however, doubted that the party ascended Peak 5. Miss Tuzo (Mrs. Wilson) considered Peak 7, which she ascended in 1906, as the "last unconquered of the Ten Peaks." Ulrichs found no summit record.

VIEW TO SOUTHEAST

Mt Tuzo

Peak 5

Peak 4

Graham Cooper Hut

Mt Bowlen

Mt Fay

Wenkchemna Glacier

E. Cooper

Moraine Lake

Mt. Allen (*Peak Six; Shappee*) (10830)

2¼ mi SW of Moraine Lake; SW of Peak Five; SE of Mt. Tuzo.

F. A. July 1904, Miss G. E. Benham, *C. Kaufmann*. From Moraine Lake ascend the long couloir to the 3–4 col — 9450' (see Mt. Little). From the col, head SW across the S glacier, passing Peaks 4 and 5 on the S, and traverse around to W slopes. Follow steep, rotten rock to summit (See Mt. Tuzo) (AJ 22–334).

The S side of Mt. Allen may also be reached from Middle Pass crossing the S glacier, and from the valley above Kaufmann Lake in Prospectors Valley.

Mt. Tuzo (*Peak Seven, Sagowa*) (10650)

2 mi SW of Moraine Lake; 2 mi N of Kaufmann Lake; NW of Mt. Allen; E of Deltaform Mtn.

F. A. 1906 by Miss H. Tuzo, *C. Kaufmann*. **SE Ridge.** From Moraine Lake, ascend couloir to the 3–4 col (Graham Cooper Hut) Pass Peaks Four and Five on the S and cross ice slope to scree pass between Mt. Allen and Peak Five. Thence traverse around Mt. Allen to glacier adjacent to Mt. Tuzo. When Kaufmann Lake is visible ascend the easy S ridge to summit. Moraine Lake to col, 4 hr; col to summit 7 hr. Descent 8 hr.

2 — S Glacier. From Fay Hut. This is a route which has been repeated many times over very easy going.

3 — W Ridge. From the Deltaform-Tuzo col — 9850' — (see Deltaform) ascend steep snow and ice to summit. Ascent from col, 1¼ hr. The col may be reached via Deltaform Mtn. Route 2, descent (which see).

Deltaform Mtn (*Peak Eight, Saknowa*) (11235)

W of Mt. Tuzo; SE of Neptuak Mtn; 1½ mi SE of Wenkchemna Pass.

F. A. July 1903, A. Eggers, H. C. Parker, *C. Kaufmann, H. Kaufmann*. **S Ridge.** From camp in Prospectors Valley — 7500' — at SW foot of Neptuak Mtn. Cross boulder and scree to the large basin between the SW and S ridges of Deltaform. A long, broad, snow couloir leads toward S ridge.

Ascend this couloir, partly using rocks along its sides, to steep but not difficult ledges and cliff band. A 40' chimney with few holds and many loose stones leads to more ledges, rising to a talus and scree slope and the S ridge at 10250' opposite Mt. Tuzo. Ascend the S ridge for about 700', passing several gendarmes. Traverse W, crossing the SW face and an ice couloir, to reach the SW ridge by a short chimney. A cliff band about 200' below summit is climbed by a narrow 80' crack (crux). Thence easy snow slopes lead to a pinnacle summit. The mountain is renowned for its loose rock. Ascent from camp, 8 hr. Descent 6½ hr (App 10–295) (Variant approach CAJ 4–143).

2 — NW Ridge. Aug 1961; G. W. Boles, B. Greenwood. From Moraine Lake via Wenkchemna Pass — 5 mi, to Neptuak Mtn (Route One). Descend over broken rock bands, chimneys and scree to Neptuak-Deltaform Col — 10200' (see Neptuak, Route 2). Moraine Lake to Neptuak summit, 7 to 8 hr; to col ¾ hr if clear of snow. The Deltaform Ridge consists of a series of 100' steps, with progressively shorter level ledges between, until the cone is reached, 500' below the summit. Rope used from this point. Climbing to S is still easy and three rope lengths lead to the N summit, separated from the higher S peak by a gap 50' deep. Ascent from col, 2½ hr Descent to col, 2½ hr (CAJ 45–121).

3 — Traverse In 1963 the above route was continued by T. B. Mason, G. Prinz. Descend the E ridge to the Deltaform-Tuzo Col (two 150' rappels required). Bivouac in the col under the lower cliffs of Mt. Tuzo. The latter was ascended in ¾ hr on steep snow and ice. Thence descend to the Tuzo-Allen Col via poor rock and 50° ice face of the SE ridge. Mt. Allen was ascended within 200' but the summit bypassed. Peak Five traversed; Peak Four bypassed via S snowfields to reach 3–4 col. Thence the couloir was glissaded, interrupted by occasional cliffs, to Moraine Lake (CAJ 47–111).

4 — E Ridge (from Mt. Tuzo) Aug 1965 — D. Gardner, C. Locke. A two-thousand-foot ridge whose main defense is four gendarmes. These are circumvented on the left. Surmounting the second gendarme requires two rope-lengths and a few delicate off-balance moves. Above gendarmes easy unroped climbing up good rock to summit.

172

5 — N Glacier, June 1968, G. W. Boles, J. Farrand, B. Greenwood, C. Locke. A long sustained ice climb. From the Wenkchemna Pass Trail, shortly before Eiffel Lake, cross the Wenkchemna Glacier to foot of climb. The glacier contains two steep icefalls with uniform slopes between. The first, shorter icefall is climbed in the center, the second, about 600' of steep climbing, by the W margin. The entire climb is through a vertical rise of approximately 2500' with an average angle close to 50° and seldom less than 40°. The first ascent was made under easy conditions, the snow at the time allowing a maximum of step-kicking; even so 7 hr were required for the ascent. With drier conditions the climb could be very exacting (CAJ 52–68).

Neptuak Mtn (*Peak Nine*) (10620)
3½ mi W of Moraine Lake; SE of Wenkchemna Pass; NW of Deltaform Mtn.

F. A. Aug 1902, J. N. Collie, H. E. M. Stutfield, G. M. Weed, H. Wooley, *C. Kaufmann*. **NW Ridge.** From Wenkchemna Pass follow the jagged crest of the NW ridge with occasional traverses on S side to summit rocks which are usually snow-covered. Ascend final rocks from the S. 6 hr up (AJ *21*–376) Variant 1923 (CAJ *14*–48).
It is possible to traverse ledges on the Prospectors Valley side to a prominent couloir of steep firm rock, ascending to the top of the nose above Wenkchemna Pass. Thence follow NW ridge as described above. The "nose" may also be climbed directly (1939: Miss G. Englehard, F. S. North). 6 hr from Moraine Lake. From Wenkchemna Pass, 2 hr.

2 — S Face. 1931, W. Gardiner, H. C. Jenkins, *C. Häsler*. From camp in upper Prospectors Valley below Neptuak SW face. Enter the cirque between Neptuak and Deltaform and observe a large obvious gully leading toward the Neptuak-Deltaform Col (10250). Ascend this gully for 150', then onto the rib to the right, and ascend easy slabs to the cliff of yellow rock. Traverse left across slabs and enter a "Y" gully, taking the right fork up to a difficult 30' wall. At top of this wall leave the gully toward the right by means of a short chimney. Thence climb a steep 70' face to the Neptuak-Deltaform Col. From col traverse left onto scree ledges on the S face until

VIEW TO SOUTHEAST

Ball Range

Peak 5

Mt Tuzo

Neptuak Mt

Foster Pk

Wenkchemna Pass

E. Cooper

Horseshoe Glacier

Wastach Pass

Paradise Valley

slabs can be climbed to summit. Camp to col — 4½ hr; col to summit, one hr. Descent via Wenkchemna Pass to camp: 3¼ hr (CAJ *20*–165).

Wenkchemna Pk (Peak Ten) (10411)
   3 mi SE of Lake O'Hara; SE shoulder of Hungabee Mtn; N of Wenkchemna Pass; 1½ mi E of Mt. Biddle.
   F. A. 1923, F. C. Bell, A. W. Drinnan, H. Herriot, T. B. Moffat, R. Neil, Miss E. Thompson, R. Williams, *C. Häsler*. From Wenkchemna Pass, the S ridge can be followed without difficulty over slabs and ledges, and occasional short traverses on the E side. The ridge crest may be followed direct to summit with two minor difficult pitches: a 15' overhang and a smooth 60' chimney (both rappeled on descent). Ascent from pass: 4 hr. Further progress toward Hungabee was considered unfeasible (CAJ *24*–53), but has since been done (See Hungabee — Route 5).

Mt. Hungabee (11457) (See under O'Hara)

Unnamed (9250)
   E of Wenkchemna Peak, W of Wastach Pass, are 3 unnamed lesser points.

Eiffel Peak (10120)
   2½ mi W of Moraine Lake Lodge; SW of Pinnacle Mtn; E of Wastach pass. Excellent views. (AJ *18*–112).
   F. A. July 1901, C. S. Thompson, G. M. Weed, *H. Kaufmann*. **SE Ridge.** From Moraine Lake follow trail to Sentinel Pass as far as Larch Valley. Thence ascend the slopes of the SE ridge (scree and talus) without difficulty to the summit. Ascent from Moraine Lake 5½ hr (App *10*–89).
This route can also be ascended in a circular tour from Paradise Valley via Sentinel Pass, with return via Wastach Pass.

Eiffel Tower (10100)
   Just N of Eiffel Peak separated by a 400' notch.
   F. A. June 1952 by J. E. Murphy, T. A. Mutch. Via chimney

system on W. From Eiffel Peak summit (which see) the prominent chimney on the SW side of the Tower is clearly visible. Descent was made from Eiffel Peak toward the Tower by two 150′ rappels. This gap may also be reached from Sentinel Pass ascending to the Eiffel-Pinnacle col — 9300′ (See Pinnacle Rt One). Thence traverse W circling the Tower to reach the base of the SW chimney. An easy lead of 100′ is followed by an overhanging wall of wet, holdless rock and requires aid over 30′. Three more 60′ leads, while less severe, require pitons for protection. From the top of the chimney, a short scramble to the summit platform. Ascent from notch, 9 hr. Descend on rappel to notch and return to Eiffel-Pinnacle col (AAJ 8–563).

Pinnacle Mtn (10062)

2 mi SW of Moraine Lake; NE of Eiffel Peak; W of Sentinel Pass; 1¼ mi SW of Mt. Temple (AJ *18*–112; CAJ *1*–197).

F. A. 1909, J. W. A. Hickson, *E. Feuz, Jr.*, *R. Aemmer*. **SW Ridge.** Not recommended, rotten rock. From Moraine Lake to Larch Valley and the Eiffel-Pinnacle col — 9300′. Thence traverse ledges NE on Moraine Lake side of ridge for 300′ (fixed rope, 1965) to a steep pitch to regain the ridge. Follow ridge with occasional traverses on the Moraine Lake side to a black tower, split by a 60′ chimney. Climb chimney and ascend scree to summit. The chimney may be avoided by traversing N on very rotten rock to a snow filled gully leading to the summit. From Moraine Lake 6 hr (CAJ *2*, 2–45; 8–71; *10*–8).

2 — E Face. July 1933, R. C. Hind, R. Neave. From Sentinel Pass the bottom of a diagonal break half way across the SE face is reached, ¾ hr. A short vertical chimney capped by a slight overhang leads to an easy couloir, above which is a short wall. To the right above, climb several easy rope-lengths to a wide scree ledge. Cross this to the right and complete the climb by the NE ridge (CAJ 22–213).

The 150′ gendarme, **Sword,** on the SE shoulder of Pinnacle Mtn is immediately above the couloir and short wall of Route 2. Ascent is made by the inside corner on the side facing Pinnacle Mtn (SW) and can easily be made during an ascent of

Route 2. 120′ rappel required for descent. If this route is not completed an easy descent can be made by this couloir leading SW to Larch Valley. Sept 1962, by P. Fuhrmann, G. Prinz (CAJ *46*–87, photo).

Unnamed (*Grand Sentinel*)

The largest pillar just below Sentinel Pass on the Paradise Valley side. It rises about 400′ above the scree, and its longest face is 1000′ (CAJ *14*–118).

First ascent party and date unknown. Via an inside corner on the E (facing Sentinel Pass). This is presumably the route of the first ascent. On a later ascent the corner was climbed to where a large overhang blocked the way (presumably this can be climbed using aid). From the overhang a traverse was made round three sides of the pinnacle to a large ledge on the N face whence the summit was reached by a chimney.

N Face. 1960, B. Greenwood, J. Steen, A. Washington. From the snow couloir below the W face climb up and around the corner left to a ledge on the N face. Follow a series of corners and cracks for 250′ to a large ledge (as on Route One). Climb the chimney or steep wall right of the chimney to a good ledge just below the summit; II, F5.

Unnamed pinnacle on SW ridge of Temple, above Sentinel Pass. P. Fuhrmann, G. Geber. SW corner easily reached over scree from pass. Two 100′ leads to summit. Belay at fixed anchor. Running belays and aid. Fixed rappel sling on summit.

Mt. Temple (11626)

2 mi NW of Moraine Lake; 4½ mi S of Lake Louise; highest of Bow Range (Outram–142). The ascent of this summit, without guides, was the first ascent of any peak in Canada over 11000′.

F. A. Aug 1894, S. E. S. Allen, L. F. Frissel, W. D. Wilcox. **SW face** — (the tourist route) — From Sentinel Pass traverse E into the huge steep scree slope between the SW and S ridges. Ascend this slope, snowfields, couloirs and scree to the summit ridge at 11000′. Follow the W side of the SW ridge (cornices on the Moraine Lake side) to summit. Ascent from Moraine Lake: 7½ hr.II, F3–4. (App 7–281; Wilcox–

243, CAJ *22*–148; *29*–11). Unstable snow caused 5 deaths on this slope in 1955.

Variant. 1954, R. Kruszyna, E. Whipple. From Sentinel Pass trail, before reaching Larch Valley, ascend long talus slope at bottom of S ridge. Then climb a snow gully, and one rope-length on rock crest of S ridge. Span a spectacular gap and traverse left on SW face to join with Route One above. See App *11*–72 for original variant.

NOTE: On the Moraine Lake side of Mt. Temple there are four major ridges descending SE from the summit crest. From S to N these ridges may be identified as follows: (**A**) SE Spur joining the S Ridge at 9800'; this spur begins directly up the fall line from Moraine Lake Lodge; (**B**) SSE ridge curving S then SE from the summit; this ridge lies NE from Moraine Lake Lodge, ½ mi by trail; (**C**) ESE ridge curving E from the summit; this ridge (Route 3) begins NE of Moraine Lake Lodge one mi by trail; (**D**) E Spur to the very complicated NE buttress.

2 — SE Cirque and ESE Ridge. Aug 1918, V. A. Fynn, *R. Aemmer*. From Moraine Lake walk NE on trail about one mi until below the center of the SE Cirque (the basin enclosed by the SSE ridge and the ESE ridge). Ascend to the base of the face rising 4000' to the summit and reach a small moraine. On the S of this large cirque is a prominent rock rib rising toward the summit. Climb this rib for 2000' until it ends in a steep wall. Traverse NE to a large snow couloir which is climbed. Thence diagonally up to NE to break in final wall. Above this wall, traverse right up to the ESE ridge and follow ridge to summit. Ascent from Moraine Lake: 7½ hr. This route subject to rockfall in center portion III, F4 (AJ *32*–309; CAJ *10*–14).

3 — SE Cirque, right side and **ESE Ridge.** July 1962: A. Gran, J. R. Hudson. Follow description above to the small moraine at base of the face. Ascend ice cone rising from the moraine to a rock rib that leads upward to the right. Climb rib to where it ends in a short steep cliff band. Move left and climb band at first obvious weakness. Another rib to the left is followed to its end at a large vertical wall. Again move left (S) and climb to a small ledge on which traverse right

E Spur

G. Boles

ESE Ridge

Moraine Lake Rd

Black Towers

SSE Ridge

SOUTHEAST SIDE of MT TEMPLE

Mt Aberdeen

Sentinel Pass

Mt Bowlen

to the top of the vertical wall, above the starting point for this wall. Climb to a large blank wall, and traverse up and left around a corner to a steep chute leading to a vertical pillar having an overhanging chimney on the left. The first pitch is on the face of the pillar; the second pitch circles to the right until behind a short rock spike at the top of the pillar. Thence up crest of ESE ridge to summit. Ascent from Moraine Lake: 12½ hr; 8 assorted horizontals; 8 assorted angles; 2 ice screws. IV, F7, A3 (AAJ *13*–407).

4 — E Spur (D) Aug 1931, O. Stegmaier, H. Wittich. From a point on the road about a mile from Moraine Lake a very large tooth of rock (300′–400′ high) marks the start of the route. Climb a wide easy couloir S of this tooth and from its top move right to a second couloir. From the top of this move right again to a third couloir. A broad flat ridge leads to a 300′ vertical buttress (F6). Above this "Big Step" are two alternatives. Earlier parties went up a second shorter step immediately, easy scrambling from the top of this to the grey rock of the final ridge. Follow the ridge easily at first to where it steepens in a series of tedious, exacting rock towers in the black band below the final long snow ridge. More recent parties have traversed left on scree ledges to a prominent notch (visible from the top of the Big Step) in the summit ridge. III F5 (CAJ *21*–80).

Variant. The grey rock ridge above the steep rock buttress is frequently reached by climbing a steep snow couloir on the N side of the mountain; this can be approached from Lake Annette or by skirting the E side of Mt. Temple from the Moraine Lake road (CAJ *46*–96).

NOTE: Mt. Temple can be described as having 4 major ridges facing N and Lake Annette. From W to E; (**F**) NW Spur to the W ridge; (**G**) NW ridge, circling W from the summit then N, and lying E from the NW Spur, and separated from it by a very deep couloir; (**H**) N Ridge rising from Lake Annette direct to the summit, — the NW ridge and the N ridge enclose the NW face; and (**I**) the N Spur to the NE buttress. The N face with its huge hanging glacier is enclosed by the N ridge and the N Spur.

5 — N Face of NW Ridge (G) 1966, B. Greenwood, C. Locke. The upper rocks may be heavily coated with verglace

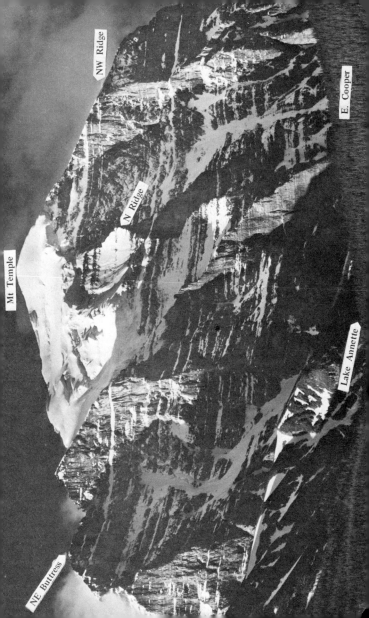

adding appreciably to the difficulty of the climb. An early start is advised because of the danger from stonefall in the lower section. One of the first of the major N face routes in the Rockies. From Lake Annette climb a snow couloir to the W of the main snow couloir (The Dolphin). Move to the rocks between this couloir and the Dolphin as soon as feasible, continue over rocks and snow up the W edge of the Dolphin. This section ends on a short sharp arete which is blocked by a steep rock buttress. Traverse to the right (W) below it until the rocks can be climbed to a wide snow ledge which crosses the entire face. Traverse left 2 leads along the top of this snow to where the rocks above may be climbed more easily. The route continues in a fairly direct line up to the NW ridge; sustained F6–7. In the upper part the route lies to the right of a deep black chimney. Follow the NW ridge easily to the summit. IV, F7 (since done in 11 hr) (CAJ 54–85).

6 — N Ridge (H). 1969, H. Abrons, D. Roberts; partial ascent. Aug 1970. G. & J. Lowe; Complete ascent. From Lake Annette climb the ridge directly below the summit; generally easy with occasional leads of F5. Where the ridge curves away to the right, after about 1500', climb straight up to the beginning of a second ridge which leads to the N glacier below the summit; generally moderate climbing except for steep rock (F7) below the rock band which crosses the face. The 1969 party traversed E off the face above this point because of dangerous conditions and joined Route 6. The 1970 party continued up the ridge, climbing the icecap where aid was required for 60' and continuing over the glacier to the summit. (AAJ 17–384) IV.

7 — NE Buttress (1). The safest and easiest of the N Face routes. 1969, B. Greenwood, J. Jones. A vertical pillar of rock leading to the lower E corner of the summit glacier. From Lake Annette the initial rocks of the face present some difficulty, mainly in deciding just where to start. These are followed by easy scrambling over broken ledges to the first steep step of pillar. Climb on the left at first, then back to the edge for the last pitches of this step. Again broken ledges covered with loose rock and shale give easy climbing to the final step. Traverse to the left (loose) and climb on the E side of the

pillar. On the fourth lead a small bay was crossed to a belay with steep slabs to the right. Continue straight up using aid at a small overhang into an inside corner, climb this for 20' then move around the corner right onto the slabs. One additional lead ends at the glacier which is climbed to the NE ridge and the summit. III, F7, A2 (AAJ *17*–148).

8 — **W Face.** Aug 1957, Mr. & Mrs. J. D. Mendenhall. From Paradise Valley (ca 6600') approach the L (N) side of the W face. Ascend loose cracks and ice gullies (pitons) reaching the upper portion of the SW ridge. Thence follow the ridge (talus, snow and glacier) to summit (CAJ *41*–79).

Winter ascent: Jan 3, 1968, D. Haley, J. Jones (AAJ *16*–412) Ascent followed Route One with variations to the SW ridge.

Glacier Peak (see under Lake O'Hara)

The Mitre (see under Lake Louise)

Mt. Aberdeen (*Hazel Peak*) (10340)
2 mi SW of head of Lake Louise; 2½ mi NW of Mt. Temple; NE of the Mitre; SW of Haddo Peak.

F. A. July 1894 by S. E. S. Allen, L. F. Frissel, W. D. Wilcox. **S Ridge** — about one mi from E Mitre Pass to the summit. From Paradise Valley a mile or so above the creek from Lake Annette, choose a convenient line of ascent leading toward the low point in the S ridge. Ascend slopes of shale, scree and rock slopes to a short chimney (sometimes icy) just below the S ridge at 9250' Thence follow the gentle snowy ridge to the summit. Ascent from Paradise valley; 5–6 hr Descent via same route (CAJ *1*–330; AJ *18*–109).

2 — W Slope. July 1908, Miss W. E. Creech, A. A. McCoubrey, *G. Feuz.* From the delta at S end of Lake Louise up scree and snow to notch between pinnacle of Castle Crags. Descend to reach Aberdeen Glacier, which is ascended to the summit. The Aberdeen Glacier may be ascended direct or circumvented on the lower rocks of Haddo. The Haddo-Aberdeen saddle is gained in 6½ hr from Lake Louise (CAJ *19*–160).

This route is capable of considerable variation, since the

Aberdeen Glacier may also be reached from Saddleback or Paradise Valley trails. The Aberdeen Glacier may be ascended direct, or circumvented on the lower rocks of Haddo, the Haddo-Aberdeen Saddle being gained in 6½ hr from Lake Louise.

3 — N Arete. Aug 1917, V. A. Fynn *alone*. From summit of Haddo Peak (which see) descend to Aberdeen Glacier and reach summit of Mt. Aberdeen — one hr over steep snow and ice of N arete. Descent as in Route One, to Paradise Valley, or over W slopes to Lefroy Glacier and Lake Louise. Total time 13 hr (CAJ 9–140).

John II
  9, 10
  If a man walks in the day, he does not stumble, because he sees the light of this world. But if he walks in the night, he stumbles, because the light is not in him.

LAKE LOUISE ROUTES

Here in are described, as in the section preceding, those peaks and routes best approached via Lake Louise. Parking at lot E of Chateau; trail (crowded in summer) along W side of Lake — 3¼ mi to Teahouse.

HUTS

The Teahouse at the Plain of Six Glaciers above the head of Lake Louise has limited accommodations, but shortens by 2 hr the climbs adjacent to Mt. Victoria. The hut in Abbot Pass has accommodations for 20. Blankets and gas stove are there but supplies must be taken. 2–3 hr from Teahouse. From the Teahouse a good trail also leads to the upper Victoria Glacier.

MAJOR FEATURES

Lake Louise is one of the best known alpine lakes in the world having been widely photographed and advertised by the CPR for over 80 years. The impressive array of peaks at the head of the glacial valley feeding this lake has been an object of attention from mountaineers since 1890. This is one of the two original centers of alpine activity in North America, the other being the Glacier House, W of Rogers Pass in the Selkirks. When the Glacier House was closed in 1928, largely as a result of retreat of "the Great Glacier", the CPR transferred its full guide staff and climbing locus to Lake Louise and Banff.

Abbot Pass was first crossed in 1898, by J. Brewster, R. F. Curtis and C. E. Fay (App 9–31), from Lake Louise to Hector. The pass, however, had been reached from the Lake O'Hara side by S.E.S. Allen and Yule Carryer in 1894, and from the Lake Louise side in 1896 by Abbot, Fay, Little and Thompson in their attempt on Mt. Lefroy. The first crossing of Mitre Pass was made in 1894 by S. E. S. Allen, Y. Henderson, G. Warrington and W. D. Wilcox, from Lake Louise to Paradise Valley (CAJ 22–133).

The peaks at the N end of the Victoria massif, W of Lake Louise are best approached by the Lake Agnes trail which ascends from the Lake Louise Chateau. 2 mi to Teahouse, Beehive Lookout 3 mi.

Fairview Mtn — (9001) — forms the SE shore of Lake Louise, its long SW ridge forms Castle Crags (AJ *18*–104; App *8*–128). The mountain has been ascended on many occasions by the prominent scree gully SE from the Chateau. The route is somewhat exposed to falling stones and has little to recommend it. It is better to climb rocks to right of the gully and then follow the ridge, 4 hr from Lake Louise. Excellent views.

2 — Follow marked trail from Lake Louise to the Saddleback shelter at 7500 — 2 hr. Thence faintly marked trail leads through larch trees to zigzag over scree on S face which may be followed to summit. Good view of Bow Valley from Pilot Mtn to Hector Lake. Snowslopes to SE may be glissaded in descending. The excursion may be combined with a walk to nearby **Saddle Mtn** — 7983, affording splendid views of Paradise valley, Mt. Temple and part of the Wenkchemna group. Marked trail descends from Saddleback through Surprise Valley to Paradise Valley, by which Lake Louise may be regained, or Sentinel Pass crossed to Moraine Lake.

Haddo Peak (10073)

½ mi NE of Mt. Aberdeen; between Lake Louise and Paradise Valley.

F. A. 1903 by E. Tewes, *C. Bohren.* (The peak ascended by Tewes, he called *Sheol,* but it is evident that he climbed Mt. Haddo). Via SW arete over snow and ice from summit of Mt. Aberdeen (which see).

2 — **N. Glacier** Aug 1917, V. A. Fynn, alone. From Saddleback via rock rib dividing the N glacier between Mts Haddo and Aberdeen. Ascend glacier to foot of couloir on the W. Ascend rocks N of couloir to E face of final peak and thence to summit. Some difficulties may be avoided by ascending the left side of the lower glacier to a steep narrow couloir 50 yards below the neve, which cuts the first band of cliff on the N face, giving access to level ground above. The left side of the couloir offers moderately difficult pitches. Above this, turn diagonally right toward the summit ridge, which is reached 500 yards W of the top, after further steep bluffs are ascended or circumvented by a long traverse to the right nearer the snow (CAJ 9–140; AJ 32–73).

3 — **E Ridge**, 1951, J. Miller, *E. Petrig*. From the Sheol — Haddo col following ridge throughout. 6 hr from Lake Louise.

Sheol Mtn (9118)

Culminates arete extending E from Haddo Peak; NW side of Paradise Valley (AJ *18*–111).

FA 1903 by the Topographical Survey. 1905, P. S. Thompson, *C. Kaufmann* (AAJ 5–152).

A cairn on the summit is visible from Saddleback and may be reached by following the arete from Haddo Peak (which see). Ascent from Lake Louise 7 hr; descent 5 hr.

Mt. Aberdeen (see under Moraine Lake)

The Mitre (9480)

Between Mts Lefroy and Aberdeen; head of Lefroy Glacier. This is an attractive climb on which many variations have been made.

FA 1901 by *C. Kaufmann, J. Pollinger*. 1903, G. Collier, E. Tewes, *G. Bohren*. From below Six Glaciers Teahouse cross Victoria Glacier and skirt N margin of Lefroy Glacier to base of SW slopes of Mt. Aberdeen. Ascend steep ledges and broken rock to E Mitre Pass. Cross the col and traverse horizontally around the base of the cliff on loose stone towards S. A wet, slanting couloir blocked by a chockstone is ascended for 100′ and a second (Y) couloir crossed below its branches. A "letter-box" gives access through the rib to a third deep couloir that cuts the whole E cliff from the top of the shoulder to the basal scree slopes (stonefall here). The vertical edge of this couloir can be climbed for 75′ and the horizontal top of the N arete gained and followed to the summit — (several narrow chimneys and steep pitches). The E Mitre Pass is also easily reached over steep scree slopes from Paradise Valley. Col to summit 1½ hr; descent 1½ hr. Chateau to summit, 5 hr.

2 — Traverse — N Arete to S Face — July 1944. E. Brooks, P. Vallance. From Paradise Valley ascend steep scree to E Mitre Pass and follow Route One to summit. Thence descend to S in the large couloir which ends in a 50' cliff (lower 20' overhangs) in a band of brown rock. Descend cliff to snow-covered scree. Thence down scree and ledges to the 500' cliffs that circle the base of the mountain from the E face to the Lefroy-Mitre col. Two difficult overhangs descended on small but adequate holds ending at the tip of the E lateral moraine of the Horseshoe Glacier. Route is exposed to falling stone, and has few suitable places for belaying. Ascent from Paradise Valley: 3 hr; descent to valley floor; 5½ hr. Loose rocks caused accident in 1944. Not suitable for a large party (AAJ 5–436; CAJ 29–162). This description is given as a descent. However, in 1961, G. W. Boles and B. Greenwood started from Paradise Valley at the lowest rocks of the S face and found easy, though rather tortuous, climbing to ledges leading to a large couloir descending to the SW. Climb the couloir to its top where steep rock bands force a traverse across the W face to the NW ridge which is followed to the summit.

3 — NW Face 1950, Miss F. D. Chamberlin, *E. Petrig.* From Lake Louise to the glacier. Instead of continuing to E Mitre Pass, ascend directly by the NW face. At the start (falling stones) a gully is traversed from left to right, the ascent thence being directly in the summit line. Ascent from glacier 3 hr.

Mt. Lefroy (11230)
E buttress of Abbot Pass; N of Glacier Peak; W of The Mitre (App 8–122, 133).

FA Aug 1897, H. B. Dixon, D. E. Fay, *P. Sarbach*, A. Michel, J. R. Vanderlip, C. L. Noyes, C. S. Thompson, H. C. Parker, J. N. Collie. From Abbot Pass via W face a direct ascent is made toward the summit, over snow, ice and outcropping rock, the difficulty being directly dependent on snow conditions. The route is frequently varied by ascending the face diagonally to gain the N arete several hundred yards N of the summit. In late season ice is often exposed and the ascent is more easily made slanting S to reach the summit

Mt LeFroy

The Mitre

Mt Aberdeen

E Mitre Pass

Route 2

G. Boles

FROM FOOT OF HORSESHOE GLACIER

via S ridge. 6 hr from Lake O'Hara in good conditions. Lake Louise to Abbot Pass, 4–5 hr; pass to summit, 3–4 hr. The ascent has been combined with that of the main peak of Mt. Victoria in 22 hr RT from Lake Louise; Aug 1918, Fynn, *Aemmer* (AJ *32*–74 CAJ *9*–140). In 1896, P. S. Abbot was killed while on this route, the first recorded alpine fatality in this range (AJ *18*–548; *19*–105; CAJ *1*–80). **Winter ascent,** March 1966 by F. Beckey, R. Burgener, J. Madsen. 2½ hr up from Abbot Pass (CAJ *50*–67).

2 — **NW Buttress.** 1913, L. Honigman, *R. Aemmer.* By the couloir leading through the lower cliff band from the Victoria Glacier to the snow of the NW ridge and lower W face. The arete is gained N of the summit. This route is parallel to the Abbot Pass route, and avoids the danger of avalanches from Mt. Victoria. The rock of the couloir is difficult and made more so by water and occasional ice. In late season there may be ice exposed in place of the snow. Chateau to base of couloir 2¼ hr. 2 hr.to snow above, one hr more to arete (AJ *35*–41; CAJ *12*–177; *22*–136, *41*–79).

3 — **E Face.** 1971, P. Lemire and friend. Climb first major rib to left of col between the Mitre and Lefroy. About ½ way up steep wall is reached. Pendulum to right and climb difficult crack. Continue up rib to summit snowfield.

4 — **S Ridge.** W Face 1971, S. King, P. Vermuelen. Following ascent of Glacier Peak, party continued along iced ridge to Mt. Lefroy. Traverse left without descent on steep, loose dirt and scree slope at junction of uppermost yellow cliffs and the black band at 10500'. The traverse ends in a vertical wall of which the N couloir was ascended on its right side. Crest of rib gained as soon as possible. Where rib merges into W face, party traversed right across another major couloir to a chimney which leads out to summit ridge. Reasonably good rock. 5 hr from Glacier Peak (CAJ *55*–80).

Glacier Peak (see under Lake O'Hara)

Mt. Victoria (S 11365)
NW of Abbot Pass and Mt. Lefroy; between Lakes Louise and O'Hara (AJ *18*–100). A plaque marks a crest directly above Abbot Pass 1½ hr distant from main S summit.

Mt Victoria

The Sickle

Ringrose Pk

Mt Hungabee

Glacier Pk

LeFroy

Abbott Pass

FROM POPES PK

G. Boles

F. A. Aug 1897 by J. N. Collie, C. E. Fay, A. Michael, *P. Sarbach*. **SE Arete:** From Lake Louise by trail and lower Victoria Glacier to Abbot Pass 4–5 hr; thence NW over broken rock until main arete is reached. This is followed to the summit, traversing the top of the snow slopes on the Lake Louise side where necessary. Ascent from Lake Louise, 8 hr; descent, 6 hr (App 9–1). This remains a popular route of ascent, though the area below Abbot Pass is justly referred to in much of the literature as "The Death Trap". The most recent proof came in 1954 when a roped party of four Mexicans, three of them women, lost their lives while descending from the S peak in soft snow of the NE face, falling over the cliffs onto the Victoria Glacier (CAJ 38–79). For combined route see Mt. Lefroy.

2 — S Face. July 1955, D. K. Morrison, J. F. Tarrant. From Lake O'Hara diagonally up and across moraine at floor of valley below Huber and Victoria; then up the S cliffs to the band which appears to overhang its base all along. Contour to right (E) and up the cliffs to the black band, a chimney of three pitches bringing one through to the prominent step on Route One (1200' above Abbot Pass) which is followed to the summit. The route offers more and better climbing than the regular O'Hara route to the SW arete (AAJ 10–125; CAJ 39–86).

3 — SW Arete. Aug 1909, J. P. Forde, M. Goddard, A. M. Gordon, Mrs. A. H. MacCarthy. From E end of Lake O'Hara ascend to saddle between Mt. Huber and Wiwaxy Peaks. Follow the usual route to Mt. Huber (W face; which see) and swing left (N) into valley between Mts. Huber and Victoria. Round the head of the valley to the bergschrund on SW side of Mt. Victoria; traverse to foot of rock wall and ascend beside a snow chimney about 400' high to Victoria SE arete which is followed to summit. This coincides with the route of first ascent for Mt. Huber. Ascent from Lake O'Hara, 6 hr, descent 4½ hr (CAJ 2, 2–100).

4 — W Face. July 1970. H. Dougall, T. Erdman, Miss S. Poole, D. Vockeroth. Approach up Huber Glacier to below rib running to centre peak, 2 hr. Attain base of rib from left over ledges and scree to gray band. Ensuing gray and black bands are good rock. Lighter-colored rocks are loose. 5 hr on rib. Descent via E face to Lake Louise, 2 hr. III, F6 (CAJ *54*–85).

5 — NE Face. July 1922, V. A. Fynn, *R. Aemmer*. The severity of this route depends greatly on the quality of the snow. Upper Victoria Glacier is attained at a point 2 mi N of Abbot Pass in 3 hr from Lake Louise. The bergschrund offers some challenge, followed by steep ice. A belt of black rock and a second ice slope are encountered, the latter leading to the arete slightly N of the summit. To foot of final wall 2 hr; to top of rock belt 600′ below summit 2½ hr; arete, 3 hr; summit, ½ hr. Total time of ascent 12 hr (AJ *34*–479; CAJ *13*–257). 1952, D. P. Graham, E. Petrig, direct to summit, the last steep several hundred feet was avoided by the 1922 party. 6½ hr up from Plain of Six Glaciers.

Winter Ascent NE Face Feb 1968 by D. Gardner, E. Grassman, B. Greenwood, C. Locke (to main peak).

Mt. Victoria N (11116)

Between S Peak and Mt. Collier.

F. A. Aug 1900 by J. Outram, W. Outram, J. H. Scattergood, *C. Clarke, H. Zurfluh*. Follow Lake Louise trail to Plain of Six Glaciers Teahouse, then trail to the upper Victoria Glacier which is ascended past Mt. Collier. Cross bergschrund, steeper snowslopes then rock to col. Late in the year there may be as much as 300′ of rock, sometimes wet and dripping, to get to the col. This rock is the prominent, locally wide-spread black band, the top of which is the col. The band rises to the S and E forming the towers on the E ridges of Mt. Temple and the summit block of Mt. Hungabee. From the col follow the N arete to the summit. Ascent from Victoria-Collier col, 2 hr; total time from Lake Louise, 12–13 hr (see Mr. Collier) (Outram–85).

2 — NW Ridge. Route not recommended because of unstable rock. Aug 1951, E. C. Porter, *Ern Feuz*. From O'Hara Road and Watch Tower Creek, a goat trail leads to the rusty rock. Above the first band of smooth black limestone is a band of scree which is traversed to the right (S) to a gully; up the right side of this to the next wall. Thence a traverse across loose rock under an immense rectangular gendarme. Descend

Mt Collier

Victoria N

Victoria S

Upper Victoria Gl

Sickle

Mt LeFroy

Abbott Pass

Route 2

Teahouse

Lower Victoria Gl

From Mt Fairview

G. Boles

and go over a crack to the N face. Steep and good climbing, eventually returning to the NW ridge, which is followed to the summit. 7 hr up (App 29–104; CAJ 35–159).

3 — N Face. May 1969, U. Kallen, C. Locke, F. Roth, M. Tott. Ascend Watch Tower Creek to glacier. Up glacier all the way, front-pointing as far as upper ice band. Difficult ice work near top. Descent by NE ridge. (CAJ 53–42).

4 — Traverse of N and S Peaks. Sept 1909, G. W. Culver, E. Feuz, Jr, R. Aemmer. To N peak as in Route One. The crest of the arete is followed with a few traverses on the Lake Louise side. This is a long ridge with numerous gendarmes, steps and rappels. The first traverse required 24 hr from Lake Louise via N Peak to Abbot Pass. Later done in much less. (AJ 32–307; CAJ 2–2; 92; 10–12; 21–19; 22–106; 24–54; AAJ 2–222). It has been done in both directions and in combination with Mt. Collier and Popes Peak (CAJ 24–54; 44–94, photo).

Mt. Collier (10550)

Between N Peak of Mt. Victoria and Popes Peak (AAJ 5–150).

F. A. 1903 by G. Collier and brother, C. Kaufmann.

The mountain has been included in a traverse from Abbot Hut across the entire Victoria Ridge and Popes Peak to Plain of Six Glaciers. Via Lake Louise trail and upper Victoria Glacier to col between Victoria N Peak and Mt. Collier; thence by SW rock arete to summit. The SE face may be descended to the upper Victoria Glacier. Ascent may be combined with that of Victoria N or Popes Peak (which see) (AJ 32–73; CAJ 10–7). Ascent from Victoria-Collier Saddle ½ hr, total time from Lake Louise 12 hr; combined with Victoria N 15 hr.

3 — NW Glacier. 1941 E. Cromwell, Miss G. Engelhard, through cirque N of the Watch Tower. Crampons on steep ice of NW (Collier) glacier to NE ridge just below summit. Ascent 7½ hr (AAJ 4–493).

Winter Ascent March 1972, D. Forest, S. King, J. Pomeroy, M. Toft: Ski the Upper Victoria Glacier to point short of Victoria-Collier Col. From here party roped up and climbed the steep rock of SE face meeting SW ridge ½ way up, thence to summit.

Unnamed (10350)

½ mi S of Popes Peak. This is readily traversed either way from Mt. Collier or Popes Peak. This and other subsidiary points N of Popes Peak are not of significant challenge. Various route combinations have been done.

Popes Peak (10376)

3½ mi S of Kicking Horse Pass; between Cataract Brook and Victoria Glacier (AAJ 5–151).

F. A 1903 by G. Collier and brother, *C. Kaufmann*. Via Ross Lake and N glacier. There is confusion about early ascents since the name was first applied to the present Mt. Niblock.

2 — E Face 1926, Mrs. R. Best, Mrs. A. Shippam, *C. Häsler*. From Plain of Six Glaciers up big draw to black cliff band on left of Popes Glacier. 80′ chimney narrowing to crack at top. Thence up E rock rib, with good climbing to summit of snow ridge. Ascent 4½ hr (CAJ 23–98). This is the most direct route, now generally in use. The mountain has been traversed in many combinations, including that of the Victoria Ridge and Mt. Collier from Abbot Hut. Immediately NE of Popes Peak is a minor point on the watershed — 9550′ (AAJ 4–494).

3 — SE Face. From upper Victoria Glacier. Plain reached from Lake Louise by trail.

4 — S Arete. From summit of Mt. Collier (which see). Ascent from Lake Louise via Plain of Six Glaciers with traverse of Mt. Collier, 12 hr.

Mt. Whyte (9786)

Between Popes Peak and Mt. Niblock; SW of Lake Agnes.

F. A. 1901 by *C. Kaufmann, C. Klucker, J. Pollinger*. From Lake Louise via trail to Lake Agnes; thence via scree and broken rock to Whyte-Niblock Saddle. Follow N arete to base of peak; a narrow ice-lined couloir involves about four steps, following which turn right into small, slanting chimney above the top of the couloir. The route leads back onto N ridge above the bluff, the summit rocks being a short distance further on. Ascent from Lake Louise, 5 hr (CAJ 19–158).

2 — Traverse. 1917. Descend SE face between main peak and subsidiary summit to S, a couloir leading down to Plain of Six Glaciers. (First ascent 1907 of S summit by J. W. A. Hickson, *E. Feuz, Jr.*) From Victoria Glacier, with traverse of main peak. Total time from Chateau Lake Louise, 8 hr (CAJ 9–140).

3 — E Ridge. 1951, W. Perren, alone. From the Needles (see Devils Thumb) via E ridge to the summit. The last cliff is particularly overhanging and seven pitons were placed. This may be avoided by crossing to the left and ascending the corner to regain the ridge. Ascent from Lake Louise, 5½ hr.

Devils Thumb (8066)

A minor elevation on the E arete of Mt. Whyte; W of Big Beehive.

F. A. 1891 by S. E. S. Allen *alone*.

The rock is firm, the views of Lake Louise and Lakes in the Clouds unusually fine, and the climb ideal for training purposes. From Lake Louise follow trail to Lake Agnes — one hr via trail to ridge of Beehive, whence the objective point is reached over easy ledges, 3 hr from Lake Louise. The short but steep N Buttress affords a pleasant climb. Rope advisable for inexperienced climbers. A short but interesting traverse of the Three Needles — 8500′ — on E arete of Mt. Whyte may be combined with the ascent of Devils Thumb in 2 hr additional. From summit of Devils Thumb cross scree slopes on S side of Whyte E arete to a dry couloir which leads to the ridge just W of the W needle. The E cairn is gained by traversing the W and central points over a sharp and precipitous arete. (AJ *18*–99).

2 — NE Corner. Oct 1963, T. B. Mason, *P. Fuhrmann*. Lower section climbed by diagonal couloir from right to left, turning into a 150′ chimney in its upper section. A platform is reached and a traverse left brings one to the direct NE corner below the main visible overhang. Straight up are several difficult pitches, the overhang being bypassed to right. The ridge is followed to the big platform below the summit. Ascent 3½ hr from Lake Agnes (CAJ *48*–150).

Mt. Niblock (9764)

N of Mt. Whyte; W of Lake Agnes.

F. A. 1899 by W. D. Wilcox. From Lake Agnes into Whyte-

Niblock cirque, ascending scree and broken rock to lowest point of S arete which is followed to the summit. Ascent from Lake Louise, 4½ hr.

2 — E Arete. 1903, M. P. Bridgland, J. Simpson, H. G. Wheeler. From Lake Agnes by way of the Niblock-St. Piran Col.

It may be questionable whether, upon the whole, mountain-climbing is more destructive than various other pursuits in the way of recreation which perhaps have no justification to plead so respectable as that which may be alleged on behalf of mountain expeditions.

W. Gladstone

ROUTES FROM LAKE O'HARA

Most of the peaks herein described are best approached from the valley of Cataract Creek. A road is maintained for 8 mi from Wapta Lake on the Trans-Canada to the Lake O'Hara Lodge, but is open only to Brewster bus or special permit vehicles. A good network of trails exists in the vicinity as well as along Cataract Brook. To the E a trail passes both sides of Lake O'Hara en route to Lake Oesa — 2 mi — and shows the finest example of trail craftsmanship in North America, the work of the guide and artisan, Lawrence Grassi. Above Oesa towards Abbot Pass, for obvious reasons, the trail is indistinct. See App 9–31, 97 for Abbot Pass crossings.

To the SE trail is excellent to below Opabin Glacier, where it peters out in moraine. To the SW a trail runs from near the ACC cabins over McArthur Pass — one mi — and down McArthur Creek to the Ottertail (see Ottertail Range). A trail runs NW towards Duchesnay Pass passing Lake Linda and others, providing access towards the imposing N face of Odaray Mtn and the Cathedral massif.

The Elizabeth Parker Huts on the Lake O'Hara meadows, facilitate ascents and are the junction point of many trails through this area. (CAJ 30–159). They are fully equipped and there is usually a custodian during the summer. The **delicate alpine environment** in this vicinity requires care and understanding by the visitor; it is seriously close to overuse.

Most routes of the Cathedral-Stephen massif are best approached from the vicinity of Field. Dennis Pass is situated below the SW shoulder of Mt. Stephen and is reached from Field by a continuation of the trail to the fossil bed, which begins directly behind the quarters of the RCMP. It rises between Mts. Stephen and Dennis, and leads over to the head of Boulder Creek, whence Duchesnay Pass may be crossed between Mts. Stephen and Duchesnay, rounding the N slopes of Mt. Odaray to Cataract Brook and Lake O'Hara.

Cathedral Pass is a more direct route from Field to Lake O'Hara and crosses between Mts. Stephen and Cathedral, a route followed in 1903 by C. E. Fay, E. Tewes, *C. Bohren,*

C. Kaufmann. The valley of Monarch Creek, 3 mi E of Field, leads to steep snow and rock slopes of the pass and down easy slopes to Linda Valley (AAJ 4–309; CAJ 27–127). Map 82N3.

Narao Peak (9757)
Culminates NW arete of Popes Peak; E of Cataract Brook; 2½ mi SSE of Wapta Lake.

F. A. 1913 by the Boundary Commission. From Cataract Brook by the W slope.

In Aug 1951 E. C. Porter, *Ern. Feuz* made the first traverse from Narao Peak to Popes Peak. From Wapta to latter summit, 7 hr.

In the summer of 1970, P. Carman and Y. Chouinard ascended the S of the two ice gullies on the E face. The actual ice was 800′, the only hazard being some loose rock which overhung the sides. In the same year T. Auger and D. Gardner ascended the N gully.

Watch Tower (8340)
A striking obelisk of rock isolated by stream flowing NW from Mt. Victoria and Popes Peak; at W tip of ridge running NW from Mt. Collier halfway between Wapta Lake and Lake O'Hara.

F. A. Aug 1932 by J. A. Corry, B. B. Gilman, H. S. Whitney. From trail near Cataract Brook through valley N of Watch Tower, ¾ hr. Circle E and S to point 15′ N of the gap separating the Tower from the ridge to E — one hr more. On delicate holds climb up and left to platform capping rock shoulder which leans against E side of Tower (130′). Next 20′ of overhang were surmounted by lassoing a projecting rock spike, 1½ hr (pitons are now in place, and spike is not). An exposed traverse to N and W has been successfully used (1935, H. S. Whitney, Miss E. D. Woolsey) to surmount this overhang. 100′ of steep firm rock above can be ascended in ½ hr to broad summit platform (AAJ 2–125; CAJ 21–25), F6.

2 — W Face. July 1962, G. W. Boles, B. Greenwood. From the old road camp halfway between Wapta and Lake O'Hara, follow creek S of Watch Tower above the bush, then over shale and ledges to shoulder below W face, the final 300' being almost directly up the center of the face. A chimney to a large ledge, 60', then a short traverse left to foot of twin cracks. In the upper part they appear difficult, but it is possible to continue left by a little wall, 70'. The short wall above and a chimney lead to a small ledge, 60'. Ascend the steep corner to a slab which is climbed to its upper left corner. The wall to left is traversed to a crack that finishes the climb, 110'. Descent by Route One (CAJ 46–95).

Wiwaxy Peaks (8870)

Double summit immediately N of Lake O'Hara, E of Cataract Brook.

Ascended without difficulty by a prominent gully directly above Lake O'Hara, with a short chimney below the summit. A minor training climb with fine panorama.

2 — NW Ridge. July 1951, by T. Church, D. Pullin, W. Raubenheimer, T. Whalley. From the road 1½ mi N of O'Hara Meadows towards ridge. Two main cliff lines must be passed. The lower is ascended by a crack on the right (W) face. The upper can be passed on the crest, or by the right of two prominent chimneys on NE face. No further difficulties to summit on broad ridge. It has also been ascended by the W couloir between the two peaks, a slightly more difficult route.

3 — S (Grassi) Ridge. 1962, B. Greenwood, Miss P. Johnson, D. Vockeroth. An outstanding rock climb on good quartzite. The route is reached by climbing ledges on the left of the prominent gully below Grassi ridge to the highest lone tree. Above the tree the climb begins on an inside corner (170') and stays near the ridge. Most all the difficulties on the ridge are bypassed by traversing to the right, then returning to the ridge as soon as possible. There is a short section of bad rock about halfway up. Very close to the top is a register, above this a steep little wall is climbed by angling to the left, then a short scramble to the top. 5½ hr from Lake O'Hara. Descent is best made by going E toward Col, round the top of a gully staying high, then bypass ridge and descend by bearing left to obvious gully.

4 — W Face. Center Rib. Aug 1964, L. Mackay, D. Voc-

GRASSI RIDGE of WIWAXY PEAK from LAKE O'HARA

G. Boles

keroth. This rib merges into the face at the top, but provides the longest line on the face. Rope up after easy rock left (N) of small stream (wet area in late season) on face. Route ascends to right but stays left of pillar to its top. Fourth pitch moves slightly left; then on rib line to scree ledge (9th pitch). Final 2 leads on good quartzite can be varied. 5 hr, III, 1700′ (CAJ 53–74).

Mt. Collier (see under Lake Louise)

Mt. Huber (11051)
NE of Lake O'Hara, between Wiwaxy Peaks and Victoria (AJ *18*–116).
F. A. 1903 by G. Collier, E. Tewes, *C. Bohren, C. Kaufmann*. Frm Lake Louise via Abbot Pass, 4½ hr. Ascend Victoria arete to below peak and descend couloir to Huber Col. Thence via N face. Return was over summit of Victoria and Abbot Pass 15½ RT (AAJ 5–151).
2 — NE Arete. 1907 by many parties of ACC. From E end of Lake O'Hara ascend scree slopes to Wiwaxy-Huber saddle (Good trail 1972) Traverse along W face of Mt. Huber and reach summit via NE arete over snow slopes (see also Mt. Victoria, Route 2, S peak) (CAJ 2, *2*–218).
Variant. 1933, S. B. Hendricks, *Ern. Feuz*. From Abbot Pass, descending and traversing above Lake Oesa into the Huber-Victoria snow-basin from which the NE arete was ascended.
3 — W Face. 1913, W. E. Stone (in a party of eight), *W. Schaufelberger*. From Lake O'Hara by the W face. A rock climb, snow and ice being encountered only in patches. As in Route 2, almost to crest of W arete; thence straight up over benches, chimneys and open rock slopes. Danger of falling stones. Ascent 7 hr (CAJ *6*–238).

Glacier Peak (10770)
S of Mt. Lefroy; N of Ringrose Peak; E of Lake Oesa. Excellent views.
F. A. Aug 1909, by V. A. Fynn, A. R. Hart, C. A. Richardson, *L. C. Wilson*. **SW Face.** From Lake O'Hara via Lake Oesa. Thence over scree and a small glacier the bergschrund of which is easily crossed to a deeply cut but not steep couloir

leading to a small gap in the main ridge between Glacier Peak and Ringrose Peak. Keeping close to left (N) side of the couloir, take to the face just below the gap but avoid traversing N. Near the main ridge is the mouth of a steep, narrow ice couloir; gain the crest of the rib on the N side of this couloir (rotten rock) and bearing slightly N attain the main arete turning the last rocks on the N over an ice slope covered with hard snow. Traverse to faintly-marked SW arete of final peak and reach corniced summit. Ascent from Lake Oesa, 4½ hr; descent 2½ hr. Total time from Lake O'Hara 10½ hr (AJ 25–85; CAJ 2, 2–84).

2 — NW Face. Aug 1935, Miss L. Gest, *C. Häsler*. From Abbot Pass Hut down scree to glacier, then up ice to rock rib left of ice and up rib to end of same. Thence ascending to right. Step-cutting to summit ridge. Danger of rockfall in afternoon. Ascent 4 hr (CAJ 23–98).

3 — N Ridge and N-S Traverse. July 1936, Miss G. Engelhard, *Ern. Feuz*. From Plain of Six Glaciers, ascending to Abbot Pass, and up several hundred feet on W face of Mt. Lefroy to prominent band of yellow scree leading continuously across this face to NW ice wall of Glacier Peak. Thence via icy ridge (crampons) and broken rock to summit in 2 hr. Descent by way of broken S ridge, with traverses on W face to couloir between Ringrose and Glacier Peaks. As this is subject to stone-falls, the rock on its N side was descended until snow can be glissaded (CAJ 24–50).

4 — E Couloir, July 1918, V. A. Fynn, *R. Aemmer*. From Paradise Valley cross the Horseshoe Glacier and head for the snow couloir descending from the Ringrose-Glacier col. Cross bergschrund and climb the steep snowslopes to the rock ribs on the left (S) side of the couloir. Climb rib and near the upper portion traverse N, crossing the couloir to the right and continue ascent along the right margin of the couloir. The main SW ridge is reached slightly N of the col to join Route 2 and followed to the summit. Ascent from Paradise Valley; 8 hr. Return is tedious (CAJ 10–9).

Variant. 1969, J. Jones, C. Locke. From glacier ascend snow couloir to Ringrose-Glacier col, thence via S ridge.

Ringrose Peak (10765)

SE of Lake Oesa; Between Glacier Peak and Hungabee Mtn. S of higher summit is a prominent gendarme on the main arete which drops abruptly to Ringrose-Hungabee col (AJ *18*–116).

F. A. Aug 1909 by V. A. Fynn, E. F. Pilkington, both summits. **SW Face.** Ascend rib between two prominent couloirs of SW face to above first cliff band, then move right (S) across couloir to rocks beside a curving gully descending from gendarme on S ridge. Ascend rocks, crossing gully higher, to rocks on left. Where main S couloir divides, cross the near branch and ascend to the main arete by the buttress, striking arete between the gendarme and the S peak. An easy wall is followed by a narrow, nearly level arete to the summit, the last difficulty being an 8′ wide gap, about 25′ deep, which requires care on account of loose rock. 6½ hr from Lake O'Hara; 4½ down (AJ *25*–81; CAJ *2*–2, 81).

2 — W Ridge. From Lake O'Hara via Lake Oesa, cross moraines and climb glacier to Yukness-Ringrose col (can also be reached over shale and scree slopes from Opabin Valley). The easy W ridge can be followed most of the way. Near the top cross a gully to the left and climb up to a wall which is bypassed on the right (S). A short scramble leads to the N summit. 5–6 hr from Lake O'Hara. A short descent on rotten rock (needing care), then a ridge may be followed to the slightly higher S summit which appears as a large flat block from the N.

3 — NW Face. From Lake Oesa cross moraine to snow below the rock buttress to the left of the glacier leading to the Ringrose-Yukness col. Climb is on steep, fairly good rock, hard in places, but with many variations. Gullies lead up to the right to easier climbing if so inclined. Halfway up the slope eases off and becomes easy scrambling with a few steeper rock bands near top.

4 — S Ridge. (to S Peak) 1965, D. Gardner, C. Locke. Ascent from Hungabee col is quite straightforward. Only difficulty is a short 15′ wall of very brittle rock. 6–7 hr from Lake O'Hara (CAJ *49*–136).

Hungabee Mtn (11457)

2 mi S of Mt. Lefroy; E. buttress of Opabin Pass; at head of Paradise Valley (App 10—91).

F. A. Aug 1903 by H. C. Parker, *C. Kaufmann, H. Kaufmann.* (App *10*–29; CAJ *1*–80). The original approaches to this outstanding summit were made via Prospectors Valley on the S. Severe danger of rockfall down S couloirs in the SW face made the routes of 1st and 3rd ascent unsafe and unused (App *12*–231; AJ *22*–75; *25*–88, 561; CAJ *2*, 2–78; *24*–51).

2 — W Ridge. 1909, V. A. Fynn, E. O. Wheeler. From Opabin Pass the W arete is ascended, keeping on crest until first band of quartzite cliffs bars progress. Traverse N across two shallow couloirs on easy ledges, then turn up mountain on ridge forming S border of the broad, often snowy NW face. One hour higher, where this ridge ends in cliffs, traverse to right and ascend a series of short traverses and chimneys to the black rock strata on the crest of the main N arete overlooking Paradise Valley. Thence ½ mi on N arete to summit. Ascent from Opabin Pass, 4 hr under good conditions. (AJ *54*–402).

Winter Ascent Dec 1966, B. Greenwood, C. Locke, C. Scott. Ski from Parket Hut to Opabin Pass. At big step move right (S) to bivouac. Thence up couloir to regain W arete. Crux is 40′ icy chimney just below N ridge. Descent by same route. (AAJ *15*–372).

3 — W Face — N Ridge. July 1925, V. A. Fynn, *R. Aemmer.* From camp at Lake O'Hara to a point below summit of Ringrose — 2½ hr. Thence bear slightly S ascending towards the Ringrose-Hungabee col. "No difficulties at all up to the gap", 3 hr. The N ridge was followed to the summit along wide flat slabs and interesting scrambles to the "treacherous" block rocks. Col to summit 3 hr. Descent via W ridge in 5 hr to Lake O'Hara. (AJ *37*–376; CAJ *15*–132).

4 — NE Face. July 1970, B. Greenwood, C. Jones, J. Moss, O. Woolcock. Approach over Wastach Pass to just right of center. Lower, gentler pitches very loose. Bivouac made 4 pitches below upper black band. Band passed by traverse right to chimney beyond wet gully. Above band, this difficult route eases onto N ridge (CAJ *54*–84).

MT HUNGABEE FROM GLACIER PK

Route 5

Route 4

G. Boles

5 — SE Ridge. Aug 1963, W. Schrauth, *R. Lofthouse*. Approached from the summit of Wenkchemna Peak. Climb down and into the gap between the two peaks and up onto the ridge of Hungabee by a 100' rock wall. After a short easy section a steep 40' wall leads to a huge plateau on the ridge (first ascent party bivouacked here). More easy climbing leads to the steep black band, about 250' high. This is the crux of the climb. It is easier to climb this towards the W combining ice and rock pitches, ending with a vertical 80' corner. The rock is generally very loose and affords little protection ending in a series of crumbling black towers. (AAJ *14*–204).

Yukness Mtn (9342)

Culminates W arete of Ringrose Peak; S of Lake Oesa.

F. A. 1918 by the Boundary Commission. May be ascended without difficulty from Lake O'Hara via the W face. Ascend boulder-field above Seven Sisters waterfall, then open gully above. Traverse heads of three deep gullies on substantial rock ledges, from the third of which an easy rock climb leads to summit. Descent may be made to Opabin Valley trail and Lake O'Hara. Yukness-Ringrose col is reached easily from Opabin meadows. Thence direct ascent to main (S) summit over loose rock, the best route being somewhat to the right of the actual ridge. Good views of major peaks.
Winter Ascent, March 1971. D. Skidmore, S. & T. Udall. W Face to N Summit; 5 hr up. (CAJ 55–86).

Mt. Oke (9581)

W of Prospectors Valley; E of Misko Creek-Ottertail junction. On N lies Misko Pass; on S lies Ottertail Pass.

F. A. 1904 by the Topographical Survey.

July 1931, K. G. Betts, A. H. Dalgleish. From head of Prospectors Valley down trail on Tokumm Creek for 2 mi to creek from Misko Pass. Cross this and ascend ridge running W to main ridge of Mt. Oke at 8500', one mi S of peak. Last 1000' of main ridge followed without difficulty. Descent by E face. Ascent 4 hr (CAJ *20*–166).

Curtis Peak (10010)

S shoulder of Mt. Biddle; one mi W of Wenkchemma Pass.

Mt. Biddle (10888)

SW buttress of Opabin Pass; between it and Lake McArthur; NE Face is totally rotten (AJ *18*–116).

F. A. Sept 1903 by A. Eggers, H. C. Parker, *C. Kaufmann, H. Kaufmann*. From camp near head of Prospectors Valley descend considerably and cross several ridges to S Arete. Follow this arete which overlooks Prospectors Valley and affords strenuous but not difficult climbing. Below final cliffs, an easy traverse over rock and snow leads to the W face above Lake McArthur. Last few hundred feet consists of very steep snow and rock which is often ice-glazed. A short but easy rock chimney is climbed just below the summit (App *10*–298).

2 — SW Face. Aug 1909, J. P. Forde, M. Goddard, J. J. Torey, J. Watt, *G. Feuz*. From Lake O'Hara follow trail to Lake McArthur, and from W end of the lake take S bank and ascend E of Park Mtn, via easy rocks and a short couloir, to the W arete, 3 hr between the lake and Misko Creek. Continue a short distance toward the mountain, then descend a few hundred feet and cross to SW ridge, which in turn is crossed and slopes traversed to the S arete overlooking Prospectors Valley whence the mountain is ascended as in Route One. 5 hr from W saddle to summit, 6 hr back to camp (CAJ *2*–2, 99).

3 — W Arete. Aug 1915, A. Carpe, *R. Aemmer*. This is the route of choice, the rock being good, and the arete fairly difficult near the top. As in Route 2 to col between Park Mtn and Mt. Biddle; thence ascend straight up W arete, traversing on SW face where necessary. 12–14 hr, including descent by Route 2 (CAJ *13*–257).

4 — W Face. July 1968, C. Locke, D. Vockeroth. From Wapta Lake via McArthur Lake to glacier, staying on left side to highest ice. 150' rising traverse to pass first cliff. Chimney on left side of brown band 700' higher. 300' above brown band are 2 smaller cliffs; upper is difficult. Party bivouacked here. Black band was passed via the prominent rib left of center. Final cliff surmounted on left using snow and ice. Descent via Route 3. Much loose and falling rock (CAJ *53*–72).

5 — N Arete. 1961, G. Prinz, D. Raubach, W. Twerker, *B. Greenwood*. From lowest point of the Biddle-Schaffer Gap. Easy scree slopes to within 800' below summit, giving way

Mt Biddle

Park Mtn

S Goodsir Tower N

Yukness Mtn

E. Cooper

Lake Oesa

to rock steps. To left (E) of ridge a shallow chimney is followed by a short exposed pitch and a thin ridge-walk over the first step. The second step has very loose rock, but 20′ to left a wide gully is an easy alternative. 7 hr from Lake O'Hara (CAJ 45–122).

Traverse including Mt. Schaffer and Park Mtn, July 1968. T. Auger, D. Whitburn. 16 hr RT from Lake O'Hara (CAJ 53–72).

Misko Mtn (9523)

3 mi S of Park Mt; between McArthur and Misko Creeks. F. A. 1904 by the Topographical Survey.

Park Mtn (9761)

Forms SW bank of Lake McArthur; culminates W ridge of Mt. Biddle.

F. A. 1904 by the Topographical Survey. Trail from Lake O'Hara to Lake McArthur, 1¼ hr. Ascend directly up NE face from NW end of lake, over rotten but not difficult rock. In descending a harder but more interesting route may be found down the W end of the peak. Ascent from Lake McArthur, 2 hr; descent, 1½ hr.

2 — E Ridge. 1907, L. Frost, *P. Kaufmann*. From Lake McArthur ascend rock and snow couloir in NE face to Biddle Pass and follow scree arete to summit. Descent by S arete (CAJ 2–2, 86).

Traverse, inc. Mt. Schaffer — see Mt. Biddle.

Mt. Schaffer (8834)

E buttress of McArthur Pass; S of Lake O'Hara, culminating NW arete of Mt. Biddle. (CAJ 24–83, ski ascent).

F. A. Aug 1909 by M. Goddard, W. S. Richardson. Ascent along entire **NW Arete** from McArthur Pass presents little difficulty, although several short bluffs are interesting. The peak may be traversed by descending the S face toward Mt. Biddle until a vertical wall is reached. Care must be taken to use the right (W) of two couloirs. This couloir has little snow in summer, and it is better not to descend to the glacier. Work to right across grassy slopes, never descending right to lake, the shore of which cannot be followed below first bluffs. (CAJ 2, 2–196)

The **N Peak** is a favorite short climb from Lake O'Hara, via the N buttress from the meadows just S of the Elizabeth Parker cabins, with descent along the W arete to McArthur Pass. NE Face has many interesting possibilities. Little Smoke Buttress, climbed in 1969 by M. Wisnicki & E. Whipple, rises towards center of this long face. (CAJ 53–74) III, 5.7

Traverse inc Park Mtn (see Biddle).

Mt. Owen (10128)

3 mi SSE of Mt. Duchesnay; NW angle between McArthur Creek and Ottertail River.

F. A. 1892 by J. J. McArthur, from Ottertail Creek via SW slope.

2 — NE Ridge and Traverse. 1940 E. Cromwell, Miss G. Engelhard. From Lake O'Hara via McArthur Pass and Creek, thence up E face to NE ridge at timberline, this being followed to the summit snow. Descent by easy broken rock of S ridge and SE face. Ascent 6½ hr Round trip 12 hr (AAJ 4–310).

Odaray Mtn (10365)

2 mi W of Lake O'Hara; NW buttress of McArthur Pass (AJ 25–27).

F. A. 1887 by J. J. McArthur. From Lake O'Hara follow trail SW toward McArthur Pass (Lake O'Hara-Ottertail River), turning NW to reach a small glacier which is crossed. Circle low SE peak and ascend to depression between it and the higher NW peak. The **SE Arete** is followed to the summit. In the arete are two short rock faces broken by chimneys. The first is avoided by a short traverse to the S; the second, just below the summit, must be ascended. (CAJ 2, 2–136; AJ 25–27).

2 — NE Ridge. July 1955, D. K. Morrison, J. F. Tarrant. From between Morning Glory and Linda Lakes. A combination of ridge and face, a series of 20′ – 60′ rock bands, the lower ledges wide. Rock generally good, all climbing quite difficult; belays are scarce. Diagonally upward to right (W) leads to the face above Linda Lake. The fourth pitch is straight up to a grassy ledge. Thence right, to another ledge 40' higher. Follow this to right around a corner, then diagonally up and across a bulge of looser rock into a depression running up the face. Ascend this to a shelf and an overhang, the first "hard" lead. A small but awkward overhang, the second difficult pitch, followed by three pitches to left toward the ridge proper and a steep ice-filled gully. Ascend easy rocks on to lower part, cross ice to rocks on right, up edge of ice 80', then straight up right wall of gully another 40' to sloping ledge with good belay. Regain the ridge by crossing back to left side and climbing a 30' wall. Two more difficult pitches and a narrow chimney; then to right up 200' of steep snow. Thence easy rock to the point where the ridge rests in its rise to the summit block. The black band is passed by a narrow chimney on right. Black rubble to final slope, a knife-edge of snow. Over 3000' of rock on this route. 10¾ hr from base to summit. (AAJ *10*–124; CAJ *34*–84) III, F6.

Vanguard Peak (8086)

W side of Cataract Valley; E buttress of Cathedral Mtn. F. A. 1913 by the Boundary Commission.
An interesting rock climb by the E face. The main peak is separated from Cathedral Mtn by the steep glacier by which the latter was first ascended.

Cathedral Crags (10083)

The NW summits of the Cathedral massif (App *9*–379).
F. A. Sept 1900 by J. Outram, W. Outram, *C. Häsler.* From Wapta camp through open, bushy slopes N of Vanguard Peak, following goat trails higher up over scree and easy cliff bands to E glacier, which rises gradually to the E face of the Crags. Skirt N along base of cliffs and up snow couloir to foot of rocks, whence 200' of climbing on steep slabs and narrow ledges leads to summit. Outram's couloir now contains no snow and is very steep, requiring rappels in descending, and several hundred feet of rock work to ascend (App *10*–88). The mountain was ascended in 1908 by E. Cowdray, *G. Feuz,* from the Kicking Horse side (CAJ *15*–133). Ascent from Wapta camp 6½ hr; descent 3½ hr (AJ *35*–200; CAJ *14*–10).

FROM HUBER GLACIER

Mt Duchesnay

Mt Odaray

Mt Hurd

Mt Ennis

Route 2

Wiwaxy Pk

Route 1

McArthur Pass

Wiwaxy Peak

G. Boles

N Crag. F. A. 1940 by Miss J. Atkin, D. R. Crosby. From Monarch Mine at Spiral Tunnels up brook W of Cathedral Crags, ascending by W couloir. The final pinnacle was attained from the col between it and the slightly higher tower immediately S, a cairn on the latter being noted (AAJ 4–309).

Cathedral Mtn (10464)

SE and highest peak of massif lying in SW angle between Cataract Brook and Kicking Horse River; E of Mt. Stephen (App 9–370; CAJ 2–2, 141).

F. A. Aug 1901 by J. Outram, *J. Bossonney, C. Klucker*. Ascend valley of Monarch Creek, traversing long slopes of debris and boulders, gullies and rock ribs, and then up steep couloir of snow and loose rocks to col between Cathedral Crags and Cathedral Mtn., thence following the narrow snow (N) arete to summit, ½ hr. Retracing route to col, descent was made to E glacier and Cataract Brook Trail in 2 hr, this now being the usual route of ascent. Ascent from Field 5 hr; descent to Wapta Lake 2½ hr (App 10–33; 20–544).

2 — **E ridge.** Partial ascent 1940 E. Cromwell, Miss G. Engelhard. From Wapta via O'Hara trail for 2½ mi. Ford brook and through open woods to S scree slopes of Vanguard Pk. Ascend to E ridge W of Survey point (Vanguard). Party attained a higher crest at 9600' (AAJ 4–310) 5½ hr up.

3 — **SE Ridge.** July 1951 by T. Church, D. Pullin, T. Whalley. From Lake O'Hara meadows pass E of Linda Lake, crossing Duchesnay Brook. Ascend steep bush and rockslide to alps. Ascend W side of first S buttress. From crest of buttress where it merges into face, move left (W) across two gullies to crest of next arete. Ascend to final tower of E summit. Ledges on right lead to easier ground and highest point. 12 hr round trip. This route was marked with cairns by H. A. V. Green, *W. Perren* 10 days later (CAJ 35–72).

4 — **SW Ridge.** Aug 1969. T. Auger, M. Wisnicki. Attain ridge via scree at W head of Cathedral basin. Lower big step gained via steep narrow gullies on E. Then along narrow arete to gully in final black band. Then steep, loose face (crux) to summit. 5 hr (CAJ 53–72).

Mt. Stephen (10495)

Above and directly E of Field (App 7–288).

F. A. Sept 9 1887 by J. J. McArthur, T. Riley, from Field. Trail starts in grounds of RCMP and goes past the fossil beds to SW arete which is followed over shale and ledges to a cliff 600' below summit. This is surmounted by a short chimney, a steep snow slope and a broken narrow arete leading to the summit. 5 hr up, 3 hr down.

This ascent is the earliest climb above 10000' in the Canadian Rocky Mountains of which there is authentic record. Starting at 4:30 AM they required 4 hr to penetrate dense forest to timberline. The first rocks were reached 3 hr later. They bore this inscription written in lamp-black: "Hill, Whately, Ross, September 6, 1886." An ice couloir above the rock with the names was ascended; it took all their nerve to traverse a knife-edge arete near the summit, 6385' above the railroad. A cairn nine feet high was built. Between this and the ascent of 1892, the character of the upper portion of the peak was greatly changed and made easier by a fall of rock, estimated by McArthur at 200,000 cubic feet. T. E. Wilson, in a list sent to Mrs. Schaffer, claimed to have ascended the peak in 1882. (CAJ *1*–118; *2*, 136)

2 — NW Face. 1927, H. F. Ulrichs, alone. From Field along CPR tracks for one mi; thence through undergrowth, fallen trees and loose rocks to base of cliffs (black rock) encircling this side of the mountain. Two general systems of couloirs divide the N face roughly into thirds, the left-hand system descending directly from the summit ridge, and the right-hand system running down from a great mass of rock jutting from the face below the W ridge. The left (E) system was ascended, the couloir breaking through the black rock and allowing this to be easily overcome. The bed of the couloir is followed over excellent rock, taking to the ribs when ice appears, following the right-hand fork toward the center of the face. The upper portions of the face were steep and icy. A small cornice was cut through to the arete, ¼ hr W of the summit. The ascent is continuous and exposed, but no falling stones were encountered. 7¾ hr; from Field, descent by Route One (CAJ *21*–42).

In July 1966 C. Locke, C. Scott, G. Walsh ascended the

Mt Stephen

Monarch Creek

View to South

Yoho River

E. Cooper

difficult lower third of the N ridge by ascending the buttress past the Monarch Mine. 1500' of climbing to easier ground. Thence traverse left to icy couloir and regain ridges, upper overhangs passed by traverse on right. Descent towards Dennis Pass. II, F6 (CAJ 50–72).

3 — N Glacier. May 1970, C. Locke, R. Saunders, N. Smith, J. Tanner. Climb cliffs below glacier, moving generally from lower left to upper right until glacier is reached. Attain and pass glacier through couloir on left side and then to top over easy climbing (CAJ 54–85).

4 — SE Ridge. July 1904. An unusual ascent by Miss G. E. Benham, *C. Kaufmann, H. Kaufmann* from Lake Louise. Starting at midnight, they crossed Abbot Pass to Lake O'Hara and skirting Odaray Mtn, ascended Cataract Valley to base of Mt Stephen below Duchesnay Pass. Mounting a snow slope they reached the SE ridge leading them to the summit — 19 hr from Lake Louise. The usual route was followed down to Field. Total time, 27 hr (AJ 22–334).

Winter Ascent N Ridge. Feb 1972, C. Locke, C. Scott, D. Smith.

Mt Duchesnay (9602)
    3 mi S of Mt Stephen; W of Odaray Mtn; head of NW fork of McArthur Creek. (Outram-184).
    F. A. in 1905 by the Topographical Survey. From camp at forks of Float Creek.

Mt Dennis (8330)
    S of Field, 3 mi SW of Mt Stephen.
    NW Face. C. Locke, alone. From just S of Power Station in Field, walk up avalanche slope to where it is pierced by buttress. Once on rocks move diagonally up to the left and work up a series of short pitches until summit is reached. Enjoyable afternoon climb.

OTTERTAIL RANGE

Lying entirely in British Columbia, this group is bounded by Ottertail, Kickinghorse and Beaverfoot Rivers. Ottertail Pass separates this range from the Bow Range to the NE and Wolverine Pass from the Vermilion Range to the SE. The highest summit is Goodsir, S Tower.

The range contains numerous snowfields; the best known is between Hanbury Peak and Mt. Vaux. Hanbury Glacier (appearing in earlier literature as Vaux Glacier) being the source of Ice River, about 3 sq mi. At the head of Goodsir Creek (Ottertail) the Goodsir Glacier has largely retreated above its lower icefall and lies between the South Tower and Sharp Mtn. On the W drainage and forming the source of Moose Creek, Beaverfoot River is the Washmawapta Glacier, SW of Limestone Mtn, about 4 sq mi.

The peaks are reached from Kicking Horse River by way of Ottertail River on the N, or via Beaverfoot and Ice River valleys on the S.

From near the highway bridge over the Kicking Horse River a fire road extends up Beaverfoot valley for 10 mi to a warden's cabin near the mouth of Ice River. Good trail continues, crossing a bridge to the true left (W) bank, another cabin being found 4 mi further. The head of Ice River trail is 6 mi from the end of the road. The ACC camps of 1939 and 1961 were placed at the junction of Ice River and Martins Valley, with a fly-camp in Zinc Gulch.

A trail runs up (SE) the Ottertail from the highway 5 mi SW of Field. At 10 mi a branch turns up (NE) McArthur Creek and goes over McArthur Pass to Lake O'Hara, connecting with trails from Lake O'Hara and Vermilion Pass. The main trail continues (S) up Goodsir Creek and ascends steeply, passing NE of Sharp Mtn to the Helmet Creek drainage-10 mi more. From NW, Marble Canyon Campground on the Vermilion River, a trail goes past the Ochre beds and up Ochre Creek with one branch going NW over Ottertail Pass — 8 mi, and one going SW up Helmet Creek to a cabin — 10 mi, where it joins the Goodsir Creek trail and continues SE an additional 5 mi beneath impressive clifflines below Limestone Peak and Mt. Drysdale, to Wolverine Pass. Wolverine Pass may also be reached by the trail branching off the Ochre Creek trail whence it follows Tumbling Creek.

The first mountaineer to visit Ice River was J. H. Scattergood, in 1900, on whose map (App 9–289) present nomenclature appears for the first time. The NE walls of this Range have received little attention from climbers and offer some of the finest challenges in the Rockies. The nature of the rock in this range is different from those to the E, being largely metamorphic.

Maps: 82N7; 82N8; 82N2; 82N1.

Aquila Mtn (9450)

One mi SSE of Butwell Peak; between Kicking Horse and Ice Rivers. S ridge extends towards mouth of Ice River; **Clawson Peak** (8780) being culminating point.

F. A. Aug 1954 by E. Plumpton, M. Rucklidge. Via Garnet Mtn and its W ridge to junction with the ridge S from Butwell Peak following the latter to the objective summit; 5 hr from Garnet. Descent via S ridge (CAJ 38–111).

Butwell Peak (9650)

One mi S of Chancellor Peak; between Kicking Horse and Ice Rivers; loftiest point on ridge extending S from Chancellor Peak toward Ice-River-Beaverfoot junction. **Garnet Mtn** is E ridge, Point "K" of Scattergood (App 9–376), whose party of C. E. Fay, J. Outram and C. Hasler made several attempts and exploratory trips in this area in 1901 (AJ 20–541). The peak was reached without difficulty in 1939, except for undergrowth on lower slopes, by ACC parties from camp near head of Ice River.

Chancellor Peak (10761)

E of Leanchoil between Beaverfoot and Ice River valleys. Ten minor peaks extend S from Chancellor Peak toward the Ice River-Beaverfoot junction.

F. A. July 1901 by J. Outram, J. H. Scattergood, G. M.

Weed, *C. Hasler*. A previous attempt a few days earlier by the same party failed on the S ridge. **S Arete,** W Approach. Camp at timberline on SW slopes at 6500'. Ascend scree and short cliffs to a deep snow-filled couloir leading to depression in the S arete just S of the summit. This is followed to the top, traversing to avoid small gendarmes and stretches of ice which often make the last part difficult. Ascent from timberline, 6 hr; descent 5 hr (AJ *20*–541).

2 — **W Arete.** July 1931, Miss G. Engelhard, *Ern. Feuz.* Through timber past Outram's bivouac, over scree and grass to W arete at 7000'. Thence steep climbing on loose rock to 9000'. A traverse (200') of smooth rock was made to buttress up which main W arete was regained and followed over many pinnacles to summit. Ascent 8½ hr; descent by Route One, 4 hr (AAJ *1*–533; CAJ *20*–36).

3 — **N Face.** 1972, L. MacKay, K. Baker, J. White. Ascend avalanche slopes to N Face. Class 4 climbing most of way. Some ice and loose rock. Long climb.

4 — **S Arete. E Approach.** July 1954, G. Camm, D. Lloyd, G. McGibbon, *W. Perren.* From camp in Ice River via basin N of Garnet Mtn to S arete; (5½ hr) (CAJ *38*–113).

Unnamed (9720)
One mi N of Chancellor Peak; a minor eminence at W of Hanbury Glacier.

Mt. Vaux (10891)
SE of Mt Hurd; between Kicking Horse and Ottertail valleys at NW corner of Hanbury snowfield (App *9*–376).

F. A. July 1901 by C. E. Fay, J. Outram, J. H. Scattergood, *C. Häsler.* **N Ridge.** From Ottertail River, camp at source of Haskins Creek, E of Mt. Hurd. Ascend over easy rock and steep snow slopes to Hurd Pass; 2 hr. Thence S along broken arete one hr to col at base of snow dome below the final peak. Steep slopes are ascended for 1800' to the snow dome at 10240'. Cross neve sweeping to SE, and circle large crevasses to reach narrow summit ridge. In descending, on arriving at dip between final peak and snow dome, the Hanbury snowfield may be followed SE to cirque at head of Ice River. Steeper slopes and rocky ledges are descended to the valley floor (see Route 2) (App *10*–6; CAJ *1*–74).

2 — **SE Snow**. 1939, parties of ACC. The main icefall, adjacent to Hanbury Peak, used in descending from Mt. Vaux (Route One), has now so retreated as to be impracticable. The 1939 ascents were made by the·W branch (nearest Mt. Vaux) where a fly-camp (not needed) was placed on the edge of the Hanbury snowfield at 9000'. This was reached in 3 hr from main camp at junction of Ice River and Martins Valley by ascending ledges on true left W side of stream. The ascent is continued across the snowfield (small crevasses), with a sharp final snow ridge (CAJ *27*–35).

3 — **SW Face**. 1933, Miss G. Engelhard, *E. Feuz, Jr.* From highway by a broad scree gully and broken cliffs of SW face. Descent by the Hanbury snowfield and a rock couloir to the basin of Hoodoo Creek, between Mts Vaux and Chancellor; thence by steep goat trails through timber to road. Ascent 6½ hr; descent 5 hr.

Mt. Hurd (9820)

NW outpost of Ottertail Group; N of Mt Vaux.

F. A. July 1948 by Mr. & Mrs. E. Cromwell. From motor road between Field and Leanchoil via game trails and open meadows to 7000'. Move right by further game trails around SW buttress to wide couloir cutting through S face. This is followed over boulders, ledges, and slabs to small summit. Rope not required. Ascent 5½ hr; descent 2½ hr (CAJ *33*–147).

Mt. Ennis (10277)

NW of Hanbury Peak; E of Mt. Vaux; culminating E crest of principal (W) Hanbury Glacier cirque (CAJ *22*–95).

F. A. 1906 by the Topographical Survey. In Aug 1933, Miss K. Gardiner, Miss L. Gest, *C. Häsler*, reaching Hanbury snowfield (see Mt. Vaux, Route 3) traversed the peak from SE to NW, descending from the Ennis-Vaux saddle. From head of Ice River valley through scrub timber to Hanbury Glacier, the snowfield being crossed to the S face, whence steep shelves and several small rock pitches lead to the summit. Ascent 8 hr.

Aug 1909 the col (Ice Pass) immediately E of Mt Ennis and between it and Allan Peak, was crossed by M. Goddard, W. S. Richardson, *R. Aemmer*, from the head of Ice River down the difficult icefall to Haskins Creek. From camp in Ice River valley to Field, 30½ hr (AJ 25–526).

Allan Peak (9550)
Immediately NE of Mt Ennis at head of E Hanbury Glacier; source of Ice River; N wall rises sheer for 3000' above Ottertail River.

F. A. July 1954 by W. Angus, Miss M. Jury, Miss M. Kirk, E. Plumpton, Miss J. Schultz, Miss H. Stewart, *W. Perren*. From edge of Hanbury Glacier via the SE ridge to the E summit, a sharp crest being crossed to the higher (CAJ 38–112).

2 — S Face. July 1961, B. J. de Vos, R. Neave, D. Redman, Miss G. L. Smith. Cross lower Hanbury Glacier to middle of S face, where two couloirs form a V. The left branch is followed to a small snow patch high on the mountain. A short traverse left leads to a 15' vertical crack, above which a traverse to left and broken rock leads to the summit. Descent by W ridge (AAJ 13–238).

Hanbury Peak (9550)
N angle between Martins Valley and Hanbury snowfield.

F. A. Aug 1935 by Mr. & Mrs. K. Fraser, *E. Feuz, Jr.* From camp in angle between Ice River and Martins Valley, an easy rock climb by way of its SE face. Ascent 4½ hr.

2 — W Face. 1939, A. J. Cooper, Miss E. DesBrisay, V. R. Fritz, Miss L. Gest, A. M. Harding, M. B. Howorth, A. D. MacPherson, Miss K. Prescott, Miss P. Prescott, W. G. Rook, *Ern Feuz*. Traverse. Party went up to Hanbury Glacier expecting to climb NW ridge, but was stopped by cliffs, so traversed to and up W face. Continuous climbing and three difficult pitches to lower peak. Thence down to col and up higher (S) summit. Descent by easy scree ledges and snow (Route 1) to Martins Creek.

Unnamed (*Martins Peak*) (9930)

One mi S of col (Wilson Pass); between heads of Martins Valley and Goodsir Creek.

F. A. July 1939 by C. Beattie, B. Curry, R. Neave, Miss P. Prescott. From camp at junction of Ice River and Martins Valley, by game trail on left bank of latter valley to col at its head—3⅓ hr. Easy going but loose rock up first part of ridge, with sound blocks and several steep pitches near top. Ascent 6½ hr.

In 1909, (Wilson Pass) 3 mi N of Goodsir N tower, was crossed by J. P. Forde, Mrs. A. H. MacCarthy, P. D. McTavish, from Martins Valley to Goodsir Creek (CAJ *2*, 2–95).

Unnamed (*Teepee*) (10230)

A tent-shaped peak on the NW shoulder of Goodsir N tower.

F. A. Aug 1933 by Miss K. Gardiner, Miss L. Gest, W. *Feuz*, C. *Häsler*. Ascend Martins Creek to the glacier, whence a gully leads S toward W ridge, reached after climbing some steep ledges, gently ascending to the summit — 6 hr up. (CAJ *27–36*).

2 — W Ridge. July 1939 by A. Bruce-Robertson, Mrs. B. De Lacy, Miss M. Gullion, Mrs. F. Neave, Mr. & Mrs. R. Neave, A. H. Rolph, D. Williams, Miss H. Zillmer. From camp at head of Ice River through bush to foot of peak. Up open slide to 7000' on NW branch, below which two difficult pitches are ascended. Follow ridge for a short distance and traverse right to the more southerly ridge at the gray band of rocks, continuing to summit. By keeping more to the N in descent, the difficult pitches are avoided, easy ledges leading down to timber (CAJ *22–96*).

Mt. Goodsir (N Tower) (11565)

One mi NW of S Tower at heads of Goodsir and Zinc Creeks.

F. A. Aug 1909 by A. Eggers, J. P. Forde, P. D. McTavish, E. *Feuz*. From camp in Ice River valley at 5100' near base of N tower, gain SW ridge as soon as possible and follow it until forced to leave on account of perpendicular bluffs. Traverse a rock slide to S to reach another SW ridge overlooking the valley between the N and S towers. Follow this arete to base of N tower at 10300′; traverse along narrow ledge covered with scree and snow (the upper leg of the V of snow distinctly visible from Ice River during summer months), ascending W face close to SW arete. On arrival at a snow-filled couloir, ascend rocks to right (good holds) for 350′, then cross to avoid a difficult cliff and continue ascent close to the couloir up steep ledges to summit snow. Ascent from camp, 9 hr (CAJ 2, 2–63; 22–95).

2 — S Face. July 1961, G. Boles, R. Dawnay, C. Fay, R. Kruszyna, J. Post. From high camp near tree line in Zinc Gulch up open slopes, then travese around base of S Tower to amphitheatre between towers. Up over scree, then hard snow to a spur at 10000′, thence sharp snow arete to base of S face. Here a broad scree band (lower leg of V) led up to the left to apex of the horizontal V of Route One. Upper leg of V followed as in Route One but party stayed to right of icy couloir (falling rock) all the way to its top (very rotten rock) coming out on top of a subsidiary pinnacle. Steps were cut across notch to main summit block. Party then made a short traverse left on steep rock, then easy scrambling to summit; 10 hr. Descent by same route, 5 hr. (CAJ 45–182).

Mt. Goodsir (S Tower) (11686)

Highest peak of massif between Ottertail and Ice River valleys. The mountain is visible from many parts of the Rockies and Selkirks (App 9–377; 10–9).

July 1901, incomplete ascent by C. E. Fay, J. Outram, J. H. Scattergood, *C. Häsler.* The route of the first complete ascent was followed, the party not crossing the final sharp arete because of dangerous cornices.

F. A. July 1903 by C. E. Fay, H. C. Parker, *C. Häsler, C. Kaufmann.* Camp at 7000′ in upper Zinc Gulch and ascend the basal W slopes of S tower over grass and scree. Ascend broken rock of SW buttress toward a conspicuous snow shoulder to E and via its narrow ridge to the base of a steep cliff at 10800′ 5 hr. The cliff was ascended over poor holds for 100′ and the narrow S arete followed for 500′ to the summit, heavily corniced on Ottertail side. Ascent from camp, 8 hr; descent 6 hr (App *10*–285; CAJ *1*–72).

The peak was traversed from SW to NW Sept 1915 by J. W. A. Hickson, *E. Feuz, Jr.* following the above route in ascending. The wall of the summit crest was skirted to the right and the summit snow gained. Descent to the N proved difficult and required a bivouac (App *19*–236; CAJ *7*–41).

In 1933 the traverse as made in the opposite direction by Miss K. Gardiner, Miss L. Gest, *E. Feuz, Jr.*, *C. Häsler*. Ascent 9¾ hr; total time 14½ hr (CAJ *22*–94).

2 — NE Face. Aug 1971, T. Auger, C. Locke, L. MacKay, D. Vockeroth. Approach from Lake O'Hara over McArthur Pass, down McArthur Creek to Ottertail River, then up Goodsir Creek. Bivouac below glacier. Party then crossed glacier, climbed 500' of good limestone to a hanging glacier, then continued up on good ice and snow. Above the second glacier is a long, drawn-out climb on very rotten rock, up chimneys, gullies, sloping ramps and open faces to the summit ridge and upper part of the E face. Easier going to summit. 10 hr. 6500 vertical feet from bivouac; pitons and ice screws used. Descent via SW ridge to Zinc Valley. V, F6 (CAJ *54*–85).

Sentry Peak (*Little Goodsir*) (10720)
½ mi SE of Goodsir S Tower; above main mass of Goodsir Glacier; at NW head of Moose Creek.

Sharp Mtn (10004)
2 mi E of Mt. Goodsir at SE head of Goodsir Creek; head of Moose Creek (App *9*–299).
F. A. 1906 by the Topographical Survey. From camp on Moose Creek via SW basin.

Zinc Mtn (9810)
2 mi S of Mt. Goodsir S Tower; S head of Zinc valley.
F. A. 1906 by the Topographical Survey.
Aug 1956, T. A. Mutch, alone. Via the S ridge from the Manganese-Zinc col (AAJ *10*, 2–160; CAJ *27*–37).

Manganese Mtn (9580)

2 mi N of Mt. Mollison; between Ice River and Moose Creek.

F. A. Aug 1956 by T. A. Mutch, alone. From the Manganese-Zinc col by N ridge (AAJ *10*, 2–160).

Buttress Peak (9030)

The substantial E buttress of Manganese Mtn; 1½ mi N of Mt. Mollison.

F. A. Aug 1956 by T. A. Mutch, alone. From Moose Creek via the SE ridge (AAJ *10*, 2–160).

Mt. Mollison (9687)

NE angle between Ice and Beaverfoot Rivers (AAJ *4*–192; App 9–376).

F. A. Aug 1900 by J. H. Scattergood, *C. Häsler, J. Muller*. From camp at 4300' E of and above Ice River-Beaverfoot junction, ascend above to first great buttress at 6100', skirting other buttresses toward base of W arete. The route then ascends the S side of the mountain over scree and rock to the crest of the arete, the summit mass being surmounted by its steep W face. Ascent from camp, 5½ hr (App 9–289).

Helmet Mtn (10297)

2 mi S of Sharp Mtn; W margin of Washmawapta snowfield; E head of Moose Creek (App 9–299).

F. A. 1906 by the Topographical Survey. From camp on Moose Creek, by E ridge, with descent down face toward creek.

Limestone Peak (9442)

2 mi E of Helmet Mtn, E margin of Washmawapta snowfield.

Mt. Drysdale (9620)

N buttress of Wolverine Pass; 6 mi SE of Goodsir S Tower.

F. A. 1963 by M. Tuttle, Mr. & Mrs. J. Peck. Via shale slopes and ledges from Wolverine Pass.

Striped Mtn (9210)

   3 mi E across Moose Creek from Mt. Mollison; 3 mi W of Wolverine Pass.

Any approach by way of the northern precipices, however, seems quite out of the question. (Ottertail)

   J. H. Scattergood

VERMILION RANGE

This is the SE extension of the Ottertail Range, being separated by Wolverine Pass. This range is not as popular with climbers as the Ottertail peaks but substantial areas of glaciation are found along the NE flank. Drainage along the SW is to the Kootenay River and on the NE to Vermilion River. The main trend of the Vermilion Range continues SE as the Mitchell Range across the Vermilion River.

Access to the E approaches of this range is varied and good. Tumbling Creek trail ascends from Marble Canyon parking lot, 9 mi to pass. From a point 4½ mi S of Marble Canyon a trail ascends Numa Creek joining with that descending from Tumbling Pass and connecting with a trail going an additional 4½ mi to Numa Pass. 1½ mi S of Numa Pass is Floe Lake (cabin). From the campground at Hawk Creek on the Vermilion River a trail leads in 6 mi to Floe Lake. Map 82N1; 82K16.

Mt. Gray (9850)
    S buttress of Wolverine Pass; 7 mi SW of Marble Canyon.

Unnamed (10240)
    N of three peaks at head of Numa Creek, the S being Foster Peak. Double summit, E higher.
    F. A. Aug 1933 by Miss K. Gardiner, K. Jones, *W. Feuz*. From Vermilion River up Numa Creek, following Wolverine Pass trail for a short distance to bivouac near small lake. Cross easy pass to S of mountain and work around to W over grass and ledges to snow and steep rocks which are ascended to the S ridge and summit. Ascent 6 hr (CAJ 22–92).

Unnamed (10060)
    Head of Numa Creek, between Foster Peak and the above unnamed peak.
    F. A. 1906 by the Topographical Survey (CAJ 22–88).

Foster Peak (10511)
    4 mi SW of Vermilion River; N of Floe Lake.

F. A. July 1933 by Miss K. Gardiner, K. Jones, W. *Feuz*. From Vermilion River road via Numa Creek to camp at timberline below pass on S side of Numa valley leading over to Floe Lake. Cross saddle between Foster Peak and next peak (10060) to N, making bivouac at timberline on W (Kootenay) side. Ascend snow-filled gully to plateau and lake, whence the NW face of Foster Peak is attained, a central rock rib leading over shelving ledges and rock pitches to the narrow main ridge, ¼ hr below the summit (CAJ 22–90).

2 — NE Ridge. 1942, J. S. T. Gibson, G. Williams. From Floe Lake cross meadows and moraines, then the lower part of a small glacier followed by more scree, in an ascending traverse to col NE of mountain (extreme right as seen from Floe Lake). At col turn left and climb rocks; interesting and intricate route without difficulty, 800′ to broken ground between lower and upper cliffs. Then up smooth slabs at easy angle, steepening as they approach upper cliff. The last bit before the upper cliff is a steep slab, climbed by a crack running up its face to a knife-edge arete separated from the main face by a gully 20′ wide and 1000′ deep. The arete connects with the main E face, and another 800′ of moderately difficult climbing leads to the ridge about 100′ below the summit. Ascent from Floe Lake 4 hr; descent by same route (AAJ 6–174).

Unnamed (9990)

2 mi SE of Foster Peak. Imposing N face above Floe Lake (Cambrian limestone). 4 mi NW of Mt. Verendrye; along the ridge towards which are several points exceeing 9500′; with severe escarpment on NE.

Mt. Verendrye (10125)

SE major peak of Vermilion Range; W of and in the curve of Vermilion River, at head of Verendrye Creek; 4 mi SW of Banff-Windermere road.

F. A. 1922 by the Topographical Survey. From camp on small creek to SW by way of the SW arete.

2 — SE Ridge. July 1952. J. Dodds, J. Duncan, M. Hicks, J. Tarrant, *H. Gmoser*. After two previous attempts foiled by snow and rainstorms, party hiked up Verendrye Creek from Vermilion Crossing. Trail ends in gravel flats but creek can be followed into a canyon where avalanche snow leads up to open slopes then gravel and scree to Verendrye-Whitetail col. Follow broad SE ridge over a succession of minor peaks to the final subsidiary which drops off 50′ to the base of a 60′ wall below the main summit. Wall climbed to the left over a bulge then traversed right. From here up diagonally to its right edge which is followed to top of wall and good belay. Then a scramble to summit. 9 hr. Rope needed on three pitches. Descent on W ridge to a large snow slope on its S side. Thence down to meadows W of Mtn at head of Whitetail Creek — ¾ hr. Party then ascended to col S of Verendrye and out. (CAJ 36–142).

3 — **NE Face.** 1966, F. Beckey, J. Fuller. From camp below face cross glacier to minor rib clear of falling rock. Thence straightforward to E summit.

Unnamed (10050)

One mi SE of Mt. Verendrye (665488).

F. A. July 1959 by J. Board, P. Pearson, R. R. Riches. By trail from Vermilion Crossing. A small glacier is traversed to the base of the SE ridge. For 500′ ascend to the S of the ridge and then by the ridge itself, to a cliff band 500′ below the summit, which is surmounted through several couloirs (CAJ 43–80).

2 — **E Face.** 1967, K. Baker, L. MacKay. F7.

Unnamed (*White Tail*) (9750)

SE of Mt. Verendrye; 2 mi NNW of Mt. Wardle: Two widely separated summits with a large gap between (674480) (SW).

F. A. Aug 1953 by B. A. Fraser, R. C. Hind, J. F. Tarrant. From Vermilion Crossing up the trail along creek draining the E sides of Mt. Verendrye and the objective peak. Where the trail ends the creek was filled with avalanche snow and a small glacier on the SW side was reached. Rope at this point and ascend to the col between SW White Tail and another peak to S. Thence up the S ridge, over one difficult pitch, until a vertical cliff forces a traverse to left on a wide ledge to a long couloir; firm rock with a few snow patches. The ascent from this point leads back to the ridge above the cliffs. The impressive final tower presents little difficulty. 7½ hr from Vermilion Crossing. The NE peak could best be climbed from the Verendyre col (CAJ 37–99-directions confused).

Mt Wardle (9218)
    4 mi SE of Mt. Verendyre; N angle between Vermilion and Kootenay Rivers; 6 mi NW of Split Peak.
    F. A. 1922 by the Topographical Survey.

Bridgland and I occupied three peaks on three successive days near the mouth of the Otterhead – quite a strain this was.

C. B. Sissons

VAN HORNE RANGE

Entirely on the British Columbia slope, this irregular group has no glaciers or snowfields of importance. It is bounded by the Kickinghorse on the S, the Amiskwi on the E, and the Blaeberry on the N and W. Mt. Sealion is the highest summit. This is an unimportant group with little interest to mountaineers.

On August 29, 1858, Dr. Hector wrote ". . . Peter [Erasmus, guide] I sent up the mountain in the angle of the valley, to take bearings, and to see what the mountains were like to the west. He ascended 3,500 feet by the aneroid, but did not get to the highest part of the mountain, which is quite a low one compared to those north of the valley. It is composed of the grey limestone, and splintery iron shale, all dipping 35° to the E N E. The mountains seen to the NW were high and snow clad, but beyond those forming the side of the valley there were more seen to the SE . . . "

Access from the NW is unrewarding due to thick brush, but the road up the Blaeberry River is good and leads to within a few miles of Howse Pass, and many of these scattered peaks are close to the N limit of the group. A road and trail leads up Amiskwi River from 2 mi W of Field, N over Amiskwi Pass (20 mi) to the upper Blaeberry River. Maps 82N7; 82N10.

Mt. King (9488)
N angle between Porcupine Creek and Kickinghorse River; 7 mi WSW of Field.

F. A. 1892 by J. J. McArthur. Via Otterhead Creek and tributary midway between two groups of cabins to a high basin; cross a shoulder to N and descend on far side into upper basin of creek flowing from Mt. King to Otterhead Creek. Thence follow steep NE arete to summit.

Mt. Deville (9594)
3 mi NW of Mt. King; between Otterhead and Porcupine Creeks.

F. A. in 1891 by W. S. Drewry.

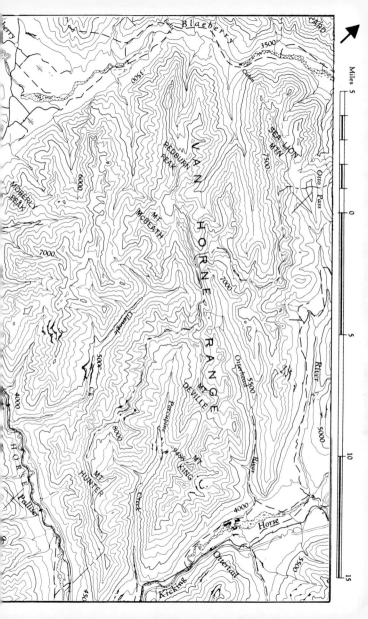

Spike Peak (9573)

S buttress of pass between Split and Otterhead Creeks. Higher points to W culminating in **Redburn Peak** (9350) 7 mi E of Blaeberry; 4 mi NW of Spike Peak.

Mt. Horsey (9350)

S of two peaks on ridge between Otto and Split Creeks; 4 mi NE of Split Peak.

F. A. June 1957 by P. J. B. Duffy, W. R. Henson. From the road at Otto Creek sawmill, through bush to small tarn NE of the peak — one hr. A smooth rib of rock is turned by a descent of 50' on the Amiskwi (SE) side to gain an open gully, which is ascended partly over snow to the final ridge about 50' E of the summit (CAJ *41*–79).

Unnamed (9388)

NW peak on ridge between Otto and Split Creeks.

F. A. Aug 1958 by P. J. B. Duffy, J. Leesing, R. D. Lyons, R. MacFarlane, K. E. Ricker, C. M. Smith. From timberline via the SE ridge, traversing sharp rock ribs and scree slopes on the S face to gain the broad, steep couloir that splits the summit block, the W point being the higher (CAJ *42*–51, marked photo).

Mt. Sealion (9650)

E angle between Split Creek and Blaeberry River; 2 mi W of Otto Pass.

F. A. 1906 by M. P. Bridgland, C. B. Sissons.

Amiskwi Peak (9259)

W of Amiskwi River; 4 mi W of Mt. McArthur; NE of Otto Pass.

F. A. 1906 by M. P. Bridgland, C. B. Sissons. From camp in Amiskwi valley, the final part of the ascent being up the E face above the river.

Ogre Peak (9311)

2 mi NW of Amiskwi Peak; NW of Twin Lakes. **Mt. Keays** (8840) is high point one mi W across Martin Creek.

WAPUTIK GROUPS

These form a long isoceles triangle with its apex to the N, bounded on W by Blaeberry and Amiskwi and on the S by Kickinghorse River (Columbia tributaries), and on the E by Bow and Mistaya Rivers. The N section of the W boundary is formed by Howse River, the apex of the group projecting into the Howse-Mistaya angle.

The irregular but connected icefields on and near the Divide in the central portion of the group cover an area of more than 40 sq mi. Balfour Pass is the division point between the Wapta Icefield to the N and the Waputik Icefield (20 sq mi, CAJ 33–86; sketch map). On the Divide, Howse Peak and Mt. Balfour are the highest peaks. Bow Pass, on the E of the group, separates Bow from Mistaya River, draining respectively into the S and the N Saskatchewan and following widely divergent courses before rejoining.

A noteworthy characteristic of this group is its unbroken E escarpment, rising above a series of magnificent lakes (Hector, Bow, Peyto, Mistaya, Chephren, Upper and Lower Waterfowl) in the terminal branches of the Saskatchewan River. Along this escarpment in recent years have been located some of the most challenging and spectacular lines in the Rockies. The rock is firmer than in most parts of these ranges. Its severity and height — ranging up to 4000' — offers numerous untried lines for the more adventurous.

Some interesting lines have been done in recent years in the Yoho Valley. Most spectacular was the 1966 route just N of Takakkaw Falls by S. Marty and B. Schiesser. The possibilities for similar short but severe climbs are extensive (CAJ 55–86).

To reach the W side of the northern peaks, not all of which are easily accessible from the highway, cross Mistaya River 2 mi S of Saskatchewan Crossing, then swing around N of Mt. Sarbach on trail to Howse River (old warden's cabin), thus affording approach to the W side of the group. Direct approach from opposite NPS Warden is unwise.

Kickinghorse Pass, traversed by the main line of the CPR and the Trans-Canada Highway, was discovered (from the W) by Dr. Hector, of the Palliser Expedition, in 1858, who then crossed Bow Pass to the N Saskatchewan. Howse Pass was discovered by David Thompson, of the North-West Company, in 1807, and used as a route to the Columbia until the opening of Athabaska Pass, four years later; it was examined in 1871 by Walter Moberly, for the CPR. Yoho Valley was first explored in 1897 by Jean Habel, who entered it via Emerald Lake and Yoho Pass (App 8–327; 9–20, 314; CAJ 30–58). An excellent historical summary of exploration of the passes in the Waputik Range is found in AAJ 1–405.

Thompson's Narrative states that Charles Lagasse and LeBlanc, in 1800, were sent W with Kootenay Indians. They were probably the first white men to cross the mountains at the head of the N Saskatchewan (Howse Pass) to the upper Columbia. Thompson sent the half-breed, Jacques Raphael Finlay, to the mouth of Blaeberry River in 1806. See also Henry Thompson Journals-704. Maps 82N7, 82N9, 82N10, 82N15.

HUTS

Good campsites are maintained by the NPS along the Bow and Mistaya Rivers adjacent to the Banff-Jasper Highway. Campground and chalets are at the mouth of Yoho Valley, and near Takakkaw Falls; the ACC Stanley Mitchell Hut is 4 mi up the Little Yoho Valley on the N side of the stream. Twin Falls chalet is above Marpole Lake near the head of main Yoho River. Balfour Hut (a wood structure) is at Balfour Pass and may be reached from Yoho Valley on the W or from Hector or Bow Lakes on the E (CAJ 33–86, map). Num-Ti-Jah Lodge on Bow Lake is a center for ascents and the home of the famous guide, poacher and old-time raconteur, the late Jim Simpson. A fiber glass igloo is located on the N slope of Mt. Thompson above Peyto Glacier.

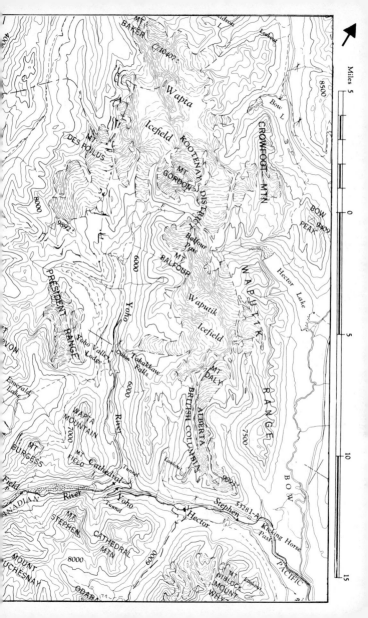

TRAILS

Burgess Pass trail ascends 3000′ from Warden Station at Field in 4 mi — 2 hr — providing access to peaks of President Range, although these are reached more easily by road to Emerald Lake. This connects with the Yoho Pass trail below which on the E is Yoho Lake — 4¼ mi from Emerald Lake. The **Highline Trail** runs along the E side of the President Range from a point 2½ mi SE by trail from Takakkaw Falls, in 7 mi reaching Twin Falls. The little Yoho Valley circuit branches off 3½ mi. N of Yoho Lake ascending to Kiwetinok Pass and the Stanley Mitchell Hut. These are more easily reached by the Yoho Valley Trail which continues from road end. The peaks of the main President Range can be readily and in part more easily reached from the Stanley Mitchell Hut in Little Yoho Valley.

On the E trails run from the highway up beside the major lakes: from Num-Ti-Jah Lodge to Bow Glacier Falls; one mi along Peyto Lake from a point 1¾ mi N of Bow Pass; one mi along Hector Lake from a point ½ mi N of viewpoint. On the S, a trail from just W of Wapta Lodge runs up E of Sherbrooke Lake and gives access over Niles Pass with Takakkaw campground. The Yoho Valley has been a favorite locale for ski mountaineering, the base for many ACC ski camps. Many climbs of the less demanding routes have been done under winter conditions and on skis.

In 1898 Vulture Col was reached by H. P. Nichols, C. S. Noyes, C. S. Thompson, from the N via Peyto Glacier, the party descending to Bow Lake. The first crossing from Bow Lake to Yoho Valley was in 1910 by E. S. Darling, T. G. Longstaff, A. O. Wheeler, E. O. Wheeler, *C. Kain*. The ice of the S slope, above Balfour Pass, has altered and become more difficult in recent years (CAJ 3–164; Thorington-26).

The **President Range** is a minor SW division of the Waputik Mtns entirely on the Columbia drainage and bounded on the E by the Yoho Valley draining S from the Wapta Glacier system. On the N the little Yoho River heads at Kiwetinok Pass with Kiwetinok River, which latter turns S and forms the W border of the range. On the S, drainage is to Emerald Lake (lodge with road access, from just W of Field). A good trail system connects Emerald Lake with the Yoho Valley over Yoho Pass and bounds the E and N side of these peaks some 1500' above the Yoho River. The trail up Amiskwi River runs for 20 mi to Amiskwi Pass.

Mt Burgess (8526)

W buttress of Burgess Pass; 2 mi NNW of Field.

F. A. July 1892 by J. J. McArthur, Miss H. L. Tuzo. From Burgess Pass (¾ mi NE of summit) over broken rock on NE ridge; laborious but not difficult (CAJ *1*–53).

2 — NW Face. 1966 by C. Locke, I. Stout. From Emerald Lake climb scree to lowest point of rock face. Climb for 600' to base of crack. One moderate pitch is followed by 6 pitches of scrambling to ridge (rotten rock). From ridge move diagonally left and up another crack over small overhang. From flat platform traverse right 200' and then up to summit. 10 hr, F6.

Wapta Mtn (9116)

Between Yoho River and Emerald Lake; between Yoho and Burgess Passes. **Mt. Field** (8650) is SSE extension of this mtn E of Burgess Pass (Outram–178).

F. A. July 1901 by J. Outram, J. H. Scattergood, *C. Bohren.* From Yoho Pass ascend N slopes with no difficulty (App *10*–85).

2 — NE Face. 1906, Miss H. L. Tuzo, *C. Kaufmann.* From Yoho Pass traverse SE over the long scree slopes to snow banks at foot of NE cliffs. The general line of ascent is from the lower right to the upper left of the face. Work up from snow through a narrow gully to foot of a wide chimney near NE angle of the cliff. Ascend left over steep rock with small holds. Traverse up toward the E outline of cliffs, for ¾ of the distance to the crest, to a level bench at the foot of several steep chimneys. Ascend chimney on right, 50' of good rock leads to cornice whence summit is easily reached. 2½ hr from foot of NE face (CAJ *11*–217).

3 — SW Face. From Burgess Pass or Yoho Pass a large snow-filled couloir in the SW face can be reached and ascended for 200'. Thence traverse ledges to E past the foot of a chimney and around a buttress to a broad dry couloir. Ascend this to top of cliff-belt. Thence over scree to second line of cliff which is surmounted by ledges leading to E extremity of final ridge. From Field or Emerald Lake, 5 hr; from base of S couloir, 2 hr.

Michael Peak (8844)

NW buttress of Yoho Pass; 3 mi NNE of Emerald Lake; 2 mi SE of Mt. President. Not really a separate summit. The high point is actually "Point 9500" (9950') situated one mi towards Vice President along the intervening ridge. This would also appear to be the "Angle Peak" of App *10*–86. The lower SE extremity was first reached in 1900 by J. Outram, *C. Kaufmann* who ascended easily from Yoho Pass. In that same year A. Michael, *C. Häsler* ascended the SW arete from Emerald Lake to the crest at 9950'. In 1901, J. Outram with *C. Kaufmann* and *J. Pollinger* followed a more strenuous route over the summit of President (*Emerald Mtn*) traversing the ridge SE to Angle Peak. This ridge has been traversed from Yoho Pass to President Pass by various parties in both directions (AJ *46*–85; CAJ *28*–236).

The Vice President (10059)

ENE of The President; S wall of Little Yoho Valley; an eminence on the long SE arete is known as Angle Peak (App *10*–86; CAJ *1*–171; *21*–123, ski ascent).

F. A. July 1901 by J. Outram, *C. Kaufmann, J. Pollinger*. From Little Yoho Valley via centre and W bank of glacier below N side of President Pass. From the pass (9750') ascend over rock and snow to summit. Only difficulty is with bergschrund below pass. Extremely rotten rock on W ridge. Ascent 3½ hr. The first party ascended the glacier for 1½ hr, but did not go to the pass, taking to the rock on the left and thence over steep snow of the NW face.

Also see under Michael Peak.

The President (*Emerald Mtn*) (10297)

SSW of The Vice-President and separated from it by President Pass; 4 mi NNW of Emerald Lake. Can be ascended in 6 hr from Takakkaw Falls.

F. A. July 1901, by J. Outram, *C. Kaufmann, J. Pollinger*. **N Glacier to E face.** From camp in Little Yoho Valley by the glacier to President Pass, and thence by easy rock and snow to the summit. 3½ hr up from Stanley Mitchell Hut (AJ *20*–541; App *10*–86). In this same year President Pass was crossed by E. Whymper, *C. Klucker* from Little Yoho Valley to Emerald Lake and Field.

2 — W Slope. From Little Yoho Valley, rounding the W side of the mountain to Emerald Pass, the W slopes can be ascended, but the snow is steep and unstable on the face. SW ridge is straight-forward and safe.

3 — N Ridge. 1909, L. C. Wilson and other members of ACC, *C. Kain* went from Little Yoho Valley up the N ridge to the summit, thence across to the Vice-President and following the SE arete of the latter to Yoho Pass. Ridge is long and rotten. II, 5.2

4 — Traverse. 1908 A traverse of President, Vice President and Michael Peak was made from Emerald Lake via Emerald Pass by C. Q. Bey, T. Kidd, A. A. McCoubrey, *G. Feuz*, but the elevation of the lake is too low to make this excursion popular (AJ *54*–401; CAJ *27*–217). Can be readily done from Stanley Mitchell Hut.

Mt. Carnarvon (9974)

S of Mt. Marpole; 3 mi NW of Emerald Lake. **Emerald Peak** (8380) is one mi SE as shoulder of this summit (Outram–201).

F. A. 1904, by the Topographical Survey.

May be reached easily from Emerald Lake by way of the Carnarvon-Marpole saddle and N ridge.

S Ridge and traverse. 1941, E. Cromwell, Miss G. Engelhard. From Emerald Lake via trail W to Hamilton Lake (7000'), thence up scree to S ridge, which is followed throughout, a few steep pitches alternating with broken ledges. Descent by N ridge to Carnarvon-Marpole saddle. Total time 9¾ hr.

Mt. Marpole (9832)

SW of the President; N of Mt. Carnavon; 4 mi NNW of Emerald Lake. Dangerously rotten rock.

F. A. 1901 by E. Whymper, *J. Bossonay, C. Kaufmann, C. Klucker, J. Pollinger*. From camp in Little Yoho Valley, via the glacier between Mt. Marpole and President. Steep rock of N arete leads to summit in one hr — 5.2. The E arete, from Emerald Pass, is steep, difficult and has been substantially altered by rockfall in recent years.

Amgadamo (8950); a minor point, culminates W ridge of Mt. Marpole.

F. A. 1906 by A. M. Gordon, A. Dunn, A. O. McCrae, *E. Feuz, Jr, G. Feuz*. From Yoho Pass by way of the Carnarvon-Marpole col, whence N to the E ridge of the objective over broken rock. A traverse may be made of the main peak of Mt. Marpole, with descent to glacier between Mts. Marpole and President whence Little Yoho Valley or Emerald Lake may be reached. (CAJ *1*–115, 175).

Mt. Kerr (9394)

S buttress of Kiwetinok Pass (CAJ 27–222, ski ascent).

F. A. 1901 by E. Whymper, *J. Bossoney, C. Kaufmann, C. Klucker, J. Pollinger*. From Little Yoho Valley, by the way of either Kiwetinok Pass or Emerald Pass. Not a significant summit.

Kiwetinok Peak (9522)

N buttress of Kiwetinok Pass; 4 mi NW of President; W of Mt. Pollinger. In 1901 Kiwetinok Pass was crossed by E. Whymper, T. Wilson, *C. Klucker* from Little Yoho Valley to Amiskwi Valley and Field in 17 hr.

F. A. July 1901 by J. Outram, *C. Kaufmann, J. Pollinger*. **NE Ridge.** From Little Yoho Valley ascend to Kiwetinok Lake (8037') at the pass. From lake ascend snow couloir at N to ridge connecting with Mt. Pollinger. Thence up steep snow of NE ridge to summit. Ascent 4 hr (AJ *20*–542).

Mt. Pollinger (9240)

One mi S of Mt. McArthur; 5½ mi WNW of Takakkaw Falls (CAJ *22*–165; ski ascent).

F. A. Aug 1902 by J. Outram, C. Kaufmann. **N Ridge.** From Little Yoho Valley enter the basin E of Mt. Pollinger to reach the Pollinger-McArthur col (rockfall). Thence to summit. The peak can be more easily ascended via gully from Kiwetinok Lake. An easy ascent. It is one of the subsidiary points traversed in passing from Kiwetinok Pk. to Mt. McArthur (which see) and was originally ascended this way (Outram–200). E ridge is short.

Mt. McArthur (9892)

One mi W of Isolated Peak; SW margin of Des Poilus Glacier; 3 mi SW of Yoho Pk; 5½ mi NW of Takakkaw Falls (CAJ 2-2, 150, 22–165; ski ascent).

F. A. 1891 by W. S. Drewry. **N Ridge.** From Twin Falls Chalet by way of Twin Falls Creek and Des Poilus Glacier and N ridge, which is accessible in many places and followed on its W side to summit. Ascent 5 hr.

2 — S Ridge. From Little Yoho Valley traverse Kiwetinok Peak and Mt. Pollinger (which see); ascend Mt. McArthur by way of the S ridge in one hr.

3 — E Face. Aug 1972 J. K. Fox, R. A. Lambe. From Stanley Mitchell Hut by trail to meadows S of Isolated Pk. Cross W on glacier to steep ice and snow of summit. One rock pitch at top. 6 hr up.

Isolated Peak (9334)

S margin of Des Poilus Glacier; E of Mt. McArthur; 3 mi N of The President; 2 mi SW of Yoho Peak. **Whaleback Mtn** is the SE ridge (CAJ 22–164; ski ascent).

F. A. Aug 1901 by J. Outram, E. Whymper, *J. Bossoney, C. Kaufmann, C. Klucker, J. Pollinger.* **W Ridge.** From camp in Little Yoho Valley, via scree and dry glacier W, of Whaleback to snowslopes and shale, leading to rocky summit. This ridge offers the easiest route, but the S face has also been ascended. (In 1901 it was reached by J. Outram, *C. Kaufmann,* traversing the crest from Kiwetinok Pass (Kiwetinok-Pollinger-McArthur). Ascent 2½ hr (App *10*–85).

2 — E Ridge. July 1943, F. Neave, R. Neave. From Mitchell Hut via Isolated-Whaleback col, thence N of gendarmes via the lower E ridge. Loose and rotten rock. 4 hr up (CAJ 28–277). II, 5.1

Yoho Peak (9056)

7 mi NW of Takakkaw Falls; 5 mi N of President at head of Yoho River (App *10*–87; CAJ *21*–122 ski ascent; AAJ *2*–209, traverse).

F. A. Aug 1901 by R. Campbell, H. W. Dubois, A. Palmer. From Twin Falls chalet the mountain may be easily reached by way of Yoho Glacier and the broken rock of the N face; or via cliffs N of Twin Falls to narrow SE ridge which is followed to the snow summit. 1933 approach from Peyto Glacier with descent to Twin Falls, H. J. Kingman, J. M. Thorington, *C. Kain* (AAJ *2*–206).

Arête Pk (9050)

One mi NW of Mt. Des Poilus. Descending gradually but above timberline for over 5 mi this is the high point of a crest running slightly W of N towards the upper Blaeberry River from Mt. Des Poilus.

Mt. Des Poilus (*Habel*) (10371)

9 mi NW of Takakkaw Falls; SW of Mt. Collie; 2½ mi NW of Yoho Peak.

F. A. Aug 1901 by J. Outram, E. Whymper, *C. Kaufmann, C. Klucker, J. Pollinger.* **S Ridge.** From Twin Falls Chalet via Des Poilus Glacier and Wapta Neve to bergschrund and steep slopes on E leading to a col in S arete from which the summit 500′ higher may be reached. Ascent 5½ hr (AJ *20*–54; App *10*–86). The route above may be reached from Little Yoho Valley by an ascent of 2000′ to the rocky col NE of Isolated Peak, and a descent of 300′ on the far side to Des Poilus Glacier. The peak was traversed by descending the N face to the Habel-Collie col, following which Mt. Collie (which see) was ascended (AAJ *1*–534).

Mt. Collie (10225)

7 mi SW of Bow Lake Lodge; 10 mi NNW of Takakkaw Falls; NE of Mt. Des Poilus (CAJ *1*–175; *21*–124 ski ascent).

F. A. Aug 1901 by J. Outram, E. Whymper, *C. Kaufmann, C. Klucker, J. Pollinger* **S Face and Ridge.** From head of Yoho Valley by way of Yoho Glacier and neve to gain the snow saddle between Yoho Peak and Mt. Collie. Thence join the now usual route from Twin Falls Chalet, via Des Poilus Glacier and center of the S face. The crest of the S ridge is gained about 400' below the summit. Large crevasses may be avoided by keeping to the W side of the neve; a large schrund is sometimes found below the S arete. Ascent 5–6 hr (App *10*–86; AJ *20*–54).

2 — E Ridge; July 1926, M. M. Strumia, J. M. Thorington, *E. Feuz, Jr.* From Bow Lake ascend E lateral moraine of Bow Glacier; crossing Wapta Neve S of Portal Peak. Cross Rhondda-Olive snow pass — 3½ hr; and round head of Yoho Glacier to SE rocks of Mt. Collie. Ascend scree and chimneys to crest of E ridge which is crossed to snow. The E snow arete is followed from its lowest point to the summit. 6½ hr up (AJ *39*–70).

Ayesha Peak (10050)

7 mi SSW of Peyto Lake; 7 mi NNW of Twin Falls; NNW of Mt. Collie.

F. A. July 1930 by E. Cromwell, J. M. Thorington, *P. Kaufmann.* From Bow Lake via Bow Glacier and S shoulder of Mt. Rhondda, which is rounded at its highest E contact with the icefield. Descend a couloir to the snowslopes and neve, which is crossed to base of objective. Ascended a snow ridge to SE shoulder, the summit cap being pierced by a difficult chimney in the E face — loose rock. Descend by W shoulder to small high saddle, below which the route of ascent is regained by a short traverse. 8½ hr up; 5½ hr down to Twin Falls. 1948 approach was from Peyto Lake via summit of Rhondda; descending scree cirque NW of same to attain S ridge and E face. 17 hr round trip from Peyto Lake with time lost on Rhondda.

Mt. Rhondda (10025)

On Divide 5 mi WSW of Bow Lake Lodge; 5 mi N of Yoho Peak; at head of Bow Glacier (CAJ *24*–77 ski ascent).

F. A. Aug 1923 by A. Geoffrion, J. W. A. Hickson, *E. Feuz, Jr.* From Bow Pass via N edge of Peyto Glacier — 2 hr, almost to pass between Mts Baker and Rhondda. Thence ascend snow basin and rocks to the N ridge, towards the end, sharp. Descent was made on E side, mainly over snow. Ascent from camp 7 hr; descent 5 hr (AJ 35–199; CAJ 24–8). In 1948 several parties from the ACC camp at Peyto Lake made differing routes on this summit, including traverses.

Mt. Olive (10270)

NE buttress of Vulture Col; 4 mi SSW of Bow Lake; 8 mi N of Takakkaw Falls. Double summit on Divide (CAJ 21–126, ski ascent).

F. A. July 1927 and traverse by M. Cropley, G. A. Gambs, N. L. Goodrich, *L. Grassi*. From Twin Falls Chalet via head of Yoho Valley N of Gordon Creek to Balfour Pass, Vulture Glacier and broken rock of the N side of E arete of the S peak, whence the slightly higher N peak is reached — 10½ hr. An easy descent may be made on W to Vulture Col. Ascent from Yoho Glacier, 5 hr (CAJ 16–245).

2 — N Ridge. July 1930, J. M. Thorington, *P. Kaufmann*. From summit of St. Nicholas Peak (which see) to lowest point of intervening arete — ½ hr — whence Vulture Col is accessible. The N arete of Mt. Olive is followed over rock and snow to the N summit, one hr. Descent to Bow Lake 3 hr (AJ 43–76). See St. Nicholas Pk.

Mt. Gordon (10510)

7 mi W of Hector Lake; W of Mt. Olive; 3 mi NE of Yoho Pk; W buttress of Vulture Col (AJ 19–109; App 8–325, CAJ 21–125, ski ascents).

F. A. 1897 by G. Baker, J. N. Collie, H. B. Dixon, C. E. Fay, A. Michael, C. L. Noyes, H. C. Parker, C. S. Thompson, *P. Sarbach*. From Bow Lake via E lateral moraine of Bow Glacier. Cross ice and gain Wapta Neve passing S of Portal Peak to Vulture Col. Thence traverse W to E snow ridge which is followed to W and highest point (AJ 19–109 App 8–325; 9–26).

From Yoho Valley July 1904, Miss G. E. Benham, *C. Kaufmann*. This peak has also been climbed via Balfour Pass and Vulture Col.

Mt. Balfour (10734)

5 mi W of Hector Lake; 5 mi N of Takakkaw Falls; 3 mi SSE of Mt. Olive; N of Mt. Lilliput; head of Balfour Glacier; second elevation of Group.

The name "Balfour" was originally applied by Dr. Hector to a peak between Mistaya and Blaeberry Rivers, and it is possible that the present Mt. Chephren or Howse Peak was so designated. (C. E. Fay in Alpina American 2–14; App 8–328; 10–87; CAJ 1–151)

A plane-table survey of the Balfour sector was carried out in 1897 by H. C. Parker and G. P. Baker, the data being incorporated in Collie's map (AJ 18–549; App 9–at end). The early attempts to ascend the mountain were made from the valley of Sherbrooke Lake (D. Campbell, R. F. Curtis, C. E. Fay in Aug 1898; App 9–93) by way of Niles Pass, and were defeated by soft snow although the Lilliput-Balfour col was then attained. Ski ascent (1935, D. E. Batchelor, L. Harmon, B. G. Moodie, V. *Kutschera* CAJ 23–52).

Mt. Balfour is accessible by any of the routes to the Waputik Snowfield. In 1909 parties of the ACC crossed the snowfield from Sherbrooke Lake and Niles Pass to timberline at the edge of the most northerly icefall from Daly Glacier. Mt. Balfour was ascended thence in 4 hr by way of its SE arete. The parties continued on the next day from Daly Glacier, traversing the W slopes of Trolltinder and descending to Yoho Glacier (CAJ 2, 2–148, 221).

F. A. Aug 1898 by C. L. Noyes, C. S. Thompson, G. M. Weed. **SE Ridge.** From Hector Lake, follow S shore, ascend scree and rock on W side of valley, past Lakes Margaret and Turquoise, to foot of Balfour Glacier, 4 hr. Crevasses are passed to neve above, and the SE ridge followed from the Balfour-Lilliput depression over broken rock and steep snow to the summit, 4 hr (App 9–20; 92). The ridge is now often reached from Yoho Valley, crossing Yoho River at Takakkaw camp and ascending gully S of main falls to reach the Daly Glacier. Follow N margin to base of SE ridge. This is the usual route. Ascent from Takakkaw camp 5–6 hr.

2 — N Ridge. July 1904, Miss G. E. Benham, *C. Kauf-*

Route 2

Balfour Pass

G. Boles

Mt Balfour

Balfour Glacier

S FROM VULTURE GLACIER

Lilliput Mtn

mann. From head of Yoho Valley via Diableret Glacier. Before reaching Balfour Pass bear to right and ascend snowslopes to N ridge, attained almost at its lower end and followed to the summit (AAJ *4*–311; AJ *22*–335; *46*–84).

3 — **Winter Ascent.** May 1936, G. V. Lillienfeld, Miss M. Read, ski ascent. From Bow Lake camp ascend the lateral valley coming from the S to its head (small lake — 3 hr) and reaching the tongue of glacier, which comes down W of Crowfoot. At top of this tongue cross Vulture Glacier E of Mt Olive to Balfour Glacier, reaching Balfour-Lilliput depression (crevasses) whence the Waputik snowfield is gained and the ascent completed as in Route One. Ascent from Bow Lake, 13 hr. Descent to snout of Balfour Glacier, 2 hr, thence to Hector Lake (CAJ *24*–78).

4 — **NE Face.** Aug 1964, G. W. Boles, A. Cole, G. Geber, R. Geber. From Bow Lake via Vulture Glacier E of Mt. Olive to Balfour Pass. Thence over Balfour Glacier (crampons) to a point directly below the summit. The crevassed ice is ascended. At the second ice-fall it was necessary to ascend an almost vertical 30′ step and then bypass an overhanging ice wall to gain the summit pyramid. N ridge followed for 200′ to summit. (CAJ *48*–122). In July 1959 the mountain was traversed N–S from Twin Falls to Takakkaw in 13½ hr by S. Gregory, R. C. West, Jr. (CAJ *43*–83).

Trolltinder Mtn (9570)

Culminates SW arete of Mt. Balfour; 6 mi WSW of Hector Lake; 4½ mi N of Takakkaw Falls.

F. A. Aug 1901 by J. Outram, E. Whymper, *C. Kaufmann, C. Klucker, J. Pollinger*. From head of Yoho Valley (Twin Falls Chalet or Takakkaw Camp) cross river and attain N bank of stream from Diableret Glacier, crossing at top of ravine above Falls of the Waves to work S diagonally to W end of main ridge. Thence up flat scree and shale to base of final 100′ tower, the W side of which is broken by outward sloping ledges and short vertical faces. Ascent 4½ hr; descent 2½ hr (AJ *20*–543; App *10*–8; CAJ *2*, 2–221).

Lilliput Mtn (9540)

On Divide 3½ SW of Hector Lake; 5 mi NE of Takakkaw Falls; 2½ mi SE of Mt. Balfour.

F. A. July 1940 by A. Cox, H. F. Ulrichs. From head of Sherbrooke Valley via the Niles-Daly Col. Descend to upper Daly Glacier crossing N 3 mi to col at NW of objective. Thence over broken rock to summit via ridge (AAJ 5–434; 7–113).

Unnamed (9050)

2 mi S of Mt. Balfour; 3 mi N of Takakkaw Falls; on NW edge of Daly Glacier.

F. A. 1940 by E. Cromwell, Miss G. Engelhard. Via gully S of Takakkaw Falls to Daly Glacier, 2 hr. Cross glacier and ascend broken rock of S ridge to broad summit. Ascent 6 hr (AAJ 4–312).

Mt. Daly (10342)

On Divide 4 mi NE of Takakkaw Falls; 4½ mi SSW of Hector Lake; NE of Mt. Niles (AAJ *21*–113).

F. A. Aug 1903 by J. H. Batcheller, C. E. Fay, E. Tewes, *C. Bohren, C. Häsler*. From timberline camp at head of Sherbrooke Creek up graded trail past lake to open scree, contouring S base of Mt. Niles to Niles Glacier and Niles-Daly col, thence up broken rock of SW face. Ascent 4 hr (App *9*–94; *10*–374).

This peak may also be ascended with Yoho Valley approach. Both the N and S ridges have been climbed with little difficulty (CAJ 2, *2*–146).

Mt. Niles (9752)

SW of Mt. Daly; at head of Sherbrooke Creek; 2½ mi E of Takakkaw Falls (AAJ *22*–112).

F. A. Aug 1898 by D. Campbell, C. E. Fay. **W. Slope.** From timberline camp at head of Sherbrooke Creek to col W of objective — one hr; thence to summit by W slope — 2 hr. This is easier and about one hr shorter than Route 2 and no longer requires a camp (App *9*–96).

2 — W Approach. The Daly Neve may be reached from Takakkaw camp, in Yoho valley, via the gully ½ mi S of Takakkaw Falls, thence gaining Niles Pass at W base of objective. Ascent 4 hr.

W of Sherbrooke valley, along the ridge between Mt. Niles and Mt. Ogden are unnamed points that have been ascended with approaches from E and W (AAJ 9–494, CAJ 23–98).

Mt. Bosworth (9093)

NW buttress of Kickinghorse Pass; 2 mi NNE of Wapta Lake.

F. A. 1903 by the Topographical Survey from W.

2 — SE Face. 1940, E. Cromwell, Miss G. Engelhard. Via SE face from road one mi E of Wapta Lodge. Up scree ledges and gullies; laborious but easy to bastion on E ridge about 500′ below summit. Thence up steep cracks and rotten rock at top. Ascent 3½ hr (AAJ 4–311).

Waputik Peak (9040)

4 mi NNW of Kickinghorse Pass; 6 mi E of Takakkaw Falls; E of Bath Creek. Gentle W slope, more impressive with corries on E.

Pulpit Peak (8950)

One mi S of Hector Lake; 2 mi NE of Lilliput Mtn.

Impressive faces S of this minor point overlook Bow Valley and reach higher altitudes E of Waputik Glacier.

Bow Peak (9409)

5 mi SE of Bow Lake; 2½ mi N of Hector Lake.

F. A. 1896 by R. L. Barrett, W. D. Wilcox.

Easily climbed by its W slope from the timbered saddle between Bow and Hector Lakes, most accessible from the latter. A prominent peak of only moderate challenge.

St. Nicholas Peak (9750)

NW of Mt. Olive; 4 mi SW of Bow Lake Lodge; 5 mi NW of Hector Lake (incorrectly located on 82N9W–OK on 82N10E).

F. A. July 1930 by J. M. Thorington, *P. Kaufmann*. **NE Face.** From Bow Lake via E lateral moraine of Bow Glacier into valley NE of objective. Thence ascend steep snow of NE face. The peak was traversed, descending by way of its S rock ridge to Mt. Olive (which see) (AJ *43*–76; CAJ *22*–214). This is now generally climbed from the Bow Hut, which is just below the NE face. It and Mt. Olive are usually done in a short day from the hut.

Crowfoot Mtn (10010)

Three peaks of almost equal height 4 mi S of Bow Lake; above Crowfoot Glacier. These are gained from the snow col immediately E of lesser point NE of Mt. Olive, whence snow can be followed to the col between the central and S peaks.

The S (highest) summit was first ascended by Mr. and Mrs. E. Cromwell in 1950 in 5½ hr from Bow Lake. The central peak (9940′) was gained in July 1959 by S. Gregory, R. C. West, and the N peak (9975′) by S. Gregory, Mrs. R. C. West (CAJ *43*–81).

2 — E Face. 1963, F. Beckey, B. S. Marts. After crossing Bow River, climb through forest to Crowfoot Glacier. Keep along the right and eventually climb to the point where lower E buttress meets the upper face. This is the main E buttress of the N summit. Some difficulty in getting from glacier to rock; treacherous snow-and-rock traverses en route. Thence ascend 1000′ of steep, sound rock to the top; limestone with good holds.

Portal Peak (9150)

2½ mi SW of Bow Lake Lodge; 2½ mi ENE of Mt. Rhondda; SE of Mt. Thompson.

F. A. 1926 by D. Duncan, L. Hudson. SW slopes from Bow Lake via S Margin of Bow Glacier; cross above lower icefall and reach neve at SW angle of Portal Peak, whence summit may be easily reached over scree slopes. Ascent 4 hr.

2 — S Ridge. 1948, A. Melville (ACC party of 6). Via Peyto Glacier passing W face to gain S arete, which is followed to prominent gendarme. Thence traverse left (W) into SW face, upward on narrow ledges to regain S arete and summit. 7 hr up from camp near Peyto Lake (CAJ *32*–62).

Mt. Thompson (10050)

4 mi S of Peyto Lake; 3 mi WSW of Bow Lake Lodge; 2 mi NW of Portal Peak. Fiber glass hut on N slope above Peyto Glacier-1967 (Stutfield–142).

F. A. Sept 1898 by J. N. Collie, H. E. M. Stutfield, H. Woolley. **SW slopes.** From Bow Lake ascend E lateral moraine of Bow Glacier cross above lower icefall and gain Wapta Neve at base of Portal Peak; round base of latter and ascend Mt. Thompson over loose rocks and snow. Ascent 5 hr.

2 — N Glacier July 1948, two ropes: D. Bidwell, Mr. and Mrs. W. A. D. Munday; L. Chatwin, R. Clapp, L. M. Erskine, P. Jackson. From camp near Peyto Lake via N glacier (dirty at lower end) 2½ hr of step-cutting. Ascend diagonally to right (W) through lower icefield. Upper icefall passed on wall to left. Thence to summit, easy. 9 hr up. Descent via W face (AAJ 7–225; CAJ 32–60).

Unnamed (9750)

2½ mi SSE of Peyto Lake; 3 mi NW of Bow Lake Lodge; NE of Mt. Thompson.

F. A. 1897 by G. P. Baker, J. N. Collie, *P. Sarbach*. From Bow Pass, follow trail to fire lookout. Thence continue up broad slopes to NE summit. Traverse S along ridge.

Mt. Baker (10407)

2 mi N of Mt. Ayesha; between Baker and Peyto Glaciers; on Divide (App 9–21).

F. A. 1923 by W. D. Wilcox, *R. Aemmer*. **NE Ridge.** From camp at Bow Pass, via Peyto Glacier and to Trapper-Baker col. Thence via NE ridge long snowslopes. The peak was traversed from N to S.

2 — S Ridge & W Face. July 1948, E. R. Gibson (ACC party of 14 in 3 ropes). From Peyto Lake camp around mtn to S. Thence pleasant scrambling. Descent via SE. 6 hr up; 3 hr return. The mountain is readily accessible by various routes from this aspect.

3 — NW Ridge. July 1948, D. Bidwell, R. Clapp, L. M. Erskine, A. Griscom, P. Jackson. From Peyto Lake via Baker-Trapper col.

Trapper Peak (9890)

One mi N of Mt. Baker; head of Peyto Glacier; 5½ mi W of Bow Lake, S summit — 9650′.

F. A. July 1933 by H. S. Kingman, J. M. Thorington, *C. Kain.* **N Slope.** Following ascent of Mt. Mistaya (which see), the irregular snowslopes of the watershed were traversed to the NE col — 9100, whence the summit was attained in one hr over steep snow and broken rock. In descending, the E face was glissaded to the Peyto Neve and camp reached via the glacier (AAJ 2–206).

2 — SE Ridge. July 1948, A. Melville and ACC party of 8 from Peyto Lake. Via Peyto Glacier to Baker-Trapper col. Thence scree to lower summit following sharp ridge to highest point. Easy but interesting. Descent via NE face to Peyto Glacier. Total time 11 hr (CAJ 32–65).

Peyto Peak (9750)

3 mi SW of Peyto Lake; 4 mi W of Bow Lake Lodge; NE of Trapper Peak. (AAJ 2–206).

F. A. July 1933 by H. S. Kingman, J. M. Thorington, *C. Kain.* From camp below Peyto Glacier via glacier to S slope of peak, scree being followed thence to summit tower which presents the only difficulty. It is best rounded to its NW, whence 200′ of broken rock and a steep chimney lead directly to the summit. Ascent 5 hr. Descent by W shoulder and N glacier followed down to Caldron Lake and camp: 8 hr RT from Peyto Lake. This peak is an easy scree walk on the W.

Mistaya Mtn (10150)

SE of Barbette Mtn; 3 mi WSW of Peyto Lake; 2½ mi SSW of Mt. Patterson; excellent views.

F. A. July 1933 by H. S. Kingman, J. M. Thorington, *C. Kain.* **S Ridge.** From camp below Peyto Glacier to grass and scree slopes to Caldron Lake, 1½ hr. From NW of lake a broad snow-basin leads to S arete of peak and is followed to summit. On descent the watershed may be followed and Trapper Peak (which see) ascended. Ascent 5 hr (AAJ 2–206). This is the usual "tourist" route.

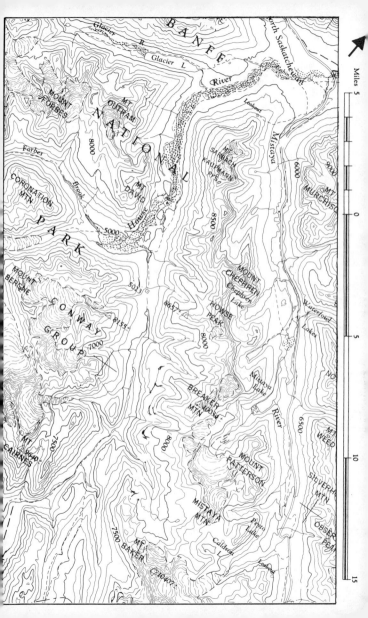

Caldron Peak (9570)

2 mi W of Bow Pass; 2 mi NNE of Caldron Lake; 2 mi SSE of Mt. Patterson.

July 1948 an ACC party of 7 led by E. R. Gibson climbed adjacent to the prominent couloir in the E face to the S summit; 2000' of fairly good rock, 7 hr. Descent by W slopes. A second route was made from the same Peyto Lake Camp a few days later by a party of 6 led by C. Beattie. This party ascended the slightly higher N peak by a route generally adjacent to a large couloir terminating on the skyline S of large gendarme. 10 hr up. Descent by W slopes.

Barbette Mtn (10080)

2½ mi SW of Mt. Patterson; 1½ mi NW of Mistaya Mtn; 4 mi W of Peyto Lake.

F. A. July 1933 by H. S. Kingman, J. M. Thorington, *C. Kain*. From camp below Peyto Glacier via N side of stream to Caldron Lake — 1½ hr; thence via scree and snowfield to Barbette-Patterson saddle, rounding to N side of the peak. Thence 500' rock buttress and 500' of steep snow above to W ridge which is followed to corniced summit. Ascent 8 hr. Descent by SE slope to 9600', thence following crest of SW cliff into basin of Wildcat Creek at 7800'. Ascend to col immediately S of Mt. Mistaya and descend snow to Caldron Lake and camp. Total time 14 hr (AAJ 2–206).

Unnamed (9950)

One mi NW of Barbette Mtn; on Divide 2 mi S of Breaker Mtn.

Mt. Patterson (10490)

3 mi NW of Peyto Lake; 3 mi SSE at Mistaya Lake; NE of Barbette Mtn.

F. A. July 1924 by F. V. Field, W. O. Field, *E. Feuz, Jr.* By raft to camp at head of Mistaya Lake. Ascend long Barbette Glacier and snowfield W of mountain, whence an easy route leads to central and highest point. Ascent 6 hr (App 16–153). July 1948 approach to W face from Peyto Glacier; 12 hr. ACC party of 7 led by A. Melville.

Mt Patterson

View to Southwest

E. Cooper

2 — E Buttress. 1962, F. Beckey, J. A. Rupley. An obvious long and straight gully cuts the lower section of the mountain. Climb up a gentle glacier to the base of the narrow rock buttress, which has three obvious steps. Begin the first step on the left (two pitches of Class 5 rock), climb the second step mainly on center. The third step is taken frontally, with zigzag traverses on left side to avoid rotten rock. Now follow the crest of a corniced ice arete, occasionally climbing on rock wall. Several exposed ice traverses near the ridge top. Steep rock and ice on final pitch through the summit wall and cornice (AAJ *13*–500).

3 — NE Face. July 1967, K. Baker, C. Locke, L. Mackay, C. Scott, and D. Vockeroth. Via Bluebird Glacier (1 AM start) 10 hr to summit from bivouac in timber at upper end of N moraine. Front-point crampon work all the way to second icefall. Thence on rocks to the left to upper basin and scrambling to notch in summit ridge (CAJ *53*–40).

Breaker Mtn (10034)

S of Ebon Peak; on Divide 3½ mi N of Barbette Mtn; SW of Mistaya Lake.

F. A. 1917 by the Boundary Commission; an easy ascent.

Ebon Peak (9550)

N of Breaker Mtn; S at Aries Pk; one mi W of Capricorn Lake.

F. A. April 1972. D. Forest, S. King, J. Pomeroy, G. Schlee, M. Toft. From highway ski across Mistaya Lake, then S to canyon below Barbette Glacier. Follow canyon to within 200 yds of its head, then exit by W wall, 2 hr. Contour to and up Barbette Glacier, then ascend through center of steep headwall, 1½ hr. Above headwall turn NW between ridge E of Parapet Glacier and 8900' peak NE of Capricorn Glacier. Gain and cross Capricorn Glacier, dropping 500', then moving farther N regain elevation passing Breaker Mtn to camp on glacier to NE, 2½ hr. Thence ski to the Breaker-Ebon col and halfway up the S slope. Here leave skis and scramble over shale to the top in 1½ hr. Return by same route.

Aries Peak (9830)

Between Ebon and Stairway Peaks; on Divide 2 mi W of Mistaya Lake.

F. A. 1944 by Mr. and Mrs. D. W. Measuroll, J. M. Thorington, *E. Feuz, Jr.* Following ascent of Stairway Peak (which see), descent was made into the S fork of Ebon Creek. Aries Peak was then gained in one hr from the high cirque to the W. Total time from camp 13 hr (App 25–141; AAJ 5–435).

Stairway Peak (9840)

Between Midway and Aries Peaks; one mi SW of Cirque Lake.

F. A. July 1944 by Mr. & Mrs. D. W. Measuroll, J. M. Thorington, *E. Feuz, Jr.* From Howse Pass, camp was established at timberline in N fork of Ebon Creek, this stream being the true source of Blaeberry River. The peak was ascended by W shale and scree slopes in 4 hr, following which a descent into the S fork of the creek led to the ascent of Aries Peak (which see) (CAJ 29–164, 193; AAJ 5–435).

Midway Peak (9570)

SE of Mt. Synge; N of Stairway Peak; one mi W of Cirque Lake.

F. A. Aug 1952 by Mr. & Mrs. J. D. Mendenhall. Following descent from Mt. Synge (which see), Midway Peak was ascended by its SW slopes, directly from snow via easy rocks (AAJ 8–562).

Mt. Synge (9750)

SE of Howse Peak; between Aiguille and Midway Peaks; one mi W of Cirque Lake.

F. A. Aug 1952 by Mr. & Mrs. J. D. Mendenhall. Approach via Howse Pass (see Freshfield Group) to timberline camp in N fork of Ebon Creek. Cross snowfield between Aiguille and Stairway to base of Aiguille Peak. Climb SW side of Mt. Synge via loose orange rocks above glacier. Ascent made by slightly lower ledges leading to base of step SE of summit. Loose, unsound ledges. Descent made by safer route described above. Ascent 4 hr. Following descent to glacier, Midway Peak (which see) was ascended (AAJ 8–562).

Aiguille Peak (9840)
One mi SE of Howse Peak; W of Mt. Synge; S of Chephren Lake.
F. A. Aug 1952 by Mr. & Mrs. J. D. Mendenhall. A round-about route. From timberline camp in N fork of Ebon Creek. Ascend easy SW ridge to edge of notch. Descend steep, sound rocks to gully on SE face. Make long traverse on unsound ledges at base of final cliffs (one piton). Ascend steep but easy chimney for one pitch leading to point SE of double summit. Traverse upward to left 50′ to base of shallow crack, slightly overhanging. The crack broadens above into chute separating the two highest points. Eight pitons used in the rotten crack, several for direct aid. Two easier pitches lead to summit. Ascent 10 hr, descent 6 hr (AAJ 8–562).

Howse Peak (10793)
E buttress of Howse Pass; 3 mi SW of Chephren Lake; highest summit of Waputik group; 2 mi S of Mt. Chephren.
F. A. Aug 1902 by J. N. Collie, H. E. M. Stutfield, G. M. Weed, H. Woolley, *H. Kaufmann*. **WNW Ridge.** From camp on Howse River, below pass, ascend through burnt timber to ridge. Thence on slopes of snow and scree (AJ 21–372).
2 — W Glacier. 1939 Miss K. Gardiner, *E. Feuz, Jr.* From bivouac at timberline in basin of stream entering Conway Creek immediately N of Howse Pass. Thence up glacier and snow slopes; (CAJ 33–72).
3 — S Face. 1958, P. A. Boswell, I. Keith, A. Mason, R. deRepentigny. From bivouac near forks of Ebon Creek towards SW face of objective. Route basically follows central buttress. Good rock over minor walls to upper snowslopes. 8 hr up, 5 hr down (CAJ 42–101).
4-NE Buttress. Aug 1967, K. Baker, L. MacKay, D. Vockeroth. From Chephren Lake via S side through boulders to E moraine. W across glacier and up 150′ of easy ledges to grey band. At lowest overhanging white rock traverse left

for 150' and slightly downwards. Climb up snow (ice) gully, then back to ridge. Follow separated ridge to top of yellow band, about half way up, then steep rock. First ascent party continued slightly ridge (N) of ridge crest to summit. V,F7, A1, 3700' (CAJ 53–36).

Variant J. Glidden, G. H. Lowe. Traverse S into central gully of E face. Ascend 300' to top of yellow band (very rotten) and traverse back to right (N). Climb black slabby face, then broken grey rock, keeping just S of buttress crest. Where angle eases climb towards crest. Near summit ice mushrooms may force move to S of crest line again, with summit attained by chopping through cornice. Bivouac likely; ice axe and crampons necessary; cable crossing at Mile 51 on highway.

White Pyramid (*West Chephren*) (10750)

Between Mistaya and Howse Rivers; 1½ mi N of Howse Peak; SW of Mt. Chephren.

F. A. July 1939 by Miss K. Gardiner, *E. Feuz, Jr.* **S Ridge.** From camp at Conway Creek and Freshfield Brook by way of N side of stream from basin between White Pyramid and Howse Peak. Thence up steep glacier to col between these two peaks, the S ridge of objective without difficulty to the summit. Descent NW ridge to the same valley. Total time 14 hr (CAJ 27–40).

2 — W Slopes. July 1962, A. Gregor, R. D. Lyon, Miss A. Prevost, C. Smith, W. Tupper. Approach to the Chephren Peaks was made from the N. Cross Mistaya River below Waterfowl Lakes and ascend parallel valley W of N ridge of Chephren Peak to col at W head of valley. From this col ascent of White Pyramid is easy via W slopes. Traverses along the ledges of E face at the level of this col are difficult, dangerous and not recommended (CAJ 55–88; 46–85).

3 — E Ridge. Aug 1971, K. Hahn, M. Toft. From Chephren-White Pyramid Col (see below) the sharp snow and ice ridge, heavily corniced early in year, was climbed for 800' to within a few feet of summit, 1½ hr from col. Descent to S (CAJ 55–86). This col, normally reached from the S can also be reached by climbing the long N ridge of Mt. Chephren to big face on the ridge, then traverse right and climb bands,

top one appears impassable, but a gully, then an excellent 100' rock pitch coming out on the glacier through small waterfall is the crux. A short trudge up the glacier to the col; 8 hr.

Mt. Chephren (*Black Pyramid*) (10715)

2 mi N of Howse Peak; ENE of White Pyramid; W of Chephren Lake (CAJ *46–85*).

F. A. Aug 1913 by J. W. A. Hickson, *E. Feuz, Jr.* From highway ford Mistaya River between Waterfowl Lakes, bridge S of upper lake, 1972, thence good trail to Chephren Lake. Cross logs at N end, and stay on E side to a moraine leading to a grassy slope of the mountain. Thence via steep rocks to saddle between White Pyramid and Mt. Chephren. From this point the peak is ascended by its W arete in ¾ hr. Ascent 7 hr; descent 6. 11, F3 (CAJ 6–94). The SE ridge can be approached via a scree cone from near NW end of Chephren Lake. Gullies to S end in overhangs and cliff bands.

2 — **E Face.** 1965, P. A. Geiser, A. Gran, J. R. Hudson. Start from glacier on left of central rib; climb the central of three parallel ramps leading up to right. Part way up follow an easy ledge system left up to the larger ramp, which is then followed to a notch in the central rib. Ascend this to an overhanging wall. Traverse left 250' and ascend to its top at the base of another overhang. Traverse right and ascend to a third overhang; traverse right to a small gendarme and climb its right side. Then up right to a ramp which leads up left and over the wall. Ascend left to a gendarme and cross gully on its left. Climb left of gully and, at its top cross back to a ledge on a steep wall. Climb groove on right; then up ramp, bearing right to base of final wall. Traverse right and up gully to top. 35 pitons, 27 hr on wall. One bivouac on ascent and one on descent. Since done in 16 hr. V, F9, A1.

Unnamed (10140)

One mi S of Epaulette Mtn; 2 mi W of Mt. Chephren on ridge W of Kaufmann Valley.

Epaulette Mtn (10150)

Immediately S of Kaufmann Peaks; 4½ mi WNW of Lower Waterfowl Lake; N and highest between Kaufmann Peaks and White Pyramid (CAJ 33–73).

F. A. July 1924 by F. V. Field, W. O. Field, *E. Feuz, Jr.* From camp on Howse River the peak was reached by the W scree and rock slopes, and traversed from NW to S; last 500′ difficult. Ascent 7 hr; total 13 hr (App *16*–153).

2 — S Ridge. July 1949, J. W. Bishop, J. F. Tarrant. From bivouac in timber W of lower S ridge, reach summit by descent route of 1924 party, 2½ hr from bivouac to S ridge; ½ hr to base of S Tower. Ascend gully and chimney to 50′ face and crest of S Tower. Descend into gully running high into main tower. 5½ hr from bivouac. Descent to bivouac 2¼ hr (CAJ 33–73).

Kaufmann Peaks (S 10200; N 10150)

Immediately S of Mt. Sarbach; separated from White Pyramid by three lower unnamed peaks. The peaks of Mt. Kaufmann are almost identical in outline and are rocky pinnacles as seen from Howse River. From Mistaya River, N Kaufmann sets back from the valley and presents a rock face; S Kaufmann shows considerable snow on NE side.

S Peak. F. A. 1927 by D. Duncan, *Ern. Feuz.* Via W slopes from Howse River to saddle between N and S peaks, and up N ridge for 900′ of interesting climbing. Ascent 5½ hr.

N Peak. F. A. Aug 1970, S. King, J. Tanner. Approach via Howse River to camp at 7000′ on W slope below Mt. Sarbach. Ascent easy over scree and cliff bands to col between summits. Thence moderate scrambling via S ridge. 3 hr up. Rope used only for one rappel on descent. Major difficulty was bypassing cliffs above valley floor (CAJ 56–86).

Mt. Sarbach (10350)

N outpost of Waputik Group; 4 mi W of Mt. Murchison in angle between Mistaya and Howse Rivers; N of Mt. Kaufmann (AJ *18*–549).

F. A. 1897 by G. P. Baker, J. N. Collie, *P. Sarbach.* From camp at mouth of Mistaya River ascend 1000′ through forest;

Kaufmann Peaks

E. Cooper

View to SW from Mt Murchison

Mistaya River

Epaulette Mtn

then up a steep gully in the limestone escarpment leading to the crest of the NW shoulder. Thence over steep scree to foot of final peak. Rock is loose and crumbling; summit ridge narrow and composed of hard limestone. Recent approaches are easier via trail towards fire lookout.

2 — **N Face.** July 1970, C. Locke, L. MacKay. Generally follow E side adjacent to gully dividing face. Rock poor at bottom, good higher up. 3 hr on cliff. Descent via W slopes (CAJ 54–86).

Could notice please be brought to the Club members in general re the littering of summits with cans, paper, etc. Baker summit is a mess.

C. M. Nicholls (1951)

MURCHISON GROUP

This includes all those peaks bounded on the N by the N Saskatchewan River, on the E by the Siffleur and Pipestone Rivers, and on the W by the Mistaya and the Bow into which latter flows the Pipestone. The Siffleur and Pipestone head in Pipestone Pass, of which the first recorded crossing was made by James Carnegie, Earl of Southesk, in 1859. The route from the Bow to the Indian meeting grounds at the mouth of the Siffleur via Bow Pass was sometimes less passable due to muskeg than the slightly higher Pipestone Pass. Thus the Pipestone route to the Kootenay Plains was often taken in preference (Coleman–244). Dr. Hector states (1858) that the Indians considered Mt. Murchison to be the highest of all the Rocky Mountains.

Access to this group is among the easiest in the entire range, being bounded along the entire W side by the new and well-marked Banff-Jasper Highway, and on the N by the newer David Thompson Highway. A park road and trail system allows access up Pipestone River to the Siffleur and connects through Pipestone Pass with trails in the Clearwater River via Clearwater Pass. Alberta Forest Service maintains a road along the S bank of the N Saskatchewan and a campground at the mouth of the Siffleur River up which a good fire break trail runs to connect with those in the Pipestone and the Clearwater. This trail starts from the forest road about ½ mi W of the Siffleur crossing. **See intro to Clearwater** for Abraham Lake and Saskatchewan River crossing.

A good trail exists in Mosquito Creek, descending on the E side of Molar Pass to join the Pipestone trail near the junction of Little Pipestone Creek. A trail is maintained by the NPS on Helen Creek over the height of Dolomite Pass, 5 mi — 3½ hr, connecting with the trail in the Siffleur Valley. This trail leaves the highway just N of the crossing of Helen Creek and climbs by an easy grade over the alpine areas past Lake Katherine and Lake Alice, thus giving good access to these interesting peaks of varied but challenging mountaineering interest. Dolomite Pass was first crossed by W. D. Wilcox in 1902. The upper Siffleur Valley may thus be reached in two easy days from the highway. All peaks in this group are on the Alberta slope (AAJ *17*–84).

There is some good rock climbing along the David Thompson Highway E of Whirlpool Point. This is a warm valley and one can climb here early and late in the season when the higher peaks are out of condition. Many of the smaller peaks along the David Thompson Highway offer fine hiking; some require difficult rock climbing by the easiest route. The 9300' peak to the north of Whirlpool Point gives a fine ridge scramble starting from the highway at Whirlpool Point. Maps:82N15; 82N16; 82N9.

Siffleur Mtn (10266)

SW angle between Siffleur and N Saskatchewan Rivers; one mi NE of Mt. Loudon (CAJ *28*–56).

F. A. 1924 by the Topographical Survey. An easy ascent from mouth of Porcupine Creek.

Mt. Loudon (10566)

SW angle between Siffleur and N Saskatchewan Rivers; head of Loudon Creek; SW of Siffleur Mtn.

F. A. 1972 by A. M. Daffern, Miss A. Ridley. From camp in Siffleur Valley to S of peak, via rock walls and ledges to col between Loudon and W Pk. Thence easy to summit.

Unnamed (10250)

One mi SW of Mt. Loudon.

F. A. 1968 by A. Daffern, P. Ford. From camp at head of the Valley of the Three Falls (lowest E tributary of Spreading Creek) via W scree slopes.

Mt. Peskett (10240)

Northerly of three peaks between Loudon Creek and Valley of the Three Falls; 2 mi W of Siffleur Mtn.

F. A. July 1970 by D. Von Hennig, *L. Grillmair*, *W. L. Putnam*. By traverse from next peak S. Bypass nose descending to E. 1½ hr RT. Descent via col S of central peak (AAJ *17*–385).

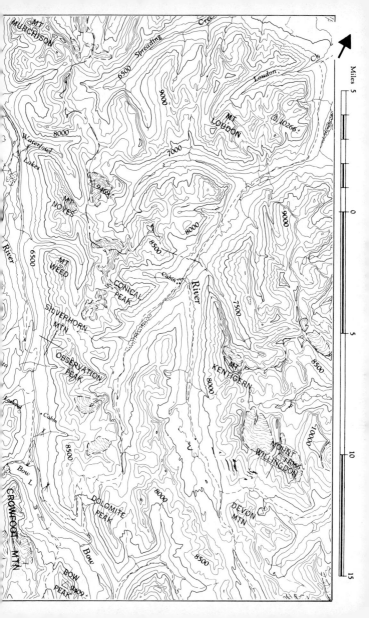

Unnamed (10250)

One mi S of Mt. Peskett.

F. A. 1968 by A. M. Daffern, P. Ford. By traverse from S peak.

2 — W Cirque. July 1970 by Mr. & Mrs. J. B. Dodge, Jr., D. Von Hennig, Dr. & Mrs. E. Holmes, V. Mahler, A. Wexler, *R. Gertsch, L. Grillmair, W. L. Putnam*. Via W slopes and cirque from camp at timberline in Valley of the Three Falls. As part of traverse with adjacent summits. 4 hr up (AAJ *17*–385).

Unnamed (10340)

Highest of 3 peaks along ridge W of Loudon Creek.

F. A. 1968 by A. M. Daffern, P. Ford. Easy ascent via S ridge and scree from camp in Valley of the Three Falls to W.

2 — N Ridge. July 1970 by Mr. & Mrs. J. B. Dodge, Jr., V. Mahler, A. Wexler, *R. Gertsch*. Via N ridge in easy traverse from next peak N in one hr (AAJ *17*–385).

Unnamed (10201)

Between Porcupine and Spreading Creeks; 2 mi W of Porcupine Lake.

F. A. 1972, A. M. Daffern, Mrs. G. M. Daffern. From Noyes Creek via easy W face. Adjacent summits one mi NW along ridge, and 2 mi SW (on Park boundary — 9300') also visited. Latter traversed up NE ridge and down NW. Lesser peaks (8000' & 9000') bounding col between Noyes and Spreading Creeks also ascended from col.

Corona Ridge (10050)

On ridge between Spreading and Corona Creeks.

F. A. July 1970 by J. B. Dodge, Jr., D. Von Henning, *W. L. Putnam*. From camp at timberline in terminus of Spreading Creek via S ridge. 6 hr RT; no technical difficulties (AAJ *17*–385).

Mt. Murchison (10936)

SE angle between Mistaya and N Saskatchewan Rivers; SE of Mt. Wilson. On the NE side of the massif a small icefield drains to the N Saskatchewan through Murchison Creek (Outram–303).

F. A. **NW Peak** only 1902 by J. N. Collie, H. E. M. Stutfield, G. M. Weed, *H. Kaufmann*. From camp at mouth of Mistaya River via W face. Follow a dry stream-bed and ascend a series of scree slopes to a narrow snow couloir and via rocks on its right (to avoid falling stones) reach NW arete over snowslopes. The highest peak is generally snowclad and invisible from Mistaya River; it is reached over long slopes of rock and scree, leading to corniced summit. Ascent 7½ hr (Stutfield–252).

The mountain is a broad massif, the two main peaks being one mi apart. S of the main crest and largely surrounding a cirque N of Totem Creek (up which a good campsite at 6500' can be reached in 2 hr from the highway) is a group of 7 conspicuous towers, unnamed and classed with Mt. Murchison, but worthy of special nomenclature. The best route up Totem Creek is on the N side to the lower lakes, crossing at outlet of the lakes; thence up the S side to the upper lake.

Tower (10450) At head of Bison Creek.

F. A. 1941 by E. Cromwell, Miss G. Engelhard, *E. Feuz, Jr*. From head of Bison Creek, thence N by steep broken ledges to base of objective. Then up steep chimneys and pitches on SW face and S ridge comparable to Mt. Louis (AAJ 4–494).

Tower (10400) W of head of Bison Creek; the second tower from W.

F. A. Aug 1937 by Miss K. Gardiner, Miss L. Gest, *E. Feuz, Jr., C. Häsler*. From road through forest to a creek (first stream N of Totem Creek) and basin above waterfall; thence over grass and scree to foot of tower. An icy W couloir is ascended skirting round a buttress to SE with a short traverse on steep rock. Another gully leads to ridge and summit. Ascent 6½ hr, total time 12 hr (CAJ 25–27).

Tower (10300) ½ mi WNW of tower ascended by Gest-Gardiner party.

F. A. 1941 by E. Cromwell, Miss G. Engelhard, *E. Feuz*,

Jr. From head of Bison Creek through a steep gully to a high col. from which three steep pitches of the SE ridge are surmounted to the summit. Ascent 4½ hr. Easy descent by SW scree face and S gully to road in 2 hr (AAJ *4*–495).

N (10530) and S (10550) Towers W of extreme head of Totem Creek.

F. A. Sept 1938 by E. Cromwell, Miss Engelhard, *E. Feuz, Jr.* Via Totem Creek to camp below lower lake directly S of the S tower. 3½ hr to base of peak. Thence one hr to S tower via the large gully which crosses the S face, descending diagonally from right to left. Party descended S tower for 600' and traversed connecting ridge to higher N tower — 1½ hr; it being necessary to rappel several times. Sound climbing with interesting slabs and chimneys. Return by same route to camp 3½ hr (AAJ *3*–366; CAJ *25*–26 marked photo).

E Tower (10550) One mi NNW of upper lake in Totem Creek.

F. A. Aug 1940 by H. S. Hall, *E. Feuz, Jr.* From camp used by Cromwell-Engelhard party by way of the glacier to col between the objective and the N tower. 5½ hr to intervening saddle (9950') one hr more to summit over easy W ridge (AAJ *4*–312).

SE Tower (10100) One mi N of lower lake in Totem Creek.

F. A. Aug 1939 by Miss G. Engelhard, F. S. North, *Ern. Feuz.* From Totem Creek camp through the cirque S of the S tower to the base of the objective summit. Scree slopes and broken ledges of W face are ascended, following a long couloir running to the base of the N ridge — 3 hr from camp. The ridge is followed to the summit in ⅔ hr with two traverses on W face (AAJ *4*–87; CAJ *27*–132).

Totem Tower (10350)

S of head of Totem Creek.

F. A. Aug 1970 by J. B. Dodge, D. Von Hennig, W. L. Putnam, A. Wexler, *L. Grillmair, R. Gertsch.* From camp at extreme timberline in Spreading Creek via E slopes to S col. Thence via S ridge & SW face. Lower notch 5.1. Second step

5.4 on ridge crest. Severe exposure. Round trip 9 hr (AAJ 17–385; CAJ 54–87). III.

Unnamed (10050)

At extreme SW head of Spreading Creek; one mi S of Totem Tower.

F. R. A. Aug 1970 by R. Gertsch (*alone*) from camp at head of Spreading Creek via N slopes & NW ridge.

May have been ascended earlier by Topographic Survey.

Unnamed (10080)

2½ mi NE of lower Waterfowl Lake; S of head of Spreading Creek.

F. A. of main summit Aug 1970 by R. Gertsch (*alone*). From camp at head of Spreading Creek E of Totem Tower via small glacier on N slopes. An easy ascent as part of one-day traverse with next peak NW.

A subsidiary point (9200′) was reached in 1939 by Miss G. Engelhard, F. S. North by way of Noyes Creek and its SW slopes. A scree gully leading to the base of a steep grey tower (rotten rock) was surmounted by two fairly difficult vertical chimneys.

Unnamed (9469)

2 mi N of Mt. Noyes with much snow on E slopes. Shown on maps as an occupied topographic survey station, hence ascended.

Mt. Noyes (10120)

E of upper Waterfowl Lake (Mistaya River); 2 mi NW of Mt. Weed. (AJ 21–374).

F. A. Aug 1902 by J. N. Collie, H. E. M. Stutfield, G. M. Weed, H. Wooley. By way of a gully on W face, above which a steep snow couloir leads up to easy rocks and scree to the summit.

Unnamed (10300)

Between Porcupine Creek and Siffleur River; 3 mi N of Conical Peak. A substantially untouched area of dolomitic cliffs lies N and E of this peak towards the lower reaches of Siffleur River. Shown on maps as occupied topographic survey station, hence ascended.

Mt. Weed (10100)

NW of Observation Peak and Mt. Silverhorn; between Mistaya River and Dolomite Creek.

F. A. Aug 1936 by Miss L. Gest, Mr. & Mrs. H. Kingman, H. S. Kingman, Jr., W. Kingman, *C. Häsler*. From camp in Mistaya valley, NW scree slopes were followed to first steep ledges. Crack of 70′ to further scree slopes at 8500′ and close to survey cairn on NW ridge. Proceed to base of summit up scree slope and a large couloir to the right, traversing W face to the ridge which is followed to top. Ascent 6 hr; descent by large couloir on S to scree slopes leading to valley 4 hr (CAJ 24–121).

Conical Peak (9320)

W of Dolomite Creek; 2 mi W of Isabella Lake.

F. A. 1924 by the Topographical Survey.

Silverhorn Mtn (9550)

N of Observation Peak; SE of Mt. Weed; between Mistaya River and Dolomite Creek (App 9–16; *21*–588).

Marmot Mtn (8520)

Lesser outlier one mi N of Observation Peak; 5 mi NNW of Dolomite Pass.

Observation Peak (10414)

NE buttress of Bow Pass.

F. A. Aug 1895 by W. Peyto, W. D. Wilcox.
A toilsome ascent from Bow Pass; scree to the main ridge S of the summit, with snow near top (App 9–19, 25; Wilcox–208).

Cirque Peak (9820)

NE of Bow Lake; NW buttress of Dolomite Pass.

F. A. Aug 1899 by H. P. Nichols, C. L. Noyes, C. S. Thompson, G. M. Weeks. From summit of Dolomite Pass by way of the S scree ridge. An easy ascent from almost any approach (App 9–91; AAJ 6–450).

Unnamed (9886)
2 mi NNW of Bobac Mtn; 3 mi SW of Mt. Kentigern.

Bobac Mtn (10130)
3 mi N of Dolomite Pass; one mi N of Lake Alice.

F. A. July 1966 by W. L. Putnam, D. Michael, L. R. Wallace. From camp below Lake Alice via long snow gully N of Lake; thence traverse and descend rotten rock ridge to E. Continue N on firm limestone to summit via dip slope. 5 hr from camp (CAJ 50–68).

Watermelon Peak (10150)
One mi E of Lake Alice.

F. A. July 1966 by D. Michael, W. V. G. Matthews, W. L. Putnam, Miss M. Stearns, L. R. Wallace. From camp below Lake Alice via glacier and snow to col SE of summit. Thence along SW ridge. 5 hr from camp. Rope seldom needed (CAJ 50–68) III.

Unnamed (10140)
2 mi E of Dolomite Pass and Lake Katherine.

F. A. 1941 by E. Cromwell, Miss G. Engelhard. From camp on Mosquito Creek skirt the E slopes of Dolomite Peak in valley between latter and objective. At head of valley turn up easy slopes to a steep, firm chimney in the whitish rocks of the SW face. Ledges and chimneys to the sloping summit ridge at about its middle; thence to summit (E) over loose slabs and boulders. Ascent 5½ hr, descent 3½ (AAJ 4–494).

Dolomite Peak (9128)
E of Bow Lake; SE buttress of Dolomite Pass (App 9–90). Highest point is 4th tower from N.

F. A. June 1930 by J. M. Thorington, *P. Kaufmann*. From Dolomite Pass traverse S along the W scree slopes until just below the third tower, a rib being ascended to the cliffs of the third tower. Traverse to the snow-filled couloir between the third and fourth towers, and ascend to the intervening notch. The objective tower is split, its highest point (SE) being gained by traversing snow bands to couloir on SW face, thence to summit. 3 hr up, 2 hr down (AAJ *1*–402; AJ *43*–77).

2 — S Approach. 1939, Miss G. Engelhard, F. S. North. From the road via trail on Helen Creek. Towers 4, 7, 8, were ascended, traversing N on ledges of W face and descending a couloir at the N end of the massif. These as well as all other main towers were found to have cairns, the ascents possibly having been made during the time of road construction. Ascent from road to #8, 4½ hr; total time 10 hr.

Route 3. July 1948, Miss P. Prescott and ACC party. Tower 3 (first tower N of main summit) was ascended.

Unnamed (9740)
SW buttress of Pipestone Pass, at head of Mosquito Creek.

Unnamed (9850)
S of Mosquito Creek, 3 mi N of Andromache.

Unnamed (*Andromache*) (9830)
N of Mt. Hector and Hector Creek.
F. A. Aug 1948 by Miss C. Cromwell, Mr. & Mrs. E. Cromwell. From highway on S bank of Noseeum Creek, flowing N of objective, ascend SE over steep scree and boulders to easy N ridge at 9000'. This is followed SE, at one point crossing upper edge of Molar Glacier, to summit. Ascent 4¾ hr; descent 1¼ hr (AAJ *7*–354; CAJ *33*–147).

Unnamed (9950)
E of preceeding and separated from it by a low col.
F. A. Aug 1948 by Mr. & Mrs. E. Cromwell. From highway via Noseeum Creek to steep waterfall. Goat trails lead up moraine to tongue of Molar Glacier. On account of fresh snow the ascent was made by the ice wall, with several hundred feet of step-cutting to col, whence boulder field was followed to flat summit. Ascent 5 hr. Descent via Andromache (CAJ *33*–148).

Molar Mtn (9915)

N angle between Molar Creek and Pipestone River; NE of Mt. Hector. Visible from Lake Louise Station (Outram–281).

F. A. 1901 by J. J. McArthur, *T. E. Wilson.* Ascended without difficulty from Molar Creek, though quite precipitous on E and NW faces.

Molar Tower (9550)

On S ridge of Molar Mtn. 1930, attempt by J. W. A. Hickson, *E. Feuz, Jr.* (CAJ *19*–40).

F. A. June 1933 by R. G. Cairns, A. A. McCoubrey, Jr., R. Neave. From camp in Pipestone Valley to lower band of cliffs E of gully between the tower and the main peak — 2½ hr. 70' of rock leads to scree above and the base of the tower. Traverse along base of cliff to rib at SW corner, and up to the W end of the highest of three ledges crossing the S face. The ledge is followed, becoming very narrow but broadening near the base of a 30' chimney, which is ascended to the SE ridge at the base of one of the gendarmes. Climb part way up this and make exposed traverse on the far side to base of the largest gendarme, a prominent feature of this ridge. The face of the gendarme is smooth and steep, and must be ascended for 50', after which a V-shaped crack leads to easier going and summit arete (much loose rock). Ascent 8¼ hr (CAJ *22*–98).

Unnamed (10250)

1¼ mi NNW of Mt Hector; W rampart of Hector Glacier; 1½ mi S of Andromache; high point on long NNW ridge of Mt. Hector.

F. A. 1967 W. Batzhuber & H. Wohlfarth. From highway up NW ridge, traversing last quarter to firm rock cliff on the left, thence loose rock to summit.

Mt. Hector (11135)

Highest peak in N angle between Bow and Pipestone Rivers; 3 mi E of Hector Lake (App *13*–1, 97; CAJ *14*–9; Outram–278).

F. A. 1895 by P. S. Abbot, C. E. Fay, C. S. Thompson. From Bow Valley opposite Hector Lake; ascend slopes of W face, N of peak, to base of shoulder separated by a large icy amphitheatre from the SW arete. Thence up the shoulder over broken rock, steep scree and snow patches to snowfield, rising steeply (40°) toward the S to summit ridge of broken rock. Ascent 8 hr; descent 4 hr.

2 — **From NE.** July 1933, R. G. Cairns, A. A. McCoubrey, Jr., R. Neave. From camp on first series of benches where the creek bed rises rapidly on Molar Creek, via side of a small stream to lowest tongue of Hector Glacier. Thence up snow-slopes of varying steepness to within 200′ of the summit, and over loose rocks to the top. Ascent 5 hr; descent 2½ hr (CAJ 22–214).

3 — **S Face.** 1902, E. W. D. Holway, *J. Muller*. From camp below S face starting at 4 AM directly up the cliff, traversing right to bypass overhangs. Some ice was encountered. This party ate lunch on the summit and descended by the SW ridge, walking back to Lake Louise by 10 PM.

Unnamed (9742)
   2 mi SSE of Mt Hector.
   F. A. 1891 J. J. McArthur, *T. E. Wilson*.

The mountain was in plain sight, we walked to its base . . . and then walked on till we reached the summit. (Hector)

P. Abbot

CLEARWATER GROUPS

This is an irregular group lying generally E of the Murchison Group. It is bounded on the W by Pipestone Creek through Pipestone Pass and the Siffleur River; on the N by the North Saskatchewan River; on the NE by Ram River drainage and the Banff Park boundary; on the SE by the watershed of the Bow River. The principal drainage of the group is eastward by the Clearwater River (which rises near Clearwater Pass, connecting with the upper Siffleur) and by the Red Deer River which drains parallel to the Clearwater but some 12 mi to the S. The dominant peaks are situated in the basin of Martin Creek; Mt. Willingdon and Recondite Peak. The area contains more than 20 peaks above 10000' in height, besides several sizeable glaciers. The nearest NPS warden is located just S of the Saskatchewan Crossing on the Banff-Jasper Highway.

In 1790, Peter Pangman blazed a tree on the N Saskatchewan 4¼ mi above the mouth of the Clearwater River, from which point he was the first white man to see this portion of the Rockies. In 1799, John MacDonald (Bras Croche) of Garth, built Rocky Mountain House, 1¼ mi above the mouth of the Clearwater.

A road from Red Deer River (Ya-ha-tinda Ranch) runs up to N of Mt. White, thence S along Snow Creek to join park roads in Cuthead Creek N of Banff. A trail from the ranch extends NW following benches above Scalp Creek and crossing a local divide to Clearwater River; thence up N bank of latter to Clearwater Pass and down Siffleur River to Kootenay Plain or connecting with the Pipestone route to Lake Louise.

Although the route through the Pipestone and Siffleur Valleys across Pipestone Pass is one of the oldest in the mountains, Dr. (afterwards Sir James) Hector and Lord Southesk having traversed it in 1859, the highest peaks were not seen by them. It afforded an important short cut between the basins of the S and N Saskatchewan Rivers, serving as an alternative to the route across Bow Pass. Presently it permits access through lateral passes into the watersheds of the Red Deer, Clearwater and Ram Rivers.

The filling of Abraham Lake (4335' — Indian guide Silas Abraham) behind the Bighorn Dam has flooded the former Forest Warden Station 25 mi E of Saskatchewan Crossing. The Edwards Bridge (at Kootenay Plains) is now removed. A new footbridge across the North Saskatchewan is 1¼ mi S of the Two O'Clock Campground turnoff on the David Thompson Highway (407673). This provides access to the Siffleur Trail, etc.

Access from the N is up the Siffleur Trail (½ mi W of river) from the Alberta Forest road on the North Saskatchewan, and via its various E tributaries in which the bush is quite open. One mi N of the Pipestone Pass the Clearwater trail joins and runs 20 mi down that stream to the park boundary to the telephone line and trail up Peters Creek and S over Divide Creek to the Red Deer River.

The Cascade Fire Road runs N and NW from near Banff to provide access to a variety of trails in Stoney Creek, Sawback Creek, Panther River, and the Red Deer River. This road is not generally open to vehicles. A trail up Forty Mile Creek starts at the Mt. Norquay #3 parking lot and joins with a branch of the Cascade Fire Road in Flints Park. A trail in Johnston Creek gives one-day access to Pulsatilla and Badger Passes.

Many of the peaks were occupied by the Topographical Survey in 1919 as camera stations: 10021', 10570', and 10563' (between Martin Creek and head of Ram River); 10382', 10055', and 10030' (between Ram and Siffleur Rivers). In addition to these, and the more detailed list given in this section, the Survey ascended 23 other peaks between 9000' and 10000'.

In 1969, a party consisting of A. J. Kauffman, W. L. Putnam, L. R. Wallace, M. A. Broman and L. Putnam went S from the mouth of Siffleur River, in 16 days passing E of Mt. Willingdon and Cataract Pk. The party traversed 6 high passes and made numerous ascents, emerging through Johnson's Canyon. The entire trip was not onerous and was made without external support (AAJ 17–84).

There is a group of small peaks named by Mary Schaffer

(Old Indian Trails–172) *Kadoona Mtn* – the northernmost group of 5 peaks, between the Siffleur and Whiterabbit Creek. The smallest of these (7400') in the SW corner of the group has a fine slabby face of reasonably firm rock about 2500' high, up which A. Daffern and P. Ford put a route. There is room for more. Several of the other peaks in the group have rock faces which appear to be firm.

For ease of description we have broken this large area into subgroups along geographic lines. The principal means of access are in these valleys, from which one can reach the base of any climb in one or two days backpacking.

The last few steps to a mountain pass are attended by a pleasurable excitement equalled only by the conquest of a new mountain. The curtain is about to be raised, as it were, on a new scene, and the reward of many hours of climbing comes at one magical revelation.

W. D. Wilcox

PEAKS NORTH OF CLEARWATER RIVER
Maps 82N16; 83C1

Wampum Peak (9396)
Between heads of Ranger and Indianhead Creeks (Clearwater River).
F. A. 1919 by the Topographical Survey.
Many pleasant ascents can be made in the largely unvisited country N and E of this peak. Little serious mountaineering challenge exists, but there is much high alpine terrain in this area N of the Clearwater valley.

Unnamed (10062)
E of head of Whiterabbit Creek; on divide to Ram River.

Unnamed (10390)
A double summit; lower NE point being 10346'; On ridge E of Escarpment River toward Ram River. Much fine climbing can be found on the faces N and W from these peaks towards Kadoona Mtn.

Unnamed (10350)
A double summit E of Escarpment River; 3 mi N of Icefall Mtn.

Nordic Ridge (9880)
N of Icefall Mtn; at W of Ram River Glacier.

Unnamed (10589)
2 mi NW of Mt. Malloch; at head of Malloch Creek.

Icefall Mtn (10570)
At extreme head of Ram River Glacier; SE of head of Escarpment River.

Mt. Huestis (10050)
E of Ram River Glacier; SW of 10589'.

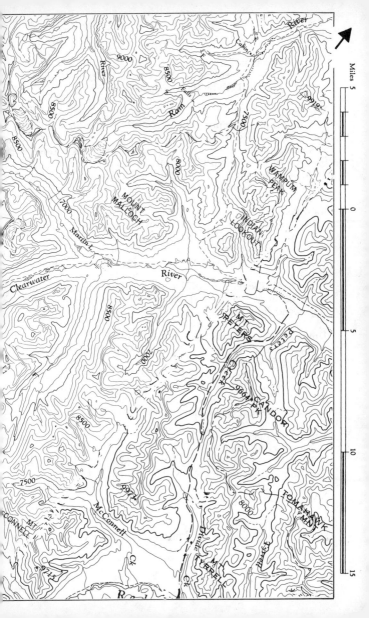

Mt. Malloch (10167)

In W angle between Malloch Creek and Clearwater River. F. A. prior to 1919 by the Geological Survey.

Mt. Fuhrer (10050)

A long ridge, precipitous to E, N of 10818′ towards Siffleur River; three lakes in valley to E.

A minor point (9500′) E of the main peak was ascended from camp as for Kahl (2) in July 1972 via easy SW slopes by Miss F. Chapple, D. Von Hennig, E. Johann, V. Mahler, *R. Gertsch, F. Stark.* II.

Kahl Peak (10400)

One mi N of Lumbago Lake, above Escarpment River.

F. A. August 1967 by E. Whipple, L. R. Wallace, H. Thompson. From camp at head of Escarpment River via snow and ledges N of Lumbago Lake to S ridge. Thence to summit. 4 hr from lake.

2 — NW Ridge. July 1972 J. A. V. Cade, *W. L. Putnam.* From camp at top of headwall in valley to N via easy NW slopes and ridge. II.

Unnamed (*Perren*) (10818)

2 mi NW of Recondite, W. of Escarpment River, E of Laughing Bears Valley.

F. A. July 1968 by M. A. Broman, A. J. Kauffman, W. L. Putnam, L. Putnam. From camp in Laughing Bears Creek via SW slopes to W ridge. Traverse across to attain summit from SE. Descent via SE ridge. 9 hr RT, III, 5.2 (AAJ *16*–412).

Unnamed (10350)

2 mi E of Mt. Antevs.

F. A. July 1972 by J. A. V. Cade, Miss F. Chapple, D. Von Hennig, E. Johann, V. Mahler, *R. Gertsch, W. L. Putnam, F. Stark.* From camp on glacier E of Antevs via easy NW glacier to W ridge, thence to summit. II, 5 hr RT.

Mt. Antevs (10420)

2 mi SE of 10818′ at head of Laughing Bears Creek.

F. A. July 1972 by Putnam party (see Unnamed 10350')
Easily attained from col to W, which in turn has been reached
from both N and S.

Simpson Peak (10750)

One mi NNW of Recondite Pk.

F. A. July 1969 by M. A. Broman, A. J. Kauffman, W.
L. Putnam, L. Putnam, L. R. Wallace. Approach from Siffleur
River via Laughing Bears Creek to campsite at timberline N
of objective. Attain W ridge by N slopes and residual glacier.
Follow W ridge to summit. Exposure, but no technical diffi-
culty. RT 7 hr (AAJ *17*–84).

Unnamed (*Osgood*) (10050)

One mi W of Recondite Peak

F. A. 1925 by W. O. Field, J. Hubbard, C. D. McCoy.
From camp in Siffleur Valley 3 mi distant by way of SE branch
of Siffleur, ascending W slopes. Ascent 7 hr (Harvard *1*–9).

Unnamed (10590)

One mi ENE of Recondite Pk; 2 mi N of Mt. Augusta; 2
mi SE of 10818'.

Recondite Peak (11010)

9 mi N of Pipestone Pass; N of head of Martin Creek.

F. A. Aug 1927 by H. Palmer, *Ern. Feuz*. From camp in
valley of SE branch of Siffleur by way of the SW arete. At
a point 1500' below the top, a shoulder is turned by descending
a chimney in the S face. A sharp pinnacle, 700' higher, neces-
sitates an 80' rappel. Ascent 7 hr; descent 3 hr (Harvard *1*–66).

Unnamed (*Augusta*) (10784)

One mi SE of Recondite Peak; 7 mi N of Pipestone Pass;
N of head of Martin Creek. Other 10000' peaks on ridge SW
toward Mt. Kentigern.

F. A. Aug 1927 by R. H. Melcer, *Ern. Feuz*. From camp
in valley of SE branch of Siffleur by way of W slopes and
N face. Total time 9 hr (Harvard *1*–68).

Mt Anteus

Mt Murchison

Simpson Peak

10590'

Mt Forbes

Escarpment Valley

E. Johann

View to Northwest from 10350'

Mt. Kentigern (10422)

Between Siffleur River and head of Martin Creek.

F. A. 1919 by the Topographical Survey, via easy W slopes. Much fine scrambling can be found in the area between the heads of Martin Creek and the valley N of Mt. Kentigern.

Clearwater Mtn (10750)

5 mi N of Pipestone Pass; second elevation NW of Clearwater Pass, the first being 10400′.

F. A. July 1925 by W. O. Field, J. Hubbard, C. D. McCoy. From camp 3 mi below Pipestone Pass (Harvard 1–5).

Unnamed (10150)

One mi NW of Mt. Willingdon glacier terminus. The E face of this peak and the Willingdon massif is severe but promising.

Mt. Willingdon (11066)

2 mi NE of Clearwater Pass; at head of Martin Creek.

F. A. 1919 by the Topographical Survey. From Clearwater Pass proceed NE across snowfield (gone in 1969) to the W ridge of the peak, ascending steep ice slopes. Follow slabby loose rocks to summit. Ascent from pass 9 hr (Harvard 1–6). 1969 party (AAJ 17–84) found access to W (Geode) Ridge easy with approach via glacier to N from camp in valley of Martin Creek. Also made traverse of summit descending via S ridge, III.

Willingdon South (*Crown*) (10950)

One mi SE of Willingdon.

F. A. Aug 1969 by M. A. Broman, A. J. Kauffman, W. L. Putnam, L. R. Wallace. One hr from col to N (see Willingdon). Descent by traverse of SW slope of Mt. Willingdon to Geode Ridge (AAJ 17–94).

Willingdon #3 (S Tower) (10910)

The S crest of the Willingdon massif, overlooking Clearwater valley.

F. A. Aug 1969 by A. Copp, R. Gertsch and one other.

From camp below Devon Lakes at 7500', ascending traverse of thinly timbered and grassy S slopes to attain saddle at 9450' on SE ridge — 2 hr. From this point the ridge was followed throughout with only difficulty being at the crest in getting through the cornice. 5 hr up. Descent via dip slope to SW.

Mt. Harris (10825)

W angle between Martin Creek and Clearwater River.

F. A. 1919 by the Topographical Survey. From camp at Clearwater Pass (7655'), skirting W slopes to S ridge, the crest of which is attained by a chimney. The N and E faces offer spectacular needles and challenges (CAJ *18*–54).

"Nor is it strange that the mountains should attract their worshippers at all seasons of the year, for the passion, once acquired, is insatiable: you may tire of the hills for a while, but if you have once felt their power you will assuredly return to them."

H. S. Salt

PEAKS SOUTH OF CLEARWATER RIVER
Maps 82012, 82N9, 82013

Mt. Peters (9350)
3 mi NW of Condor Peak; 6 mi E of Mt. Mallock.

Condor Peak (9664)
W of head of Forbidden Creek; E of Peters Creek.

Tomahawk Mtn (9578)
NW of Wapiti Mtn; between heads of Tyrrell and Scalp Creeks (Red Deer River). Higher summits to N and E.

Wapiti Mtn (9951)
N angle between Tyrrell Creek and Red Deer River.
F. A. 1918 by the Topographical Survey.

Unnamed (10050)
5 mi S of Mt. Peter; 4 mi SW of Condor Peak.

Unnamed (10040)
One mi SSE of above; 7 mi WNW of Mt. Tyrrell.
These two peaks are part of a ridge extending for 7 mi W of Divide and Peters Creeks. The E escarpment is impressive and in many places exceeds 1000′ sheer.

Boar Station (9973)
5 mi NE of Mt. McConnell; at extreme S end of ridge with two summits above.
F. A. 1955 by Dominion Survey party under L. E. Pelton.

Mt. Tyrrell (9050)
One mi N of Red Deer River; opposite Snow Creek road and Divide Creek.

Smoky Mtn (10278)
E of Roaring Creek; 6 mi N of Mt. McConnell.
F. A. 1919 by the Topographical Survey.

Roaring Ridge (10250)

S of Smoky Mtn over 7 mi of high country towards Mt. McConnell are six high points exceeding 10000'. These points lie E of Roaring Creek and W of the N fork of McConnell Creek. This fork has three W tributaries in each of which are several very attractive lakes.

Mt. McConnell (10300)

E of Cataract Peak; 4 mi N of Mt. Drummond; W angle between McConnell Creek and Red Deer River. The N face is steep ice (CAJ 3–48).

Devon Mtn (9855)

NE buttress of Pipestone Pass.
F. A. 1919 by the Topographical Survey.

Dip Slope Mtn (10250)

At extreme N end of Cataract massif, S of Clearwater Lake, are 3 summits on ridge N of Three Brothers of equal height, two in E-W line about one mi apart, 5 mi directly E of Clearwater Pass, the third 2 mi S near the Brothers, to which the name is properly applied. A series of lesser points lie in the angle N towards Martin Lake.

Unnamed (*Three Brothers*) (S-9950; C-10440; E-10230)

5 mi SE of Clearwater Pass; immediately W of sources of Roaring Creek. The W glaciers drain W to Clearwater River (CAJ *19*–37; picture).

F. A. Sept 1937 by Miss Gardiner, *E. Feuz, Jr.* From camp near Cataract Waterfall (N side of Pipestone Valley; 20 mi N of Lake Louise) N peak was ascended through valley and forest to high lake with island; whence glacier was followed to col between objective and central peak; the W arete ascended over short steep pitches. Ascent 6 hr; total time 11 hr.

Central and S peaks. By way of next Pipestone tributary N of camp to gain glacier draining to Clearwater River. Central Peak by its slabby W face — 6 hr. Descent to glacier and reach S peak by its N arete — one hour by rock slabs. Total time 10½ hr (CAJ 25–28).

Unnamed (10420)

2 mi NW of Cataract Peak at head of Pipestone River. A sizeable lake at its SE base is a source of Roaring Creek (Clearwater River) (AAJ *17*–84).

F. A. 1937 by Miss K. Gardiner, *E. Feuz, Jr.* From camp near Cataract Waterfall (N side of Pipestone Valley; 20 mi N N of Lake Louise) through valley and forest to high lake with island. From upper end of lake ascend scree and follow steep rock band to S ridge. Several small pitches on way to summit. Ascent 7⅓ hr. Total time 10½ hr (CAJ *25*–29).

Unnamed (*Little Cataract*) (10410)

One mi NW of Cataract Peak.

F. A. July 1930 by J. W. A. Hickson, *E. Feuz, Jr.* From camp in Fossil Creek over grass and scree to the W side, mounting a gully between a prominent rock tower, in which the W ridge culminates, and the upper slab-like cliffs. From the top of the gully — 3½ hr — the slabs are ascended to the summit; 5 hr up.

Cataract Peak (10935)

W of Mt. McConnell; head of Pipestone River.

F. A. July 1930 by J. W. A. Hickson, *E. Feuz, Jr.* From camp in Fossil Creek via moraine and N glacier to upper snow on NW side — 9400′; 3 hr. NW ridge ascended easily for 700′, after which it becomes steeper, with slabs and towers to summit. Ascent 5¼ hr (CAJ *19*–36).

Unnamed (10370)

One mi S of Cataract Peak in forks of Fossil Creek; 3 mi W of Mt. McConnell.

Unnamed (10300)

W side of Drummond Glacier.

F. A. July 1930 by J. W. A. Hickson, *E. Feuz, Jr.* Via Drummond Glacier; skirting base of Cyclone Mtn, over snow and final rock ridges (CAJ *19*–42).

Unnamed (10393)

NW of Drummond Glacier; above Fossil Creek.

F. A. 1948, Mr. & Mrs. R. A. Linck, C. Couttet. Ascended without difficulty from Drummond Glacier, a summit cairn without record being found (CAJ *19*–35).

Unnamed (10310)

NE corner of Drummond Glacier, a lesser summit to W is SE of lake in Fossil Creek.

F. R. A. 1962 by D. Gardner, J. Gardner (CAJ *47*–136).

Mt. Drummond (10330)

3 mi NE of Cyclone Mtn; at sources of Red Deer River (CAJ *19*–41).

F. A. 1947 by Miss E. Rummel and party. An easy ascent from Drummond Glacier over W slopes.

Cyclone Mtn (9979)

3 mi SE of Mt. Drummond; NE of pass between Little Pipestone Creek and Red Deer River.

F. A. 1910 by J. W. A. Hickson, *E. Feuz, E. Feuz, Jr.* From Little Pipestone Valley by way of Drummond Glacier. Ascent 4½ hr.

Pipestone Mtn (9750)

S corner of Drummond Glacier; above head of Little Pipestone Creek.

PEAKS SOUTH OF RED DEER RIVER
Maps 82012, 8205

Warden Rock (8844)

On Banff Park boundary S of Red Deer River; 3 mi NW of Barrier Mtn. "A good rock climb."

Gable Mtn (9606)

4 mi W of Barrier Mtn; W angle between Red Deer and Panther Rivers.

F. A. prior to 1918 by the Geological Survey.

Barrier Mtn (9703)

E of Gable Mtn; W angle between Red Deer and Panther Rivers.

Ascents 1947 by ACC parties; possibly earlier.

Dormer Mtn (9074)

SW angle between Dormer and Panther Rivers; on Banff Park boundary.

Mt. White (9040)

5 mi W of Gable Mtn; 3 mi N of Snow Creek Pass; N end of Bare Range.

F. A. prior to 1918 by the Geological Survey.

Panther Mtn (9655)

Between sources of Panther and Dormer Rivers; S end of Bare Range; E of Wigmore Creek.

F. A. 1891 by J. J. McArthur, *T. E. Wilson.*

Prow Mtn (9377)

5 mi NW of Snow Creek Pass (7800' gravel road); E of upper Red Deer River.

F. A. 1918 by the Topographical Survey.

Unnamed (10185)

W angle of Snow Creek and Panther River; 6 mi E of Mt. Douglas.

F. A. 1918 by the Topographical Survey.

Unnamed (10150)

One mi W of Unnamed 10185'; overlooking headwaters of Red Deer River; 3 mi E of Douglas Lake.

Unnamed (10082)

3 mi N of Bonnet Peak; head of Panther River.

F. A. 1920 by the Topographical Survey (CAJ *13*–180).

Unnamed (10013)

4 mi ESE of Mt. Douglas; at head of Panther River.

F. A. 1920 by the Topographical Survey.

Mt. Douglas (10614)

N of Mt. St. Bride; W of Douglas Lake.

F. A. 1907 by L. M. Earle, *E. Feuz, G. Feuz*. From Lake Louise via Pipestone and Little Pipestone Valleys, cross pass to head of Red Deer River and camp in side valley SW of the mountain. Ascend SW face over loose but not difficult rock and gain S arete which is followed to summit. Ascent 5½ hr (CAJ *1*–318; *3*–40; *7*–58).

Mt. St. Bride (*White Douglas*) (10867)

S of Mt. Douglas; W of Douglas Creek; E of pass between Baker Creek and Red Deer River (CAJ *8*–136).

F. A. 1910 by J. W. A. Hickson, *E. Feuz, E. Feuz, Jr. From Lake Louise via Ptarmigan Valley (Corral Creek) to camp E of head of Baker Creek (7200')*. Ascend into rocky amphitheater, crossing a rock wall at the lowest point to gain large flat neve SW of the peak. Traverse to pass at right and cross descending steep snowslope and traverse base of cliffs N along the snow to a point below a notch, where there is a cave and a waterfall (falling stones). Gain the notch over snow, ice and rotten rock (varying difficulty). Cross to W side and cliffs at the corner. A difficult 20' chimney with an overhanging top required a party of three for its negotiation. Bearing diagonally across the SW face above the cave brings one to another difficult 35' chimney to the right, leading to a platform and easy rocks below a dangerous 60' chimney with poor holds and loose rock. Thence via SE arete to the flat top, 500' above (CAJ 3—40; App 12–227).

Lychnis Mtn (10350)

2 mi S of Mt. St. Bride.

F. A. 1969 by A. J. Kauffman, W. L. Putnam, L. Putnam, L. R. Wallace. From camp near Alfred Lake ascend steep snow col to glacier level E of Mtn. Thence to E ridge and SE snowslope to summit. N summit not reached. 6 hr RT (AAJ 17–95).

Bonnet Peak (NE–10150; C–10615; S–10550)

7 mi SE of Mt. Douglas; at sources of Johnson Creek and Cascade River. The massif is composed of 3 distinct peaks, the arete between the central and NE summit being not readily traversable (CAJ 19–45). The Bonnet Glacier can be reached readily from the Valley of the Hidden Lakes (Douglas Creek) to the N (CAJ 13–170), from Badger Pass to the S or over alps, rock and steep scree from Pulsatilla Pass to the SW.

S Peak; F. A. 1890 by A. St. Cyr.

Easily attained from Bonnet Glacier.

C Peak; F. A. 1914 by the Topographical Survey.

Easily attained from Bonnet Glacier.

Unnamed (10100) (*Hickson Pk.*)

2 mi W of Bonnet Peak; head of Bonnet Glacier (Red Deer River); N of Mt. Pulsatilla.

F. A. 1930 by J. W. A. Hickson, *E. Feuz, Jr.* From camp at confluence of streams from Pulsatilla Pass and Bonnet Glacier, ascend E to base of peak — ¾ hr. Game trails lead E over gravel and shale to a col, from which one turns left over more scree to reach a prominent rock band at 9100', which is surmounted without difficulty. One hr more to summit. Ascent 4 hr (CAJ 19–45).

Flints Peak (9680)
5 mi E of Bonnet Peak; SW of Cuthead Lake.

Ye who love the haunts of nature
Love the sunshine of the meadow
Love the shadow of the forest
Love the wind among the branches
And the rain-shower, and the snow-storm
And the rushing of great rivers
And the thunder in the mountains.

H. W. Longfellow

PALLISER RANGE

This subgroup lies E of the Cascade River and N of Lake Minnewanka. It is geologically part of the Clearwater Group and is generally approached from the limited access park roads on the W, and unmarked private lands to the E. This is drier country than the areas to the W and supports no glaciers. Many attractive faces and lines are to be found and much of the rock is quite sound (AAJ *17*–84). The peaks are generally a few hundred feet lower in altitude as one approaches the plains and for the most part are unnamed. The bulk of the higher summits are found along the ridge that marks the Park boundary, and the remainder to the NE of Ghost River, along which a good trail is found. Maps 8205, 8206.

Mt. Oliver (9785)
8 mi N of Mt. Aylmer; between heads of Ghost and Dormer (Red Deer) Rivers. S towards Mt. Steacie are several summits of comparable elevation.

Revenant Mtn (10050) (*Steacie*)
4 mi NW of Mt. Alymer; lower E summit is Apparition Mtn.
F. A. 1968 by T. A. Swaddle, M. Benn, T. Sorenson. From camp in valley 2 mi SE, via S ridge; traverse summits to descend from SE ridge to lakes in basin S of peak — 5½ hr (CAJ *52*–58).

Mt. Aylmer (10375)
4 mi N of curve in Lake Minnewanka; 5 mi NE of Stewart Canyon. Along the ridge towards Mt. Steacie are 3 points exceeding 9500′.
F. A. 1889 by J. J. McArthur from Lake Minnewanka (CAJ *10*–32).

Mt. Costigan (9775)
2 mi N of E end of Lake Minnewanka.

Costigan's Boil (8410)
ENE of Mt. Costigan; W of Phantom Crag; NW of Devil's Gap.
F. A. Aug 1960, P. Duffy, J. K. Gray, Mr. & Mrs. H. Kahl. From Devils Gap (Banff Park boundary) pass Phantom Lake to second canyon on the N side of the valley. (Spectacular canyons in this area). This particular one with 400′ walls was followed and climbed at its head bypassing two waterfalls to trees above canyon wall, one hr thru forest. Then steep meadows to ridge, one hr, this ridge runs E to Phantom Crag. The ridge was followed on N side and rope used again near top. Descent by same route (CAJ *44*–55).

Devils Head (9174)
8 mi E of Mt. Aylmer; 4 mi N of Mt. Costigan. This is the only named peak — and not the highest — in a group centered about the headwaters of Waiparous Creek. A number of good climbs can be found on faces reaching up to 2000′. E and N faces quite spectacular.
F. A. 1925 by L. S. Crosby, J. W. A. Hickson, *E. Feuz, Jr.* From camp near Ghost River (5500′) peak was approached over high ground S of W ridge. Thence crossing draw to S face. A system of couloirs was ascended to the W ridge. In places the going was thin and rock very coarse. Rope not used after attaining ridge. 5½ hr up; 4½ hr down (AJ *38*–67).

SLATE RANGE

This minor group lies E of the lower Pipestone River and S of the Little Pipestone. Access is easy via Pipestone road and trail to the lodge at Skoki Valley and other trails in Corral Creek and Baker Creek. The trail up Corral Creek connects with the trail via Baker Creek and over the height of land with those via Pulsatilla Pass and the Little Pipestone. Map 82N8, 82N9.

Merlin Castle (9320)
2 mi NW of Mt Richardson; 3 mi W of Skoki ski lodge.

Mt. Richardson (10125)
Between Pika Peak and Pipestone River.
F. A. 1911 by L. L. Delafield, *E. Feuz, Jr*. From camp in upper Corral Creek (Ptarmigan Valley) via S arete — 3 hr up (CAJ *4*–142).
2 — E Ridge. 1911 by L. M. Earle; *R. Aemmer*. From Ptarmigan Valley, II.

Pika Peak (9950)
Between Mt. Richardson and Ptarmigan Peak.
F. A. 1911 by L. L Delafield, L. M. Earle, *R. Aemmer, E. Feuz, Jr*. From camp S of Ptarmigan Peak, Mt. Richardson (which see) was traversed to the Richardson-Pika col and Pika Peak ascended over steep broken rock of W arete — one hr from col (CAJ *4*–142).

Ptarmigan Peak (10036)
E of Pika Peak; NW of Ptarmigan Lake and Pass; between heads of Corral Creek and Red Deer River (CAJ *21*–135, ski ascent).
F. A. 1909 by J. W. A. Hickson, *E. Feuz, Jr*. via couloir on SE side, and E ridge. 3 hr from Ptarmigan Lake (App *19*–233).
2 — E Arete. 1911, J. F. Porter and party of eight. Via S face and E arete; the last 100' narrow, with loose rock (CAJ *4*–114).

3 — N Face. 1911 by L. M. Earle, *R. Aemmer*. From the Richardson-Pika col, by a difficult traverse of the N face of Pika Peak. The route then lies above the N glacier to broken neve and steep snowslopes to the summit (CAJ 4–142).

4 — S Face. 1911 by L. L. Delafield, *E. Feuz, Jr.* From the Richardson-Pika col, traverse scree on S face of Pika Peak to col in E arete between Pika Peak and objective. Ascend a snow-filled couloir and the rock on its E side to summit ridge. Traverse for short distance on N side and regain arete several hundred feet W of summit (CAJ 4–142).

Mt. Redoubt (9520)

S of Ptarmigan Lake; between Corral Creek and Redoubt Lake (CAJ 4–111).

F. A. 1906 by the Topographical Survey. From Ptarmigan Lake via scree slopes and N arete.

Wall of Jericho (9550)

NE of Mt. Richardson; above Lake Merlin.

Anthozoan Mtn (8850)

S of Baker Lake (CAJ 4–112).

F. A. 1911 by J. F. Porter and party. From Baker Lake via scree and broken rock of NW face.

Fossil Mtn (9665)

3 mi E of Mt. Richardson; N of Baker Lake at head of Red Deer River (CAJ 4–112; *20*–144, ski ascent).

F. A. 1906 by the Topographical Survey.

Oyster Peak (9110)

W of Mt. Douglas; SE of pass between Little Pipestone Creek and Red Deer River.

F. A. 1906 by the Topographical Survey.

APPENDIX OF PASSES

ABBOT (A-P) 9598	Lake Oesa — Victoria Glacier Mt Victoria — Mt Lefroy (hut)
AKAMINA (A-P) 5850	Cameron Lake — Akamina Creek Forum Pk — Mt Rowe (trail)
ALLENBY (A) 7980	Bryant Creek — Brewster Creek Og Mtn — 9850 (trail)
AMISKWI (P) 6545	Ensign Creek — Amiskwi River Arête Peak — 8320 (trail)
ASSINIBOINE (A-P) 7152	Bryant Creek — Og Creek Cave Mtn — Cascade Rock (trail)
BADGER (A) 8330	Johnston Creek — Cascade River Bonnet Peak — 9450 (trail)
BAKER	(Amiskwi)
BALFOUR (A-P) 8050	Hector Lake — Yoho River Mt. Balfour — Mt Olive (hut)
BALL (A-P) 7250	Hawk Creek (Vermilion) — Redearth Creek Isabelle Peak — Haiduk Peak (trail)
BIDDLE (P) 8550	McArthur L. — Misko Creek Park Mtn — Mt Biddle
BOOM LAKE (A-P) 7550	Boom Lake — Vermilion River Boom Mtn — Chimney Peak
BOULDER (A) 7650	Corral Creek — Baker Lake Redoubt Mtn — Ptarmigan Peak (trail)
BOW (A) 6878	Bow River — Mistaya River Mt Thompson — Observation Peak (road)
BURGESS (P) 7160	Emerald Lake — Kickinghorse River Mt Burgess — Mt Field (trail)

CATHEDRAL (A) 8940	Monarch Creek — Duchesnay Creek Mt Stephen — Cathedral Mtn
CITADEL (A-P) 7750	Howard Douglas Creek — Simpson River Citadel Pk — Fatigue Mtn (trail)
CLEARWATER (A) 7640	Siffleur River — Clearwater River Devon Mtn — Clearwater Mtn
CONSOLATION (A) 8110	Babel Creek — Boom Lake Bident Mtn — Mt Bell (trail)
CORAL (P) 8350	Nivelle Creek — Cadorna Creek Coral Pk — Rock Tower
CROWSNEST (A-P) 4451	Summit Creek — Island Lake Loop Ridge — Crowsnest Ridge (road)
DEADMAN (A-P) 5250	Alexander Creek — Allison Creek Allison Peak — Mt Tecumseh
DECEPTION (A) 8120	Skoki Valley — Ptarmigan Lake Ptarmigan Peak — Fossil Mtn (trail)
DENNIS (P) 7418	Boulder Creek — Kickinghorse River Mt Dennis — Mt Stephen
DEVILS GAP (A) 5008	Lake Minnewanka — Ghost River Orient Point — 8000 (trail)
DOLOMITE (A) 7850	Helen Creek — Dolomite Creek Cirque Peak — Dolomite Peak (trail)
DUCHESNAY (P) 8747	Boulder Creek — Duchesnay Creek Mt Duchesnay — Mt Stephen
EDITH (A) 6380	Bow River — Forty Mile Creek Mt Edith — Mt Norquay (trail)
ELK (A-P) W 6205 (E 6510)	Kananaskis River — Elk River Mt Fox — Mt Tyrwhitt (road)
ELPOCA (A) 6850	Elbow River — Pocaterra Creek Mt Rae — Elpoca Mtn (trail)

EMERALD (P) 8899	Emerald Lake — Little Yoho Mt Marpole — The President
FATIGUE (P) 7580	Fatigue Creek — Simpson River Nasswald Peak — Fatigue Mtn (trail)
FERRO (P) 7450	Simpson River — Mitchell River Indian Peak — Nestor Peak
FLATHEAD (P) 5750	Squaw Creek — Michel Creek Centre Peak — Limestone Ridge
FORDING (A-P) 7580	Baril Creek — Aldridge Creek Mt Bolton — Mt Cornwell (trail)
GIBBON (A) 7550	Twin Lake — Redearth Creek 9950 (Ball Range) — 8980
HALSTEAD (A) 9050	Panther River — Guendolyn Lake Bonnet Peak — 10080
HARTLEY (P) 5050	Hartley Creek — Sulfur Creek Mt Hosmer — Three Sisters (road)
HARVEY (A) 8050	Bourgeau Creek — Healy Creek Mt Bourgeau — 9550
HEALY (A) 8050	Pharaoh Creek — Healy Creek Monarch Ramparts — 8250 (trail)
HIGHWOOD (A) 7250	Storm Creek — Pocaterra Creek Mt Arethusa — Mt Tyrwhitt (road)
HORNADAY (P) 5540	Brule Creek — Norboe Creek (Bull R.) Mt Roth — 9240 (trail — cabin)
HURD (P) 8650	Haskings Creek — Kickinghorse River Mt Hurd – Mt Vaux
ICE (P) 8750	Haskings Creek — Ice River Mt Ennis — Mt Allan
N KANANASKIS (A-P) 7250	Leroy Creek — Maude River Mt Maude — Mt Beatty (trail)

KICKINGHORSE (A-P) 5333	Bath Creek — Kickinghorse River Mt Bosworth — Mt Niblock (road)
KIWETINOK (P) 8250	Little Yoho River — Kiwetinok River Mt Kerr — Kiwetinok Peak
LUXOR (P) 6150	Luxor Creek — Dolly Varden Creek Through Briscoe Range
MARVEL (A-P) 6980	Aurora Creek — Marvel Creek Mt Gloria — Aurora Mtn (trail)
McARTHUR (P) 7250	Cataract Brook — McArthur Creek Mt Odaray — Mt Schaffer (trail)
MIDDLE (A-P) 9500	Tokumm Creek — Boom Lake Chimney Peak — Mt Quadra
M KOOTENAY (A-P) 6350	Middlepass — W. Castle River Mt Haig — Rainy Ridge
MILLER (P) 5520	Cross River — Albert River Tangle Peak — Mt Soderholm
MISKO (P) 8050	Misko Creek — Tokumm Creek Mt Oke — Mt Biddle
MITRE (A) 8450	Lefroy Glacier — Paradise Creek Mitre Peak — Mt Aberdeen
NILES (P) 8320	Daly Glacier — Sherbrooke Creek Mt Niles — 8368
NORTH FORK (A-P) 6450	Dutch Creek — Line Creek Mt Erris — 9030
N KOOTENAY (A-P) 6770	Carbondale — Pincher Creek Hollebeke Mtn — Centre Mtn
NUMA (P) 7710	Floe Lake — Numa Creek Numa Mtn — Foster Pk.
ODARAY (P) 8260	Duchesnay Creek — MacArthur Creek Odaray Mtn — 8910

OG (A) 9163	Og Lake — Bryant Creek Cave Mtn — Og Mtn (trail)
OPABIN (P) 8460	Lake O'Hara — Tokumm Creek Mt Biddle — Hungabee Mtn
OTTERTAIL (P) 6700	Ochre Creek — Ottertail River 8405 – 9348 (trail)
OTTO (P) 6910	Otto Creek — Marin Creek Sealion Mtn — Amiskwi Peak
PALLISER (A-P) 6850	Spray River — Palliser River Mt Williams — Mt Queen Elizabeth (trail)
PHILLIPS (A-P) 5150	Crowsnest River — Summit Creek Mt Phillips — Crowsnest Ridge
PIPESTONE (A) 8036	Siffleur River — Pipestone River Devon Mt — 8398 (trail)
PRESIDENT (P) 9469	Little Yoho River — Emerald Lake The President — The Vice President
PTOLEMY (A-P) 5630	Andy Good Creek — E. Crowsnest Creek Mt. Ptolemy - Tent Mtn
PULSATILLA (A) 7760	Johnston Creek — Wildflower Creek 9350 – 9810 (trail)
RACEHORSE (A-P) 6950	Alexander Creek — S. Racehorse Creek Mt. Ward — 8777
REDEARTH (A-P) 6700	Pharaoh Creek — Verdant Creek Monarch Ramparts — Pharaoh Peak (trail)
SADDLEBACK (A) 7650	Lake Louise — Paradise Creek Saddle Mtn — Fairview Mtn (trail)
SAGE (A-P) 7050	Bauerman Creek — Sage Creek Kishenina Peak — 7986
SENTINEL (A) 8566	Paradise Creek — Larch Valley Mt Temple — Pinnacle Mtn (trail)

SIMPSON (A-P) 6914	Healy Creek — Simpson River Monarch Ramparts — Quartz Hill
SINCLAIR (P) 5350	Swede Creek — Sinclair Creek Mt Sinclair — Lookout Peak (road)
S KANANASKIS (A-P) 7439	Beatty Creek — 3 Isle Creek Mt Worthington — Mt. Putnik
S KOOTENAY (A-P) 6850	Kishenina Creek — Blakiston Creek Festubert Mtn — Kishenina Peak
SPRAY (A-P) 6850	Spray River — Albert River Mt Leval — Mt Laman
SUNDANCE (A) 5750	Spray River — Sundance Creek Sundance Range — Sulfur Mtn
SYLVAN (P) 7670	Joffre Creek — White Riverjt Shatch Mtn — Mt Joffre (trail)
TEGART (P) 6640	Windermere Creek — Kootenay River Mt Aeneas — 8450 (trail)
TENT (A-P) 5370	Crowsnest Creek — Michel Creek Tent Mtn — Loop Ridge
TORNADO (A-P) 7050	Dutch Creek — Line Creek 8950 — Tornado Mtn.
TUMBLING (P) 7100	Tumbling Creek — Numa Creek 10150–8510
VERMILION (A-P) 5416	Altrude Creek — Vermilion River Boom Mtn — Storm Mtn (road)
VULTURE (P) 9620	Wapta Glacier — Vulture Glacier Mt Gordon — Mt Olive
WASTACH (A) 8338	Paradise Creek — Eiffel Lake Eiffel Peak — Wenkchemna Peak
WEARY CREEK (A-P) 7370	McPhail Creek — Weary Creek Mt Muir — Mt McPhail

WENKCHEMNA (A-P) 8531	Wenkchemna Glacier — Tokumm Creek Neptuak Mtn — Wenkchemna Peak
WHISTLING (A) 7520	Scarab Lake — Haiduk Lake Pharaoh Peaks — Haiduk Peak (trail)
WHITE MAN (A-P) 7050	Cross River — White Man Creek Mt White Man — Mt Red Man (trail)
WILSON (P) 8400	Martins Creek (Ice) — Goodsir Creek Goodsir N — 8827
WOLVERINE (P) 7240	Tumbling Creek (Ochre) — Dainard Creek Mt Gray — Mt Drysdale (trail)
WONDER (A-P) 7950	Magog Creek — Marvel Lake The Towers — Wonder Peak (trail)
YOHO (P) 6030	Emerald Lake — Yoho River Wapta Mtn — Michael Peak (trail)

INDEX

328

This book may need help. The editors would be grateful for specific corrections or comments. Please jot them down on this page and mail to The American Alpine Club 113 East 90th Street New York 10028.

This book may need help. The editors would be grateful for specific corrections or comments. Please jot them down on this page and mail to The American Alpine Club 113 East 90th Street New York 10028.